T0381104

Cyber Resilience
Index

Mastering Threat-Informed
Defense

Lampis Alevizos

Apress®

Cyber Resilience Index: Mastering Threat-Informed Defense

Dr. Lampis Alevizos
Amsterdam, The Netherlands

ISBN-13 (pbk): 979-8-8688-1121-0   ISBN-13 (electronic): 979-8-8688-1122-7
https://doi.org/10.1007/979-8-8688-1122-7

Managing Director, Apress Media LLC: Welmoed Spahr
Acquisitions Editor: Susan McDermott
Development Editor: Laura Berendson
Project Manager: Jessica Vakili

Cover image by Pixabay (www.pixabay.com)

Distributed to the book trade worldwide by Springer Science+Business Media New York, 1 New York Plaza, New York, NY 10004. Phone 1-800-SPRINGER, fax (201) 348-4505, e-mail orders-ny@springer-sbm.com, or visit www.springeronline.com. Apress Media, LLC is a California LLC and the sole member (owner) is Springer Science + Business Media Finance Inc (SSBM Finance Inc). SSBM Finance Inc is a **Delaware** corporation.

For information on translations, please e-mail booktranslations@springernature.com; for reprint, paperback, or audio rights, please e-mail bookpermissions@springernature.com.

Apress titles may be purchased in bulk for academic, corporate, or promotional use. eBook versions and licenses are also available for most titles. For more information, reference our Print and eBook Bulk Sales web page at http://www.apress.com/bulk-sales.

If disposing of this product, please recycle the paper

To my family, my anchors in the cyber storm.

Table of Contents

vii

About the Author

Dr. Lampis Alevizos a consistent thinker and doer, is the Head of Cyber Defense Innovation at Volvo Group. With two decades of experience in cybersecurity and a PhD, he combines academic rigor with practical expertise to empower leadership in adopting proactive and innovative strategies and leading with cyber foresight.

About the Technical Reviewer

Dr. Vinh-Thong Ta is the leader of the cybersecurity research group at the Department of Computer Science at Edge Hill University. Before that, he worked at the CrySyS Lab in Europe, which discovered the famous DuQu malware, and INRIA in France. He published numerous papers in the areas of security and privacy in reputed venues and high-impact journals, including *Vehicular Communications, IEEE Communication Magazine, IEEE Access*, and Privacy Enhancing Technologies Symposium (PETS/PoPETs), and he is the author of several software tools related to his research (e.g., DataProVe, a privacy policy verification tool). He has been a reviewer and program committee member of conferences and journals (including high-ranked venues such as the Network and Distributed System Security (NDSS) Symposium, ACM Conference on Security and Privacy in Wireless and Mobile Networks (WiSec), IEEE INFOCOM). He was part of the organization team of several international conferences such as the Third International Conference on Decision and Game Theory for Security (GameSec'12), the Sixth ACM Conference on Security and Privacy in Wireless and Mobile Networks (WiSec'13), and the Eighth International Conference on Computers, Privacy, and Data Protection (CPDP'15). He is a member of the British Computer Society and a Fellow of the Higher Education Academy.

Acknowledgments

To my wife and two young boys, whose patience and love made this book possible. To the mentors and colleagues who shaped my cybersecurity journey, your wisdom and challenges have been invaluable. And to the invisible heroes of our digital world, the cybersecurity professionals on the front lines, this book is for you. Thank you all for being part of this never-ending chess game we call cybersecurity.

Introduction

In a busy corporate office, Alex, the head of cyber resilience and a leader in the field of cybersecurity, advocated for a revolutionary approach to cyber defense. He believed that true cyber resilience was attainable for any organization willing to embrace change. He decided to approach the experienced CISO of the organization, Sophia, who was facing daily cyber threats and compliance demands while being stressed by the board to prove the division's value and return on investment. As they sat down to talk, the CISO saw only an overwhelming landscape of threats and risks, while the expert envisioned a transformative path forward through quantifiable resilience and proactive strategy.

The game-changing proposition

Sophia (CISO): You seriously believe there is a way to create a unified metric for cyber resilience, that I can explain it to the board?

Alex (Head of Cyber Resilience): Absolutely. It's effective and easier than you think.

Sophia: Easier than I think?! So, while we change our approach on the back end, we are becoming proactive instead of reactive, like you said. And we, as defenders, can finally start anticipating the attacker's next move?

Alex: Yes, we can quantify our defenses similarly to a stock market index, using it to drive decision-making at every level, operational, tactical, and strategic. Cyber threat actors do not have the first mover's advantage; it is a myth. We do, the defenders. It is simple!

Sophia: It is also simple! This is the first time I hear that, and it sounds a bit... far-fetched. I appreciate your enthusiasm, but we are swamped. Risk management is breathing down our necks, and we've got audit findings piling up. I don't see how we can take on anything new right now.

Alex: I understand your concerns, but please hear me out for two minutes. I have been researching a concept called the cyber resilience index, or CRI. Before I explain it, shall we do a quick thought experiment?

Sophia: All right, but please make it quick; I have a board meeting in 20 minutes.

Alex: Imagine we have two urns in front of us. Urn A has 10 red balls and 10 black balls. Urn B has 20 balls as well, but we do not know the mix of red and black. If you draw a black ball, you win a million euros. If you draw a red ball, you must pay a million euros. Which urn would you choose?

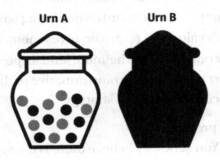

Sophia: I would choose Urn A that at least I know the odds, which is 50-50. But what does this have to do with our cybersecurity strategy?

Alex: It's called the Ellsberg paradox. In cybersecurity, like in life, we tend to prefer known risks over unknown ones, even if the unknown could be more favorable. Our current approach is like always choosing Urn A. We focus on known threats and security compliance requirements. But what about the unknown threats and risks? What if there was a way to take a sample from each urn first, analyze it, and therefore enhance our decision-making with solid, data-backed evidence?

Sophia: I get it, but we are doing fine as is. Compliance is up, we are meeting all the regulatory checkboxes, why mess with what's already working?

Alex: Indeed, we are doing well in those areas. Compliance is crucial, and I am not suggesting we ignore it. But compliance alone is not enough to stay ahead of emerging threats. We need to shift from a reactive to a proactive approach. Because if we don't, we are bound to fall behind. Adversaries are always evolving; we need a metric that helps us anticipate them.

Sophia: And how do you propose we do that? We are already running low on capacity and barely coping up with our current responsibilities.

Alex: By becoming threat intelligence driven. Remember the cyber resilience index I mentioned? It is not just another metric in a dashboard. It is a way to quantify our cybersecurity posture, considering both known and unknown threats, thus showing us a clearer picture of how prepared we really are. It goes beyond compliance and helps us anticipate and prepare for a wider range of scenarios.

Alex: And because you specifically mentioned capacity, the resilience index will significantly help us improve our effectiveness and efficiency, thereby helping in better decision-making and resource allocation.

Sophia: That sounds interesting, but also like a lot of work. How would it improve our current situation?

Alex: Think of cybersecurity as a chess game. We are often stuck playing defense, reacting to the attacker's moves. But here's where we have the advantage; they are playing on our board. We know our IT landscape better than any attacker ever could. Just like in chess, reacting alone won't win the game; we need to anticipate and use the knowledge we have to become proactive. With a threat intelligence–driven approach, we can start to anticipate moves and set the pace of the game.

Sophia: I see your point, but change is risky. We have a system that works. Introducing something new could disrupt our operations.

Alex: I understand your hesitation. Change can be scary. But the risk of not evolving our approach could be even greater. The threat landscape is constantly changing. If we do not adapt, we will always be one step behind.

Sophia (pauses, then nods slowly): I admit you've given me something to think about. I wish I had more time to discuss this now.

Alex: It's okay; I would be happy to go into more detail when you have time. There is a lot more to cover about how the CRI works and how we could implement it without disrupting our current operations.

Sophia (checks her watch, then makes a decision): You know what? This sounds intriguing, and improving effectiveness and efficiency at the same time is of utmost importance. How about we discuss this tomorrow morning? Can you block a few hours already in your calendar for me? I will ask my secretary to reschedule my meetings. I want to hear more about this cyber resilience index and how it could improve our strategy.

Alex: Sounds like a great plan! I think you will see how this could be a game changer for us, addressing not just our current challenges but preparing us for future ones as well.

Sophia: Alright. Although I am still skeptical, I am willing to listen. This better be good.

Alex: I promise you, by the end of our discussion, you will see the potential of this approach to transform our cybersecurity strategy.

CHAPTER 1

The Chess Game of Cybersecurity

The Ellsberg Paradox: A Lesson in Uncertainty

Alex: So, the Ellsberg paradox I mentioned yesterday is not just a thought experiment – it is the perfect analogy for the challenges we face in cybersecurity, because the game is not only won by knowing and managing the risks you see but also by preparing for those you can't.

Sophia: How does choosing between urns relate to our cybersecurity strategy?

Alex: Just as in the Ellsberg paradox, we are constantly making decisions with incomplete information. We have some known threats – that is, our Urn A – but we also face unknown threats, our Urn B.

Sophia: But in cybersecurity, we cannot just choose one urn. We must deal with both known and unknown threats.

Alex: Exactly. And that is where many organizations struggle. They focus too much on the known threats because they are more comfortable dealing with what they can measure and understand.

Sophia: I see your point, but how do we make decisions when we are dealing with so much uncertainty?

© Lampis Alevizos 2025
L. Alevizos, *Cyber Resilience Index*, https://doi.org/10.1007/979-8-8688-1122-7_1

Alex: In cybersecurity, we face what economists call "radical uncertainty" – situations where we can't calculate the odds of various outcomes. To deal with such situations, it requires a shift in mindset. Instead of trying to predict every possible outcome, we need to focus on building resilience and adaptability into our systems and processes.

Sophia: Can you give me an example of how this works in practice?

Alex: Take our patching strategy, for instance. A traditional approach might focus on patching known vulnerabilities in order of their CVSS scores. Some organizations act faster when the CVSS score is higher; others take a more risk-based approach. But that's like choosing Urn A; we are focused with known threats.

Sophia: And that leaves us vulnerable to unknown threats – our Urn B.

Alex: Precisely. A more resilient approach would be not just patching known vulnerabilities but also implementing broader security measures that can mitigate even unknown threats. Things like network segmentation, principle of least privilege, and robust monitoring systems, all being driven through cyber threat intelligence and based on our own information technology (IT) landscape.

Sophia: So, we are preparing for both known and unknown risks.

Alex: Exactly. Now, let's consider another analogy that builds on... chess.

Sophia: Chess? How does that fit in?

Alex: Think of cybersecurity as a chess game. We are the defenders, and the cyber threat actors are our opponents. Now, here is the key difference, and the reason I mention we, as defenders, have the advantage as opposed to attackers. An advantage that many don't realize.

Sophia: What is that?

Alex: We have much greater visibility of our own chessboard, our IT landscape. The attackers only see a limited view of our defenses and assets, like a chess player who can only see the squares immediately around their pieces.

Sophia: I see, but what do you mean practically? Our IT landscape like cloud and on-premises?

Alex: Great question, and yes that's exactly right. We are not just playing on one chessboard, but on multiple boards at once. Each board represents a different part of our IT landscape.

Sophia: Multiple boards?! As in... multiple parts of the network?

Alex: Think of it like this. The "on-premises chessboard" is our traditional infrastructure. We have full control and visibility, like being able to see and move all our pieces freely. We know the layout of our network, our servers, and our endpoints well.

Alex: Then, the "cloud chessboard" is a bit different. We still have good visibility, but some of the squares are managed by our cloud provider. It's like having an ally who controls certain pieces and helps defend those areas. We need to coordinate with them, but it also means we have additional resources at our disposal.

Alex: And lastly, with the rise of remote work, we have the "remote work chessboard." This is a board that extends beyond our traditional perimeter. It's like having some of our pieces scattered on a larger board, making defense more challenging but also giving us a wider range of moves. And that in fact signals the end of the perimeter-based defenses.

Sophia: That's interesting. How does this multiple board scenario affect our advantage?

Alex: It enhances our advantage in some ways. On one hand, it makes our job more complex, but it also means we have a much broader view of the entire "game" than our opponents. We can see how moves on one board might affect another, and we can coordinate defenses across all our environments.

Alex: The attackers, on the other hand, might only see small portions of each board. They might find a vulnerability in our cloud environment, for instance, but not understand how it connects to our on-premises systems.

Sophia: So our challenge is managing all these boards effectively?

Alex: Exactly. Our advantage lies in our comprehensive view and the ability to coordinate across all these environments. But to maintain this advantage, we need robust monitoring, consistent security policies across all environments, and the ability to quickly respond to threats wherever they appear. It certainly is complex and might sound easy in theory, but it's also our great strength as defenders.

Sophia: That's an interesting perspective. But doesn't that advantage get negated as attackers probe and explore our network?

Alex: That's true. Attackers gain more information as they probe, but we still maintain the home field advantage. We know our systems, our vulnerabilities, and our critical assets far better than any attacker ever could. The question is, are we using that knowledge effectively?

Sophia: Indeed, but how do we leverage this advantage?

Alex: By combining our deep knowledge of our own environment with threat intelligence about potential attackers. It is like playing chess with the ability to anticipate several possible moves ahead.

Sophia: But we cannot predict everything. There is still a lot of uncertainty.

Alex: Correct, and that's a crucial point. We are not aiming for perfect prediction – that is impossible. Instead, we are looking to make the best possible decisions with the information we have and then continuously adjust our strategy as we learn more.

Sophia: So, it is about being adaptable?

Alex: Exactly. It's about creating a framework that allows us to make informed decisions in the face of uncertainty and then quickly course-correct as new information comes in.

Sophia: Okay, this all sounds good in theory, but how do we implement this in our day-to-day operations?

Alex: Let's break it down into practical steps. First, we need to improve our threat intelligence capabilities. This does not mean data collection simply; it means cutting out the "noise" produced by vast datasets online, creating actionable and valuable cyber threat intelligence and analyzing it in the context of our specific environment, thus producing a "signal" out of the noise.

Sophia: Okay, that makes sense. How do we go from having that pure, actionable, and valuable signal then?

Alex: Then we need to enhance our visibility into our own systems. This means not just knowing what assets we have, but understanding how they interconnect, what data flows between them, and where our critical points of failure might be.

Sophia: That sounds like a big and challenging undertaking.

Alex: It is, but it is crucial. Think of it as mapping out our chessboard in detail. The better we understand our own position, the more effectively we can defend it.

Sophia: But isn't that a typical asset-driven approach? Given the size of our organization, wouldn't that take years to achieve?

Alex: That is an excellent observation, and you're right, a traditional asset-driven approach would indeed take years and might never be fully accurate, given how quickly our IT landscape changes.

Sophia: So how do we overcome this challenge?

Alex: We shift our approach to being threat informed, which practically means, instead of trying to map every asset from the start, we use threat intelligence to guide our exploration. Let me give you an analogy to illustrate this.

Alex: Imagine you enter a completely dark square room. You know threat actors were previously there and left a hammer somewhere. The room is surrounded by benches along the walls, and you are looking for the hammer on one of these benches. However, there are also sharp items around that could cut you accidentally.

Sophia: Okay, I am picturing it. So, what is our traditional approach in this scenario?

Alex: The traditional asset-driven approach would be like systematically feeling your way around the room, touching every bench from left to right. You would eventually cover the entire room, but probably with lots of cuts along the way. More importantly, while you are doing this, cyber threat actors could enter the room and try to steal things from your pockets!

Sophia: That doesn't sound very efficient, nor safe, neither proactive. What's the alternative?

Alex: Instead, we enter the room being "threat informed." We know what the attackers did with the hammer, for instance, which wall they targeted, and what their goal was. Now we have a rough guide on where to start and what we are looking for, rather than taking a full left-to-right approach, searching on every bench and every possible tool.

Sophia: So, we are focusing our efforts based on threat intelligence?

Alex: Exactly. In our analogy, we might go straight to the right wall and check that there is no hole. If there is not, it means we have some coverage against an attack they tried to perform but failed. Something worked well against that attack, and that is how we start building visibility on both our assets and security controls much faster.

Sophia: I see. So, we are using threat intelligence to guide our exploration of our own environment, rather than trying to map everything at once.

Alex: Precisely. This approach helps us build confidence in our cyber defense much more quickly and efficiently. We are focusing our efforts where they matter most, based on real threat data.

Sophia: Sounds reasonable. Can you give me a real-world example of how this might work?

Alex: Let's say we receive threat intelligence about a new ransomware variant targeting companies in our industry. Instead of trying to assess every single system for vulnerability, we would focus on the specific attack vectors this ransomware uses. In other words, their tactics, techniques, and procedures (TTPs). We might check our email gateways, inspect our backup systems, and verify the patch levels of the specific software the ransomware exploits.

Sophia: And this gives us a more focused and efficient way to improve our defenses?

Alex: Not just improving our defenses blindly – we are doing it in a way that directly addresses real, current, and emerging threats. And in the process, we are learning more about our own environment in the areas that matter most.

Sophia: But how do we ensure we are not missing other key areas, while we focus on these specific threats?

Alex: That's where the cyber resilience index comes in. It provides a framework for measuring and managing all these elements in a cohesive way. But before we get into that, there is one more critical aspect of dealing with uncertainty that we need to discuss to set the stage for the CRI properly.

Sophia: Okay, what is that?

Alex: The concept of known unknowns and unknown unknowns. Understanding this distinction is crucial for an effective cybersecurity strategy.

Sophia: Known unknowns and unknown unknowns... right. You have given me a lot to think about.

Alex: Sounds complicated? It is rather simple. Understanding these concepts, we will be better equipped to navigate the inherent uncertainty in cybersecurity and make more effective strategic decisions. Let me explain...

Known Unknowns and Unknown Unknowns

Alex: In cybersecurity, known unknowns are the threats or vulnerabilities we are aware exist, but we do not have complete information about.

Sophia: Please give me an example.

Alex: We know that zero-day vulnerabilities exist in software we use, but we don't know exactly what they are or when they will be discovered. That's a known unknown.

Sophia: I see. And how about unknown unknowns?

Alex: Unknown unknowns are the threats we do not even know exist. These are the surprising attacks or vulnerabilities that we could not have anticipated. It might also be a novel reaction of adversaries against a specific IT landscape or, following our chess analogy, against a custom chessboard.

Alex: We may use cyber threat intelligence and observe that eight out of ten times adversaries behave in a certain way and follow specific TTPs; however, given the individualities of each IT landscape, there are chances for novel reactions that we do not know.

Sophia: Like the next big cybersecurity incident that no one sees coming, right?

Alex: Hm, kind of; think about the SolarWinds attack. Before it was discovered, it was an unknown unknown for most organizations. Who could imagine that adversaries would use the supply chain as a way of breaching into organizations seemingly secure in the first place? Or think of a ransomware threat actor who is in possession of tooling capable of encrypting VMware-based machines, yet when they presented with Citrix-based machines, they adapted, evolved, and succeeded during uncertainty.

Sophia: Okay, I understand the distinction. How does this knowledge help us in practical terms?

Alex: Understanding these concepts helps us approach our cybersecurity strategy more comprehensively. For known unknowns, we can prepare and allocate resources more effectively and efficiently.

Sophia: How so?

Alex: Take our earlier example of zero-day vulnerabilities. We know they exist, so we implement strategies like robust patch management, network segmentation, and principle of least privilege. These helps mitigate the risk even if we do not know the specific vulnerabilities. They are general, overall good cybersecurity hygiene so to speak.

Sophia: Indeed, that makes sense. But what about unknown unknowns? How can we prepare for something we do not even know exists?

Alex: That is where resilience comes in. We cannot predict unknown unknowns, but we can build systems and processes that are adaptable and resilient to a wide range of potential threats.

Sophia: Tell me more about. Perhaps an example?

Alex: Certainly. Let's say we implement a robust incident response plan and regularly practice it, considering the individualities of our IT landscape. At the same time, we consider that adversaries will make small adjustments, if those adjustments serve their goal. This prepares us to respond effectively to a wide range of incidents, even those we have not specifically anticipated.

Alex: So, it's about thinking an entire end-to-end scenario, from the pawn opening till checkmate. A winning sequence in chess, rather than simply calculating an isolated move. There is a big difference here.

Sophia: Got it, so if we have the cyber intel and we can anticipate attack scenarios, then it becomes a matter of building interoperable cybersecurity capabilities rather than isolated defenses in silos, right?

Alex: Exactly. It is about building an interoperable cybersecurity value chain. The faster we can anticipate, withstand, and recover from new threats and their potential attack scenarios, the better we can manage our attack surface, our exposure to unknown unknowns, and evolve further.

Sophia: This all sounds good, but how do we balance our efforts between known unknowns and unknown unknowns? We cannot focus on everything equally.

Alex: That's where a unified metric becomes imperative. That's one of the key notions of the cyber resilience index. To be used as a guiding tool continually assessing our confidence in our security control effectiveness, prioritize our efforts, and allocate resources accordingly.

Sophia: And I suppose this is where threat intelligence plays a crucial role?

Alex: Threat intelligence helps us turn unknown unknowns into known unknowns and known unknowns into known knowns. It is a continual process of increasing our awareness and understanding.

Sophia: Okay, I am starting to see how this all fits together. But it still seems like a huge challenge to manage all of this effectively.

Alex: It's a challenge, yes, but that's precisely why we need a comprehensive framework like the cyber resilience index. It helps us manage these different types of uncertainties in a structured and repeatable way.

Sophia: I can see how this understanding could reshape our approach. So, how does the cyber resilience index incorporate these concepts?

Alex: Before we start discussing the cyber resilience index in detail, we need to understand the evolving battlefield of today's cybersecurity landscape. This will provide us with the foundation necessary to genuinely appreciate how the cyber resilience index can transform our approach.

Sophia: Alright, I am listening carefully. Let's talk about this evolving battlefield then.

Sophia: (Interrupting with a sigh) Oh, come on, Alex. Not the "evolving cyber landscape and threats" speech again. I've heard that a million times through countless pitches and sales meetings. Can we skip the usual doom and gloom?

Alex: (Smiling) I promise this isn't your typical fear-driven session. Bear with me for a moment. Remember when we thought a strong firewall was all we needed? It was like believing a moat around our castle would keep all the dragons out.

Sophia: (Rolling her eyes, but with a hint of amusement) And let me guess, now the dragons have learned to fly?

Alex: More like they've learned to teleport, shape-shift, and disguise themselves as our own knights. Our data now resides everywhere, and we've moved into borderless networks. That castle-and-moat approach is about as effective as bringing a catapult to a drone fight.

Sophia: Okay, you've piqued my interest. So, if we're not just building higher walls, what are we doing?

The Evolving Battlefield: Today's Cybersecurity Landscape

Alex: I will answer that, but, first, think of this digital battlefield as a chess game, where the board keeps expanding, and new pieces with different moves are constantly being introduced.

Sophia: Okay, never thought of it like that... How can we keep up with such a dynamic environment?

Alex: That's exactly the main challenge. The pace of technological change nowadays is relentless. Every technology we adopt is like adding a new square to our chessboard. It provides us with a new square to move our pieces on and enables us to develop out strategy further, but since it can be used or abused by our opponents, it also expands our attack surface.

Sophia: Like our recent move to cloud services and the increase in remote work?

Alex: Precisely. These changes have brought enormous benefits, but they have also introduced new vulnerabilities. Our data and systems are no longer confined within our physical perimeter. Thus, the old "castle-and-moat" model of cybersecurity is... obsolete.

Sophia: So, we cannot just build a wall around our assets anymore? That's what you are saying, right?

11

Alex: You got it. It is more like we are playing chess on multiple boards simultaneously, with pieces that can move between boards. That's why we need a more flexible, proactive, and adaptive approach, rather than reactive.

Sophia: And this makes traditional security approaches less effective?

Alex: Correct. We are not just defending a single castle anymore, where we could rely on guards monitoring a gate and some entry points, hoping that detection will be enough to save the castle. Mind you, I am not saying detection is not needed. We are protecting a distributed kingdom with multiple access points; therefore, a proactive and adaptive approach would be far more beneficial than simply a reactive one relying primarily on a security operations center focused on detect and respond.

Sophia: So, what are the biggest threats we are facing in this new landscape?

Alex: One notable change is the increasing sophistication of threat actors. But it is important we do not fall into the trap of being fear driven.

Sophia: What do you mean by that?

Alex: Well, there is a lot of talk about Advanced Persistent Threats (APTs) and nation-state actors. While these are real concerns, we need to be careful not to overhype them.

Sophia: So, we shouldn't worry about APTs?

Alex: It is not that we shouldn't worry, but we need to be data driven and context-aware. Let me give you an analogy. If the police reported a group of sophisticated burglars targeting homes with gold in the backyard, what is the first thing we should ask ourselves?

Sophia: Do we have gold? Oh wait, do we even have a backyard first?

Alex: Exactly! We shouldn't rush to install expensive security systems if we don't fit the target profile. The same applies in cybersecurity. We need to understand our specific context, risks, exposure, and attack surface.

Sophia: That makes sense. So how do we cut through the noise and focus on what is relevant to us?

Alex: That is where cyber threat intelligence comes in. We need to analyze the threats in the context of our specific environment. It is about producing meaningful signals from the noise as I previously mentioned.

Sophia: And I suppose this helps us avoid overspending due to fear or misjudging our security controls?

Alex: Precisely. We want to avoid both under-trusting and over-trusting our security measures. It is about finding the right balance based on data and facts.

Sophia: Okay, I see the importance of being data driven and context-aware. What other major shifts should we be aware of?

Alex: A crucial change is the shift away from centralized, perimeter-based defenses. Our workforce is distributed globally; we are using cloud services, and our networks are borderless.

Sophia: How does this impact our defensive strategy?

Alex: It means we need to be as flexible and adaptive as our adversaries. Recent threat intelligence shows that attackers are becoming more cloud-aware. They are pivoting between cloud and on-premises environments.

Sophia: So, we need to be able to defend across all these environments?

Alex: Exactly. We need to think beyond traditional network boundaries. Our chess pieces, if you will, need to be able to move and adapt just as flexibly as the attackers.'

Sophia: This all sounds quite complex. How can we possibly manage all of these moving parts effectively?

Alex: That is where the cyber resilience index comes in again, remember? The ultimate guiding tool. It is designed to help us navigate this complex, rapidly changing environment. It provides a framework for assessing and improving our overall cyber resilience, not just our compliance or our ability to prevent known threats.

Sophia: And how does it help us stay ahead of the attackers?

Alex: The cyber resilience index helps us in understanding our environment, anticipating potential moves, and being prepared to respond quickly and effectively. Just like in chess, we are trying to think several moves ahead. Following the index's signals, we become proactive rather than reactive.

Sophia: Alright, I am convinced that our current approach might not be sufficient for this new landscape; however, I want to hear more about how this cyber resilience index can help us address these challenges. That's still not clear to me.

Introducing the Cyber Resilience Index (CRI)

Alex: The cyber resilience index is a comprehensive metric that quantifies an organization's ability to prepare for, respond to, and recover from cyber threats. It is not just about prevention or detection alone – it's about overall cyber resilience.

Sophia: Okay, that sounds ambitious. How does it work exactly? You got me hanging. Tell me more about it.

Alex: It is composed of several key components. It starts with cyber threat intelligence as the primary input – although not explicitly and I will tell you more about other inputs later on – then our security control effectiveness follows, our incident response readiness, and our ability to recover from attacks. Each of these high-level areas is assessed and scored.

Sophia: How is this different from our current security metrics?

Alex: Unlike traditional metrics that often focus on compliance or the number of prevented attacks, number of detected attacks, number of incidents, and so forth, the cyber resilience index provides a holistic view of our cybersecurity posture. It helps us understand not just where we are, but where we need to improve and how we can do that.

Sophia: Okay, sounds much like a bird's-eye view metric, right? What are the main objectives of implementing that index?

Alex: Correct. The primary objectives are to improve our overall cyber resilience, enable data-driven decision-making, and provide a clear, actionable metric for both technical teams and executive leadership.

Sophia: A single metric that serves both executive leaderships and operational teams... that sounds incredibly ambitious, maybe even unrealistic. But I am curious for now; how does it incorporate threat intelligence?

Alex: Threat intelligence is the primary input and therefore a crucial component of the resilience index. It informs our understanding of the threat landscape and helps us prioritize our efforts. The index then based on this intelligence and against our existing security control effectiveness reflects and adjusts scores while highlighting areas of emerging risk and points for improvement for our defenses.

Sophia: I appreciate the explanation, but I am not entirely convinced. So, how on earth does this influence our decision-making processes?!

Alex: Because it becomes the bird's-eye view metric and the key input for strategic decisions. For instance, if it's trending downward, it means that there are certain areas for improvement in our defenses. If it's trending upward, it means we are doing something well; however, that could change anytime according to the cyber threat landscape. Moreover, even if it's trending upward, there is always room for improvement, right? Ultimately, it helps us allocate resources more effectively, prioritize security initiatives, and make informed risk management decisions.

Sophia: Okay, now I get it. It is intriguing, but how do we avoid that index becoming a black box that obscures important details?

Alex: Excellent question. The goal is for the index to be a tool that everyone understands and can use effectively, not a mysterious number handed down from on high. That said, we are committed to fill transparency in how the index works. Everyone is onboarded on the idea of score calculation, not just reading the final score. Meaning, we have documented and shared the entire calculation process, we are conducting workshops for all teams involved, and our reports break down the index into its constituent parts, showing how each area contributes to the overall score.

Sophia: Okay, that is good to know, but earlier, we talked about known and unknown threats. I am curious about that. How does the resilience index address these? Where is the connection with those notions?

Alex: That's one of the key strengths of the resilience index. For known threats, it assesses our specific controls and preparedness. For unknown threats, it evaluates our overall resilience and adaptability. This dual approach helps us prepare for both types of challenges.

Sophia: And how scalable and adaptable is the resilience index itself? We both know very well that our organization is constantly changing, similarly to the cyber threat landscape.

Alex: The index is designed to be highly adaptable. It can be customized to fit organizations of different sizes and industries. As our organization evolves, the index can be adjusted to reflect new technologies, business processes, or threat landscapes.

Sophia: This sounds like... too good to be true? What are the caveats or potential challenges in implementing something like this? What are some potential hurdles we might face?

Alex: Well, you are right to ask about challenges. The main ones tend to be initial data collection to build our own security baseline, getting buy-in across the organization, seamlessly uniting our people and thereby capabilities to form a cyber value chain, and lastly maintaining this way of working over a period of time. However, there are strategies to address each of these potential hurdles...

Sophia: Hm, I presumed something as good as such wouldn't come easy. This is a lot to grasp right now. The cyber resilience index sounds powerful, but also complex. I'm still curious, nonetheless. How do we get started with something so potentially powerful like this?

Alex: Implementing the cyber resilience index is a journey, not a destination. In principle, we would set up a solid cyber threat intelligence capability, continue by assessing our current state, defining our key risk areas, set upper and lower thresholds for the index, and gradually building out our measurement and improvement processes. The key is to start small, show value quickly, and expand from there.

Sophia: This is fascinating, but I am still trying to wrap my head around how we quantify something as complex as cyber resilience into a single index.

Alex: I understand and let me draw an analogy that might help. Think of the cyber resilience index as the equivalent of a stock market index, but for cybersecurity.

Sophia: Like the S&P 500?

Alex: Exactly! Just as the S&P 500 tracks the performance of 500 large companies in the Unites States, the CRI tracks our performance against key cyber threats.

Sophia: Aha! Interesting. How exactly does that work in cybersecurity though?

Alex: We focus on the top 5 threats applicable to our organization, and the corresponding top 10 threat actors per threat. We then measure our cyber resilience against these threats and their respective threat actors while also measuring and validating our confidence in our existing cybersecurity controls.

Sophia: Okay, so it's not just about having controls in place, but about how effective they are against specific and applicable to us threats and the respective threat actors?

Alex: Precisely. Now, imagine the Bitcoin price chart. When it goes up, a trader might want to sell and take profits. If it goes down, traders might want to buy more or cut their losses, depending on their risk tolerance, right?

Sophia: I am not a professional trader, but yes, these are fundamentals that I am aware of. How does this apply to our cyber resilience index?

Alex: If our index goes up in points, it means our validated resilience is improving. This in turn informs decisions about investments in security tools, telemetry, or people hiring, adjustments in budget, and so forth. On the other hand, if the index goes down, it might signal a need to re-prioritize work, invest in different technologies, build new processes, increase budget, or simply refine our value chain way of working.

Sophia: I see. So, we are using this bird's-eye view resilience index to track our overall resilience and for ongoing decision-making, not just a one-time assessment?

Alex: Exactly. Like the S&P 500 index, the housing market index, or any other chart, we would want to see it increasing in the long term, even if there are short-term dips.

Sophia: What might cause a dip?

Alex: It could be a new threat actor emerging with a novel TTP, targeting our company or sector. But even such event that would naturally cause a dip because we have still not assessed our resilience against that novel threat vector is valuable information. It will help us improve our decision-making and ultimately increase our cyber resilience.

Sophia: This all sounds impressive and great in theory. But do you have any real-world example of how you and your teams leverage the resilience index so far? Perhaps you had a pilot run or a minimum viable product?

Alex: Yes, we have. Let me briefly share the results of a case study we did some months ago with you. I was planning to do an official pitch to you on the matter, but since we are having a nice dialogue and momentum here, I believe it will not overwhelm you, rather help you grasp the bigger picture.

Alex: As you already know, our number one priority and problem to solve is prioritizing our cybersecurity investments and measuring the effectiveness of our cybersecurity program. Therefore, the cyber resilience index was put to the test.

Alex: We started by identifying the top 5 threats applicable for us, namely, ransomware, supply chain attacks, insider threat, distributed denial of service (DDoS) attacks, and cloud to on-premises pivoting. For each threat, we identified the top 10 threat actors and analyzed thoroughly their modus operandi. For instance, for ransomware, Lockbit, BlackBasta, Cl0p, and other infamous threat actors made it to our top 10.

Alex: Next, we assessed our existing security controls and measured their effectiveness against these specific threats and threat actors. We created a scoring system that weighted each threat based on its potential impact on the business and, lastly, implemented continuous monitoring and regular reassessments to keep the score of the index up to date.

Sophia: Okay, that's a nice one-minute pitch. It doesn't sound that complex anymore. What were your results?

Alex: Within six months, we had a clear, quantifiable measure of our cyber resilience. We identified critical gaps in defenses against supply chain attacks, which we hadn't previously prioritized. Reallocating resources based on the cyber resilience index helped us improve the cyber resilience score by 27% in the first year! We also saved two million euros annually from security-related investments that would not be the best choices to mitigate Lockbit-related issues, but we could address them equally well by refining specific configurations in our IT and security telemetry.

Alex: Moreover, when a new ransomware strain emerged, targeting financial institutions, we were able to quickly assess our readiness and make necessary adjustments. We are left at this stage now, where the cyber resilience index can become a key metric in board meetings, helping you and the rest of the leaders to justify cybersecurity investments and demonstrate progress.

Sophia: Sound like there is value in such results, but I am concerned about the real-world issues that might arise. So, tell me, did you face any challenges? I still have my doubts if that is scalable.

Alex: Initial data collection was time-consuming. We had to overcome skepticism from some departments about the value of the new approach, which was mostly... resistance to change. Collaboration and prioritization of backlogs was another issue for the teams to work seamlessly. And lastly, keeping the threats and threat actors list updated required ongoing effort and collaboration with our threat intelligence team.

Sophia: That is a compelling example and a solid list of challenges to solve onward. I can see how this could be transformative for our own cybersecurity strategy, and, although I am not entirely convinced, I believe it is worth exploring further. But tell me, how does this tie back to the chess analogy we've been using?

Alex: I thought you've already forgotten the chess analogies! It's an excellent question. There is a vital connection that will help us understand how the resilience index can guide our strategic thinking in cybersecurity. Shall we grab a coffee and continue?

The Chess Analogy: Strategy in Cybersecurity

Alex: So, in chess, the board represents the battlefield. In our case, it's our entire digital landscape – our networks, systems, data, and even our users.

Sophia: What you are saying is that our security controls are like the chess pieces?

Alex: Not only our security controls but also our security capabilities. Different security measures are like different chess pieces, each with their own strengths and ways of operating. The same applies for our teams and capabilities. Firewalls, for instance, might be like rooks, defending in straight lines, while endpoint protection could be like knights, able to bypass obstacles but also be bypassed...

Sophia: Interesting. So, what would be the equivalent of making a move in chess?

Alex: In cybersecurity, our moves are the actions we take to defend our assets or respond to threats. For instance, we could implement a new security control, patch a vulnerability, or respond to an incident.

Sophia: And the attacker's moves would be their attempts to breach our defenses?

Alex: Precisely. Just like in chess, we need to anticipate the attacker's moves and plan our strategy accordingly. This is where the resilience index comes in handy.

Sophia: How so?

Alex: The index helps us understand our "position" on the cybersecurity chessboard. It gives us a clear picture of our strengths and vulnerabilities, much like a chess player assessing their position on the board.

Sophia: Then, thinking several moves ahead is crucial in both chess and cybersecurity, right?

Alex: Spot on. In chess, grandmasters think many moves ahead, considering multiple possible scenarios. In cybersecurity, we need to do the same. The cyber resilience index helps us achieve the same. It serves as a framework for assessing potential future threats and our readiness to face them or recover from them if needed.

Sophia: That makes sense. But knowing little about chess, sometimes I know that you must sacrifice pieces to gain an advantage. How does that translate to cybersecurity?

Alex: That's a great observation, and indeed a common phenomenon in chess. In cybersecurity, we often must make trade-offs. We might need to sacrifice some convenience or performance to enhance security or the other way around. The index helps us make these decisions by quantifying and visualizing the impact on our overall resilience in a simple chart.

Sophia: Okay, I'm following. So, in short, the index helps us plan ahead and prioritize.

Sophia: But in chess, there's a clear endgame – checkmate. What's the endgame in cybersecurity?

Alex: In cybersecurity, our "endgame" is achieving and maintaining a strong security posture. You cannot win once, do a checkmate, for example, and consider it a final win. It's about continuous improvement and adaptation, so I would better call it a never-ending game instead. The resilience index, however, helps us track our progress and ensures we are in control during this never-ending game, at all times.

Sophia: Aha... now I can see how this analogy helps put things in perspective. But how does the CRI help us adapt to changing threats? In chess, the rules don't change mid-game.

Alex: That's where cybersecurity is even more challenging than chess. The "rules" are constantly changing as new threats emerge. The index helps us stay adaptable by continuously updating our understanding of the threat landscape and our resilience against it.

Sophia: This is fascinating. How do we put this into practice? How do we start thinking like chess grandmasters in our cybersecurity strategy?

Alex: Firstly, I am glad to hear that you might be convinced and want us to apply chess-like strategic thinking to our cybersecurity approach using the resilience index as our guide.

Sophia: Well, I am not convinced yet, so don't get too excited. But it certainly sounds very promising, and I see the value. Perhaps we should take a break to play a game of chess; I want to check your theoretical and practical skills.

Alex: Good idea! But first, some chess theory, let's consider the concept of "board control" in chess. In cybersecurity, this translates to having visibility and control over our entire digital landscape.

Sophia: "Board control" sounds interesting. Reminds me of the executive, but okay let's talk about the chessboard; how do we achieve that board control?

Alex (smiling): Well, the resilience index will certainly help you communicate with the executive board! The equivalent of achieving chessboard control here is like providing a comprehensive view of our assets, threats, and controls. It's like having a bird's-eye view of the chessboard, while the opponent only sits with a limited view somewhere in the back ranks. We use this concept to identify areas where we have strong "control" and areas where we're vulnerable.

Sophia: Can you give me a concrete example?

Alex: Let's say our resilience index shows that we have strong perimeter defenses, although we discussed that there is no perimeter nowadays, but for the sake of the analogy – that's like controlling the edges of the chessboard. But it also reveals that we're weak in detecting lateral movement within our network – that's like having poor control of the center of the board.

Sophia: So how do we use this information?

Alex: Just as a chess player would move pieces to strengthen their position in the center, we would allocate resources to improve our ability to detect and prevent lateral movement. This might involve implementing network segmentation or enhancing our internal monitoring capabilities by building specific, tailor-made detection rules against threat actor's tactics, techniques, and procedures (TTPs).

Sophia: I like this concept; it makes sense, as visibility is key. What other chess strategies does the cyber resilience index bring?

Alex: Another key concept is the "initiative." In chess, having the initiative means you're forcing your opponent to respond to your moves, rather than executing their own plan.

Sophia: How does that work in cybersecurity?

Alex: In our context, having the initiative means being proactive rather than reactive. The cyber resilience index helps us here by highlighting potential future threats based on current trends and our specific vulnerabilities.

Sophia: Intriguing concept, can you give me an example?

Alex: Let's say our threat intelligence, which serves as the primary input for the resilience index, indicates a rising trend in supply chain attacks within our industry. Instead of waiting to be targeted, we take the initiative. We might conduct a thorough threat intelligence–based security assessment (TIBSA) of our supply chain, implement stricter vendor security requirements, or even redesign our systems to be more resilient to this type of attacks.

Sophia: The more I hear about this proactive approach, the more I understand it. Is there more to it?

Alex: Another chess concept is "tempo." In chess, tempo refers to the time it takes to make a strong move. Losing the tempo means wasting a move, giving your opponent the advantage.

Sophia: How does this apply to us?

Alex: In cybersecurity, tempo relates to how quickly we can respond to threats or implement improvements. The resilience index helps us maintain a good "tempo," because we can prioritize our actions based on their impact on our overall cyber resilience. Therefore, increasing our accuracy of decisions, meaning achieving effectiveness and efficiency.

Sophia: That's a very interesting and relevant concept. Can you elaborate on that?

Alex: Let's say we've identified ten potential security improvements against an ineffective or inefficient security control, which is in place to mitigate a set of TTPs. The resilience index helps us calculate which of these ten improvements will have the biggest impact on our resilience score. We thereby focus on the highest-impact changes first, ensuring we're making the most of every "move" or action we take. How does that sound?

Sophia: That's helpful for prioritization and sounds exactly what we need for data-driven decision-making. Perhaps we could use that notion in our next objectives and key results (OKR) planning session. Any other chess strategies we should consider?

Alex: Excellent idea. Drafting OKRs based on the cyber resilience index is one of the best use cases. One more crucial concept, however, is the "positional play" versus "tactical play." In chess, positional play means making moves that gradually improve your position, while tactical play means short-term combinations and attacks.

Sophia: And in cybersecurity?

Alex: In our world, positional play means gradually building our overall cyber resilience by making the best available strategic, tactical, or operational decisions. This might be long-term projects like improving our security culture or implementing a comprehensive identity and access management system. Tactical play, on the other hand, means responding to immediate threats or vulnerabilities, directly addressing a specific TTP by a threat actor.

Sophia: So, the cyber resilience index helps in balancing these, oftentimes, difficult decisions. How is that possible though?

Alex: The resilience index gives us a framework to balance both, indeed. It helps us to track our long-term resilience improvements while also highlighting immediate risks that need tactical responses. It's like a chess player who's working toward a strong overall position while still staying alert for tactical opportunities or threats.

Sophia: That's insightful and impressive. Thinking like a chess player could really elevate our cybersecurity strategy. But here's where I disagree with you. There's one key difference – in chess, you can see all the pieces on the board. In cybersecurity, there's so much uncertainty. Much like as you described.

Alex: That's an excellent point, and you're right, but that's where the cyber resilience index emerges. It helps us make informed decisions even in the face of uncertainty. Remember how we talked about known unknowns and unknown unknowns?

Sophia: Yes, I do.

Alex: Well, the resilience index is designed to help us navigate both. For the known unknowns, it helps us assess and prepare for potential threats we're aware of but don't fully understand. For the unknown unknowns, it helps us build general resilience that in turn helps us respond to unexpected situations.

Sophia: I see. So, it's not about having perfect information and therefore making perfect decisions, but about being as prepared as possible and making decisions with the information we have?

Alex: Exactly! It's about making the best moves we can, based on our current understanding of the "board," while always working to improve that understanding.

Sophia: I'm intrigued. What else does the resilience index brings that's inspired from chess?

Alex: Let's talk about the concept of "zugzwang" in chess. It's a situation where any move a player makes will worsen their position.

Sophia: Hm, that sounds unpleasant. How does this relate to cybersecurity?

Alex: In cybersecurity, we sometimes face situations where every action has potential downsides. For instance, if we discover a critical vulnerability in a key system, we might face a choice between immediate patching, which could disrupt operations, or delaying the patch and risking exploitation.

Sophia: But why do I need an index for that? Why can't I just do a typical risk assessment, or even a quantitative one, and be done with it? I would still be able to make a solid decision.

Alex: Indeed, that's how we used to make decisions up until recently, primarily with asset-driven or vulnerability-driven defenses. With the threat-informed defense and the implementation of the cyber resilience index, we can perform a much better assessment of the situation because we're not looking at it as an isolated event, but rather as a sequence of events. It's much like calculating a chess sequence leading up to checkmate, rather than a single move from square to square.

Sophia: Interesting analogy. How does this change our perspective?

Alex: It's like looking from above with a drone and having an overview of the entire battlefield, thus giving you the advantage of foresight, rather than staying on the ground where you can only see a few meters around you. Eventually, your assessment will be much more strategically, tactically, and even operationally accurate.

Sophia: So you're saying the resilience index gives us a more comprehensive view of our cybersecurity landscape?

Alex: Exactly. It allows us to make decisions that are not just reactive, but proactive and aligned with our overall security strategy. Moreover, the index helps us quantify the impact of each option on our overall resilience. It allows us to make data-driven decisions even in the toughest situations, choosing the option that best maintains our security posture.

Sophia: I see. That's helpful. Are there any other chess concepts we should consider perhaps?

Alex: Yes, the concept of "prophylaxis" in chess. It's a move that prevents the opponent from taking a specific action.

Sophia: And in cybersecurity?

Alex: Prophylaxis is about anticipatory defense. It's taking actions not just to address current vulnerabilities, but to prevent future attacks. The resilience index helps us identify areas where we might be vulnerable to emerging threats, enabling us to implement preventive measures before those threats materialize.

Sophia: What would be an example?

Alex: If our threat intelligence, for instance, indicates a rise in attacks exploiting misconfigured cloud services, our current exposure and security control effectiveness will be assessed, measured, and visualized in the cyber resilience index. In this specific case, we would expect a dip in the trendline on the specific threat actor's TTPs. Thus, we might proactively review and harden the relevant cloud configurations to increase our effectiveness and thereby increase our overall resilience, even if we haven't been targeted yet. That's anticipatory defense.

Sophia: That's insightful and proactive. I am wondering if there's more.

Alex: One last very important concept. In chess, strong players often talk about "playing the board, not the player." This means focusing on making the best moves based on the position, rather than trying to guess what your opponent is thinking.

Sophia: Interesting one, and I have heard it before. But how does that translate to cybersecurity?

Alex: In our field, it means focusing on building strong, resilient systems and processes, rather than trying to predict every possible attack. The index helps us do this by providing a comprehensive view of our security posture and attack surface, allowing us to make improvements that enhance our overall resilience, regardless of the specific threats we might face.

Alex: For instance, have you heard before of MITRE ATT&CK?

Sophia: Yes, quite a few times. I think lately it's being referred to more and more as the "golden standard"?

Alex: Correct, briefly that means a curated knowledge base and model for cyber adversary behavior, reflecting the various phases of an adversary's attack life cycle and the platforms they are known to target. The tactics and techniques abstraction in the model provide a common taxonomy of individual adversary actions understood by both of our offensive and defensive teams. It also provides an appropriate level of categorization for adversary action and specific ways of defending against it.

Alex: Now, imagine our detect, prevent, and respond capabilities' coverage against the MITRE ATT&CK adversary knowledge base, all scoring high numbers, except in lateral movement. In this case, regardless of the opponent we could choose to improve our position there, if the time and resources allow, following the notion of playing the overall board rather than the player.

Sophia: That makes a lot of sense. It means we should be prepared for anything, rather than just trying to guess the next attack, right?

Alex: Exactly! And that's why the need for a unified metric becomes imperative. The cyber resilience index gives us that comprehensive view we need to "play the board" effectively in cybersecurity.

Sophia: Alright, I'm ready to hear more about this unified metric. These chess analogies really helped me understand our cybersecurity strategy in a new light. I can slowly see how the cyber resilience index could be a powerful tool for guiding our decision-making.

Alex: I'm glad it's helpful, and remember, just like in chess, mastery comes with practice. As we use the index and apply these strategic principles, we'll get better at anticipating threats, responding effectively, and continuously improving our cybersecurity posture. Having said that, how about we set up a session to review the cyber resilience index and identify our priorities?

Sophia: Sounds great, but tell me more about why we need a unified metric first.

The Need for a Unified Metric

Alex: Now that we've discussed the strategic aspects of cybersecurity, let me explain why we need a unified metric like the cyber resilience index.

Sophia: Sounds like a plan, but wait, I must ask first – why isn't our current set of metrics sufficient and we need a unified one?

Alex: Right now, we have a bunch of different metrics for various aspects of our cybersecurity. Perhaps, some of those are in busy Power BI dashboards here and there; some are lost throughout different Excel sheets, SharePoint, PowerPoints, different tooling and security telemetry, and so on and so forth. It's like trying to solve a puzzle with pieces from different sets. Each piece is valuable, but they don't quite fit together to give us the bigger picture.

Sophia: I see the pain point here, and in all honesty, you are not wrong. It is something that I am thinking from time to time as well, but it's hard to see the forest from the trees sometimes.

Alex: Exactly. A unified metric like the cyber resilience index gives us that bird's-eye view of the forest. It's like having a drone that can show us the entire landscape, not just individual trees, thereby guiding successfully the entire threat-informed defense approach in a fact-based manner.

Sophia: Okay, I can see how that could be useful. But cybersecurity is complex, and you know that as well – do you think that only one number really captures everything?

Alex: Look, the CRI doesn't replace our detailed metrics – it's more like the executive summary that ties everything together. It's designed to give us a high-level view that's informed by all those nitty-gritty details.

Sophia: Hmm, I see... I've been reading about different approaches to metrics lately. What are your thoughts on quantitative versus qualitative approaches? Each seems to have its pros and cons, but what is your take on the matter as an expert?

Alex: Indeed, there are few approaches and several opinions on the topic. Both approaches have their merits and shortcomings. Qualitative methods can provide rich, contextual information, but they can be subjective and hard to compare. Quantitative methods give us hard numbers, which are great for tracking progress, but they might miss nuances.

Sophia: So, which is better for cybersecurity?

Alex: My view is that we need both. That's why the resilience index uses a semi-quantitative approach. We quantify where we can, but we also incorporate qualitative assessments where needed. It's about finding that balance and leverage the best of both worlds.

Sophia: That makes sense. But still, I don't have a clear answer, why having this unified view is so crucial?

Alex: There are several reasons. First, it gives us a "common language" for cybersecurity across the organization. Instead of different departments speaking in their own metrics, everyone can work together, everyone can become part of the cyber value chain and start improving our overall cyber resilience score. At the end of the day, if we want to win in that uneven game against the cyber threat actors, we must seamlessly collaborate on people, process, and tooling levels.

Sophia: Indeed, that could help with alignment and perhaps streamline better our entire work within the whole cybersecurity division and beyond. What else though? You said "several" reasons.

Alex: It's also a game changer for decision-making and resource allocation. When we're deciding where to invest our cybersecurity budget, we can look at which initiatives will have the biggest positive impact on our resilience index. And that is multifaceted. Some simple detection rules might add, for instance, 200 points to our index, while investing a million euros for a new technology would increase our index by 250 points. Is that a good cost versus benefit ratio? What would you choose in this case? Is that a good return on investment or something acceptable? The cyber resilience index provides the foundation to have such dialogues based on facts and data.

Sophia: That sounds valuable. But how does this translate when we're talking to the board?

Alex: Because it allows us to speak the language of business and money. Cost versus benefit. We can show the board how our cybersecurity efforts are protecting and even creating monetary value for the company. How our cybersecurity value chain keeps the business in business.

Sophia: Now you're speaking my language! Can you give me a tangible example?

Alex: Let's say we're considering expanding our threat hunting team. With the cyber resilience index, we can quantify how much value that team is currently producing and project how much additional value the expansion would create. It's not just about preventing losses; it's about showing the positive impact on our bottom line.

Alex: Moreover, imagine someone from the executive board reading an article online stating "KillNet is preparing to launch the biggest ever distributed denial of service attack against western European banks"; what is their next action? I see you nodding; yes, you guessed correctly – you will be called immediately, right?

Sophia: Exactly.

Alex: How can you provide the executive board with reasonable assurance that we have done our utmost to be protected against this new wave of cyber-attacks? That's another reason why the unified metric is so powerful.

Sophia: That's indeed powerful. But it sounds like it could get complicated. How do we account for all the different parts of our cybersecurity operations to be captured in a single metric.

Alex: The cyber resilience index helps us understand our entire cyber value chain. For instance, we can see how much our threat hunting team contributes, how that impacts our SOC's ability to create detection rules, and how those detection rules enhance our overall resilience.

Sophia: So, it's not just about individual teams, but how they work together? Do I get that right?

Alex: Exactly. And to add to that, it helps us identify bottlenecks too. For example, if we increase our threat intelligence team's capacity, the resilience index sub-metrics might show us that our threat hunting and detection teams can't keep up with the increased workload. This insight helps us invest wisely across our entire cyber value chain.

Sophia: That could help us optimize our operations. But how does this fit with our broader business objectives?

Alex: The resilience index isn't just about technology. It's designed to align with our strategic business goals. Whether we're launching a new product and cybersecurity needs to be baked in or considering an acquisition, the index helps us understand the cybersecurity implications in business terms, translated into cost versus benefit versus required effort.

Sophia: Okay, I'm starting to see why you're so excited about this. Nonetheless, implementing a new metric like this seems like a big undertaking. How do we get started?

Alex: You are right; it is significant. But the benefits are substantial. We start by defining what factors contribute to our cyber resilience, then work on ways to measure and combine these factors into our cyber resilience index. We have already few sub-metrics and measurements in place helping the index; I can elaborate more on the sub-metrics later, if you are still interested.

Sophia: And I suppose once we have it in place, we can track our progress over time?

Alex: Yes, indeed; think of the resilience index like a stock market index for our cyber resilience. Just as traders use indices to make buy or sell decisions, we can use the cyber resilience index to make informed decisions about our cybersecurity investments, actions, and strategies.

Sophia: That's a helpful analogy; it really makes the point on how this could change our decision-making process.

Alex: Exactly, and instead of relying on assumptions or paper exercises, we're basing our decisions on hard data and validated security control effectiveness. We are making our cybersecurity as data driven as any other part of our business. Sometimes, explaining the cyber resilience index concept reminds me of how grandmasters evaluate chess positions. That's another parallel I could use.

Sophia: How so?

Alex: Look, in chess, players don't just count the number of pieces they have. They use a unified evaluation that takes into account piece position, king safety, pawn structure, and many other factors. The resilience index is similar – it's not just about counting our security tools or experts but evaluating our overall security posture altogether.

Sophia: That's an interesting parallel. So, the cyber resilience index is like our position evaluation in the cybersecurity chess game?

Alex: Spot on. And just like in chess, a good evaluation helps us make better moves. With the resilience index, we can make better strategic decisions about our cybersecurity.

Sophia: Okay, but in chess, different players might evaluate the same position differently. Isn't there a risk of subjectivity with the resilience index?

Alex: Indeed, much like in chess, there's always some element of judgment involved. But the index aims to be as objective as possible by using clearly defined criteria and data-driven assessments. It's like having a chess engine evaluate our position – it's based on algorithms and data, not just gut feeling.

Sophia: Okay, that makes sense. But I'm curious; are there any other benefits to having the resilience index as a unified metric that we haven't discussed perhaps?

Alex: Yes, one important aspect we haven't touched upon is how a unified metric can help with benchmarking.

Sophia: Benchmarking? Against what?

Alex: We can benchmark against our own historical performance. That's one of the... "best by test" ways to start building confidence on our security controls' effectiveness. Next, there is the standard way, which is to benchmark against industry standards and then discuss and compare with peer organizations, if they're using a similar framework.

Sophia: Interesting ideas. Both would be insightful for us to understand where we stand in the bigger picture.

Alex: Indeed, and here's another chess parallel. Chess players often compare their performance against rating systems like Elo, which is a method for calculating the relative strength of players in zero-sum games. The resilience index could serve a similar use case, but within the cybersecurity context. Therefore, it could become the standard cyber resilience benchmarking too, like the "Elo rating" for chess, but for cyber resilience.

Sophia: That's thought-provoking and would be indeed very useful. Perhaps we could start a working group on that!

Alex: To add to that, one more crucial point. The index can help us with scenario planning and predictive analysis.

Sophia: Oh wait, you lost me now; what does that mean?

Alex: Well, just like a chess player might think "If I move my knight here, how does that change my position?", we can use the cyber resilience index to model "If we implement this new security measure, how will it affect our overall resilience?" It allows us to play out different scenarios and see their potential impact, all visualized in a unified metric.

Sophia: Aha, that's powerful. Sounds like we're able to look a few moves ahead in our cybersecurity strategy.

Alex: Exactly! And in both chess and cybersecurity, the ability to think ahead and anticipate future scenarios is crucial for success.

Sophia: This all sounds promising, but how does this resilience index relate to other cybersecurity frameworks and approaches we've been using? Is there an overlap somewhere or a mismatch?

From CTEM to CRI: A New Approach

Alex: The cyber resilience index builds upon and enhances existing approaches like continuous threat exposure management (CTEM), which I am sure you have read a lot via Gartner. It is something we also have implemented and operationalized. In fact, I can tell you in all detail how we implemented Gartner's CTEM step by step and then enhanced it with the CRI later.

Sophia: Yes, that would be great. I recall we had an extensive CTEM program going on. How does the cyber resilience index fit into this? Is there an overlap?

Alex: CTEM has been a valuable approach, but the cyber resilience index takes it to the next level. CTEM helps us continuously evaluate our exposure to cyber threats. It has five stages: scoping, discovery, prioritization, validation, and mobilization. It's cyclical and helps us manage our attack surface, but it has some limitations.

Look at this picture to visualize it.

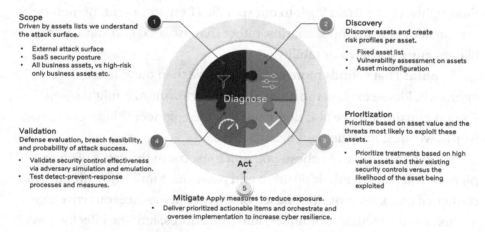

Scope
Driven by assets lists we understand the attack surface.

- External attack surface
- SaaS security posture
- All business assets, vs high-risk only business assets etc.

Discovery
Discover assets and create risk profiles per asset.

- Fixed asset list
- Vulnerability assessment on assets
- Asset misconfiguration

Diagnose

Prioritization
Prioritize based on asset value and the threats most likely to exploit these assets.

- Prioritize treatments based on high value assets and their existing security controls versus the likelihood of the asset being exploited

Validation
Defense evaluation, breach feasibility, and probability of attack success.

- Validate security control effectiveness via adversary simulation and emulation.
- Test detect-prevent-response processes and measures.

Act

Mitigate Apply measures to reduce exposure.
- Deliver prioritized actionable items and orchestrate and oversee implementation to increase cyber resilience.

Sophia: What kind of limitations?

Alex: First and foremost, CTEM is asset driven, as opposed to the cyber resilience index which is threat intelligence driven, which practically means that with the threat-intel driven approach, it's like studying your opponent's favorite openings in chess, rather than just memorizing general chess principles. In other words, instead of starting with our assets, we start with the threats and threat actors that are most relevant to our organization. It's like the difference between checking every door and window in your house versus knowing which ones a burglar is most likely to target.

Sophia: So how does this change our approach?

Alex: Instead of starting with a full inventory of our assets, we begin by understanding the threats most relevant to us. We merge the scoping and discovery phases into a single, more efficient process.

Sophia: So, we're not trying to protect every pawn on the board equally?

Alex: Exactly, no CISO or organization can allocate equal resources to protect everything evenly at once. We're prioritizing based on the opponent's most likely moves. And speaking of moves, the resilience index gives us a much more detailed playbook. We outline each phase and step thoroughly, contextualizing it to our specific IT environment. Remember, we consider end-to-end scenarios, rather than isolated and static moves like solving a single vulnerability.

Sophia: That sounds more comprehensive than our current approach. Please explain me more about prioritization. It might sound comprehensive, but we also don't need to overengineer things. Using your words, we must find the right balance here.

Alex: Great points. In chess, you don't just count the value of your pieces – you consider their position and potential. Similarly, with the cyber resilience index, we prioritize based on threat intelligence; our coverage against known tactics, techniques, and procedures; and the effectiveness of our existing controls.

Sophia: And how does this affect our validation process?

Alex: The validation phase itself is similar, but the outcomes are quite different. Instead of just identifying issues, we can now quantify them based on potential monetary impact. It's like assigning a precise value to each chess piece based on its current position and the state of the game. At the end of the day, the index should be used at all managerial and decision-making layers, even at the executive board level. Hence, we need that cost versus benefit analysis to be integrated and speak "your language." Have a look at the following figure to visualize how we are enhancing Gartner's CTEM with our cyber resilience index.

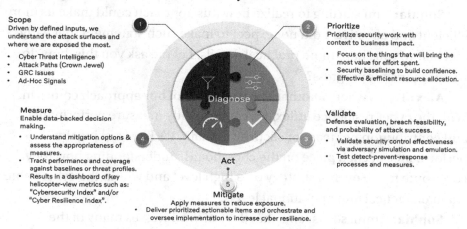

Scope
Driven by defined inputs, we understand the attack surfaces and where we are exposed the most.

- Cyber Threat Intelligence
- Attack Paths (Crown Jewel)
- GRC Issues
- Ad-Hoc Signals

Prioritize
Prioritize security work with context to business impact.

- Focus on the things that will bring the most value for effort spent.
- Security baselining to build confidence.
- Effective & efficient resource allocation.

Measure
Enable data-backed decision making.

- Understand mitigation options & assess the appropriateness of measures.
- Track performance and coverage against baselines or threat profiles.
- Results in a dashboard of key helicopter-view metrics such as: "Cybersecurity Index" and/or "Cyber Resilience Index".

Validate
Defense evaluation, breach feasibility, and probability of attack success.

- Validate security control effectiveness via adversary simulation and emulation.
- Test detect-prevent-response processes and measures.

Diagnose

Act

Mitigate
Apply measures to reduce exposure.
- Deliver prioritized actionable items and orchestrate and oversee implementation to increase cyber resilience.

Sophia: That sounds powerful for decision-making. How does this change our overall strategy?

Alex: It's a game changer indeed. We're introducing a unified metric for cybersecurity that both executives and technical teams can understand and act upon. It's like having a chess engine that not only evaluates your position but also suggests concrete improvements.

Sophia: And I suppose this affects how we prioritize our efforts?

Alex: Yes, our mitigation and prioritization are now based on this unified metric, underpinned by quantitative assessments, that we can reflect against risk tolerance and appetite. We're not just reacting to the opponent's last move; we're strategically positioning ourselves for the entire game.

Sophia: It sounds great, but it also sounds like a big shift. How do we manage this transition?

Alex: Truth be told, it is a significant change. But remember, we're not starting from scratch. We will still use our configuration management database (CMDB) initially to discover potentially impacted assets by threat, but we will achieve full visibility sequentially as dictated by the threat landscape. It's like gradually illuminating the chessboard, focusing on the most critical areas first.

Sophia: I am starting to realize how this approach could make us more efficient and effective. I did not expect to make such statement that early and before you share more practical details. Let me ask you this, how do we measure our progress?

Alex: That's where another key advantage of our approach comes in. With the cyber resilience index, we can explicitly measure performance and contribution per team or security domain. It's like tracking the performance of each piece on the chessboard, understanding how they contribute to the overall strategy on a high level and within the cyber value chain on tactical and operational levels.

Sophia: Hmm, so it seems that the index addresses many of the limitations we have experienced with CTEM. Is there anything else we should consider as we progress onward with the implementation of this approach?

Alex: A crucial point is how the index changes our risk management approach. Instead of relying on qualitative risk registers, we are moving to a quantitative model. It's like moving from subjective evaluations in chess to data-driven analysis.

Sophia: That could really help with getting buy-in from leadership. Speaking of which, how do we present this to the board?

Alex: That is where the unified metric really makes the difference and helps us to articulate our message better. We can now present a single, comprehensive measure of our cybersecurity posture that executives can easily understand. It is like giving them a clear score of our chess game, rather than trying to explain all the intricate positions on the board, avoiding all the technical jargon.

Sophia: Understood. So, what is our next move?

Alex: Sticking with our chess analogy, our next move is to assess our current position. Shall we perform a self-assessment exercise to see where we stand and where we need to focus our efforts?

Your Move: Self-Assessment Exercise

It's your move now dear reader! This self-assessment is designed to help you quickly evaluate your organization's current cybersecurity readiness for advanced approaches like continuous threat exposure management (CTEM) and the cyber resilience index (CRI). It's divided into six key areas, each with a scoring system and interpretation guide.

Instructions:

For each statement, rate your agreement on a scale of 1 to 5:

Strongly Disagree = 1 Point

Disagree = 2 Points

Neutral = 3 Points

Agree = 4 Points

Strongly Agree = 5 Points

Section 1: Threat Intelligence and Risk Management (50 points possible)	Score
We regularly consume and act upon threat intelligence.	
Threat intelligence is incorporated into our decision-making processes.	
We have a formal, regularly updated threat intelligence–based risk assessment process.	
We can quantify the potential financial impact of cyber incidents.	
Our risk assessments influence our security investments.	
We have a clear understanding of our most critical assets and data.	
We regularly assess our security posture against industry benchmarks.	

(continued)

We have processes to quickly adapt to new threat information.

Our threat intelligence covers both technical indicators and strategic trends.

We can translate threat intelligence into actionable security measures.

Total Score

Section 2: Asset and Vulnerability Management (50 points possible)   Score

We have a comprehensive, up-to-date inventory of all our digital assets, and we have confidence on our CMDB to identify our attack surface.

Our asset inventory includes cloud resources and shadow IT to the extent possible.

We continuously discover and assess new assets added to our network.

We have tools to identify vulnerabilities and misconfigurations.

We adopt a threat-based approach to vulnerability prioritization based on actual risk to our business and context.

We have processes to quickly patch or mitigate critical vulnerabilities.

We regularly review and update our security policies and procedures.

We have visibility into our entire attack surface, including third-party risks.

We can quickly assess the potential impact of newly disclosed vulnerabilities.

Our asset management processes are largely automated.

Total Score

Section 3: Security Control Effectiveness (50 points possible)   Score

We regularly test the effectiveness of our security controls.

We can quantify the impact of our security investments.

We have a process for continuously improving our security controls.

Section 3: Security Control Effectiveness (50 points possible)   Score

We use automation to test and validate our security controls' effectiveness.

We can quickly detect and respond to security incidents.

We have well-documented and regularly tested incident response plans.

We conduct regular tabletop exercises to test our response capabilities.

We have metrics to measure the effectiveness of our incident response.

We regularly conduct penetration testing or red team exercises.

We have a process for lessons learned after security incidents.

Total Score

Section 4: Metrics and Reporting (50 points possible)   Score

We have a set of clearly defined measurable security metrics.

Our metrics provide actionable insights for decision-making.

We can demonstrate the business value of our security investments.

We have an effective way to communicate security status to executives.

Our board of directors receives regular, understandable security updates.

We can quickly generate reports on our current security posture.

Our metrics cover both leading and lagging indicators of security.

We have a unified view of our security posture across all systems and assets.

We can track our security improvement over time with our metrics.

Our metrics help us predict and prevent future security issues.

Total Score

Section 5: Readiness for Advanced Approaches (50 points possible)   Score

We are familiar with the concept of continuous threat exposure management (CTEM).

We have processes in place that align with CTEM principles.

We can continuously assess our exposure to cyber threats.

We have a way to prioritize our security efforts being threat informed.

We can validate the effectiveness of our security measures against real-world threats.

We have a process for mobilizing resources to address identified security gaps.

We are considering or ready to implement more advanced security frameworks.

Our security approach is proactive rather than reactive.

We have executive support for advancing our cybersecurity approach.

Our team has the skills and resources to implement more advanced security strategies.

Total Score

Section 6: Cybersecurity Capabilities Interoperability (50 points possible)   Score

We have a clear understanding of how our different cybersecurity processes interact and depend on each other.

We have documented the inputs and outputs for each of our key cybersecurity processes (SIPOC or similar).

Our teams have common objectives (OKRs or similar) that encourage collaboration across different cybersecurity functions.

Section 6: Cybersecurity Capabilities Interoperability (50 points possible)   Score

We regularly assess and optimize the flow of information between different cybersecurity capabilities.

Our cybersecurity tools and platforms are well integrated, allowing for seamless data sharing.

We have established clear handoff procedures between different cybersecurity teams and processes.

Our threat intelligence feeds directly into our vulnerability management and incident response processes.

We have a centralized dashboard or system that provides a holistic view of our cybersecurity operations.

Our cybersecurity metrics consider the performance of the entire value chain, not just individual components.

We regularly conduct cross-functional cybersecurity exercises to test the interoperability of our capabilities.

Total Score

Scoring and Interpretation:

For each section, add up your scores. Then, add all section scores for a total out of 250 points.

Results per Section:

40–50: Excellent – You're well-positioned in this area.

30–39: Good – You have a solid foundation but there is room for improvement.

20–29: Fair – This area needs significant attention.

Below 20: Poor – This is a critical area for improvement.

Aggregated Score Results:

240–300: Advanced

- Your organization has a mature cybersecurity posture and with well-integrated capabilities.

- You're well prepared to implement advanced approaches like CTEM and CRI.

- Focus on continuous improvement and staying ahead of emerging threats.

- Consider how CTEM and CRI can further enhance your already strong posture.

180–239: Progressing

- You have a solid foundation and are well-positioned to begin implementing CTEM and CRI.

- Some capabilities may be more mature than others.

- While adopting CTEM and CRI, prioritize enhancing less developed areas.

- Use the transition to these advanced approaches as an opportunity to improve integration between capabilities.

120–179: Developing

- Your cybersecurity program has a foundation to build upon.

- While full implementation of CTEM and CRI may be challenging, you can begin incorporating elements of these approaches.

- Focus on strengthening core capabilities and their integration.

- Consider a phased approach to adopting CTEM and CRI, starting with the most mature areas of your program.

Below 120: Basic

- Your organization is in the early stages of cybersecurity maturity.

- While full CTEM and CRI implementation may be premature, you can use their principles to guide your program development.

- Prioritize building a comprehensive, integrated cybersecurity program.

- Consider seeking external expertise to help develop your capabilities and plan for future CTEM and CRI adoption.

Extra (optional) exercise:

Think about your organization's current strategy and take a moment to assess your approach. Are you only focused on known risks (Urn A), or are you preparing for the unknown (Urn B)? Write down three actions you can take today to reduce uncertainty in your cyber defenses and discuss it with your peers.

CHAPTER 2

Setting Up the Board

The Power of Cyber Threat Intelligence

Sophia: It is still unclear to me how threat intelligence fits into all of this. How does it help us "set up the board," so to speak?

Alex: You know, this reminds me of something the ancient military strategist Sun Tzu once said: "If you know the enemy and know yourself, you need not fear the result of a hundred battles."

Sophia: Sun Tzu? I thought we were talking about cybersecurity, not ancient warfare.

Alex: The principles are surprisingly similar. In both cases, knowledge is power. Threat intelligence is our way of "knowing the enemy" in cyber space.

Sophia: So, it's like studying your opponent's past games in chess?

Alex: Just as a chess grandmaster studies their opponent's favorite openings and strategies, we use cyber threat intelligence to understand the modus operandi, the tactics, techniques, and procedures of potential adversaries.

Sophia: But how do we gather and produce this intelligence? And more importantly, how do we use it effectively?

Alex: Let's start with the basics. It is very common nowadays for many organizations to confuse threat-informed defense terminology; therefore, I want to make sure we have a solid foundation to build upon and speak the same language. Imagine our cybersecurity situation is like protecting a house.

L. Alevizos, *Cyber Resilience Index*, https://doi.org/10.1007/979-8-8688-1122-7_2

Sophia: That even happens between cybersecurity, audit, and IT departments; it doesn't surprise me! But you are right; let's put down a common terminology and set things straight. That will also help me clarify things in my mind.

Alex: Great, so there are some terms casually used like threat, threat actor, threat vector, risk, impact, likelihood; I am sure you have heard all of that before.

Alex: A threat is simply the possibility that something bad could happen to our digital assets. It's like knowing there's a chance someone could break into the house. Common threats nowadays are ransomware, phishing, spear phishing, distributed denial of service, cloud to on-premises infrastructure pivoting, and others.

Sophia: And I suppose the person who might break in is the threat actor?

Alex: Correct, the threat actor is the "bad guy" – the person or group who might want to steal our information or damage our systems. In our house analogy, it's the burglar looking for a way in. For instance, if we take ransomware as an example of a threat, there are plenty of threat actors that made it to the news such as Lockbit, BlackBasta, and Cl0p. And, just like different burglars have different motives and methods, cyber threat actors range from lone hackers to state-sponsored groups targeting specific assets.

Sophia: Aha! Those names ring a bell. I got called by a member of the executive board recently and was asked about Lockbit and their activities. The next question was, how safe are we against Lockbit? Pieces are slowly falling in place now. And I don't mean chess pieces, but the cyber resilience index ones. What about threat vectors?

Alex: The threat vector is how the bad guy gets in. The modus operandi that I mentioned before. Oftentimes, threat vectors and tactics, techniques, and procedures (TTPs) are terms that we use interchangeably. If the burglar climbs in through an open window, that open window is the threat vector. In our digital world, it might be a phishing email or a software vulnerability. Think of the threat vector as the route the bad guy is using to get in, while the TTPs is their full plan, from a single vector (the window or a door) up to stealing valuables and escaping unnoticed.

Sophia: Okay, I see. I have observed however that you refer mostly to "threat-informed defense" and threats and threat actors, while audit usually talks about "risk-based approach" to cybersecurity. So, how does risk fit into all this?

Alex: Risk is about the chance that we'll be targeted and how bad it would be if we were. It's like asking, "How likely is it that my house will be robbed, and how much would it hurt if I lost my stuff?" In cybersecurity, we might ask, "How likely is it that we'll be hacked, and how much damage would it cause?"

Sophia: That makes sense. I've also heard the term "vulnerability" a lot. How does that fit in?

Alex: A vulnerability is like an unlocked door or window in your house. It's a weak spot that makes it easier for the burglar to get in. Sometimes, it can also be a low-quality door with defects. Just as some doors are sturdier than others, vulnerabilities can vary in severity, and threat intelligence helps us figure out which ones attackers are actively targeting, increasing the likelihood of a break-in. In our systems, it might be outdated software or weak passwords. Do you remember the endless hours we spent battling against Log4j or Log4Shell vulnerability? That is a nice example to grasp this term.

Sophia: This is something I would like to forget honestly and focus on the lessons learned. But how do we determine the chances of an attack?

Alex: That's where likelihood comes in. Likelihood is about how probable it is that the bad guy will try to attack us. If we have valuable data and our defenses look weak, the likelihood is high. It's like a house with expensive items visible through the windows – it's more likely to be targeted.

Sophia: And if we are attacked, how do we measure the consequences?

Alex: That's what we call impact. Impact is about how much damage could be done if we're breached. If we lose critical data or our systems are down for days, that's a high impact, roughly speaking. It's like thinking about what you'd lose if a burglary happened at your house.

Sophia: Okay, this is a great foundation, but where does threat intelligence come into all this?

Alex: Let's break it down into two parts: cyber threat information and cyber threat intelligence.

Sophia: Are they not the same thing?

Alex: Not quite. They're related, but distinct. Cyber threat information refers to raw data we collect from various sources. It might include system logs, security alerts, or simply news from various sources about recent attacks. And trust me, there are lots of news out there, so we need to be very careful while vetting information. Cyber threat information is like hearing rumors of break-ins around the neighborhood or getting alerts from your home security cameras. They are bits of information about possible threats. But, when we analyze that data, connect the dots, and figure out patterns, that's when it becomes cyber threat intelligence. So, think of this like pieces of a puzzle or facts about break-ins in the neighborhood.

Sophia: So, it's just raw data?

Alex: Exactly. It's unprocessed information – a lot to take in and it might not make sense on its own. Moreover, it might be misleading or information written entirely by blogs and news sources without much context. Remember we talked about not being fear driven? Sometimes, this is caused by some news sources for the benefit of "click," the so-called clickbaits. So, we must analyze carefully and contextualize that information; that's when we produce actionable and valuable cyber threat intelligence.

Sophia: And how is that different?

Alex: Cyber threat intelligence is what you get when you put all those pieces together. It's the completed puzzle that gives you a picture you can understand and act on. For instance, intelligence might tell us that attackers are targeting companies like ours using a specific method, at certain times of day. That's actionable insight – it tells us what to look for and how to prevent an attack.

Sophia: So, threat intelligence helps us understand not just what's happening, but what it means for us specifically?

Alex: Precisely! It's the difference between knowing that break-ins are happening in the neighborhood and knowing that burglars are targeting houses with a specific type of lock, during times when a blue van is seen in the area. The first is information; the second is intelligence.

Sophia: Fascinating, I can already see cyber threat intelligence through a different lens. But how do we use this intelligence in our cybersecurity strategy?

Alex: In a simple sentence, cyber threat intelligence allows us to become proactive rather than reactive. Instead of waiting for an attack and then responding, we can anticipate potential threats and prepare for them.

Sophia: Can you give me a tangible example?

Alex: Let's say our threat intelligence tells us that a specific type of ransomware is targeting companies in our industry. We can use that intelligence to check if we're vulnerable to that ransomware; update our systems, if necessary; create or modify detection or prevention rules; place certain decoys to deceive the adversaries and stall them down; and train our employees on what to watch out for. We're not just waiting for an attack – we're actively preparing based on what we know about the threat landscape.

Sophia: That sounds much more effective than always playing catch-up.

Alex: Exactly. And it goes beyond just prevention. Threat intelligence also helps us detect threats more quickly if they do get through our defenses. If we know what to look for, we can spot unusual activity much faster.

Sophia: Do you know of any real-world examples as well? I am curious if that's only theory or real-world happenings.

Alex: This is happening out there as we speak; it is not theory only. One notable case is the WannaCry ransomware attack in 2017. Organizations that had robust threat intelligence were able to patch the vulnerability exploited by WannaCry before the attack spread widely. They essentially closed the window before the burglar could get in.

Sophia: That's impressive. Do we have any numbers on how effective threat intelligence is overall?

Alex: Indeed, we do. According to a recent study by the Ponemon Institute, organizations with mature threat intelligence capabilities were able to reduce their average cost of a data breach by $2.26 million compared to those without such capabilities.

Sophia: Wow, that's a significant difference. But implementing a threat intelligence program must come with its own challenges, right?

Alex: One of the biggest challenges is the vast volume of data. It's like trying to find a specific chess move in a database of millions of games. Organizations often struggle with information overload and determining which threats are truly relevant to them.

Sophia: This must be probably overwhelming. How do organizations manage all that information? And how do we do it actually?

Alex: Understanding different types of threat intelligence is imperative. We generally categorize it into three types: strategic, tactical, and operational.

Sophia: Can you explain these?

Alex: Let me show you a picture, and I will briefly explain them.

Strategic

Focused on understanding high level trends and adversarial motives. Leveraging that understanding, to help strategic security and decision making.
Stakeholders: CISO, CIO, CTO, Executive Board, Strategic Advisors.

Tactical

Focused on performing malware analysis and enrichment. Ingesting atomic, static, and behavioral threat indicators into defensive cybersecurity systems.
Stakeholders: SOC Analysts, SIEM, EDR/IDS/IPS, Firewalls.

Operational

Focused on understanding adversarial capabilities, infrastructure and TTPs. Leveraging that understanding to conduct more targeted and prioritized cybersecurity operations.
Stakeholders: Threat Hunters, SOC Analysts, Monitoring, Incident Response, Vulnerability Management, Counter Insider Threats.

Alex: Strategic intelligence is high-level information about broad trends, like emerging threats in our industry and figuring out the goals of the adversaries. The typical stakeholders here would be yourself as the CISO, the CIO, the CTO, executive board, and strategic advisors. It's like understanding the overall strategy your chess opponent tends to use.

Alex: Tactical intelligence is more specific, focusing on performing malware analysis and enrichment, ingesting atomic, static, and behavioral threat indicators into defensive cybersecurity systems. The typical stakeholders here would be our SOC analysts, intel analysts, and systems such as firewalls, endpoint detection and response (EDR), intrusion detection and prevention (IDPS). This is like analyzing specific chess moves and their immediate consequences – it focuses on understanding current threats and how to counter them in the short term.

Alex: Operational intelligence is focused on understanding adversaries' capabilities, infrastructure, and TTPs. Then, leveraging that understanding to conduct targeted and prioritized cybersecurity operations through our cyber threat value chain. The typical stakeholders here would be the threat hunting team, SOC analysts, monitoring team, incident response, vulnerability management, and counter insider threat capability. It's the equivalent of studying your opponent's playing style, favorite strategies, and typical responses in chess. We understand their "playbook" and using this knowledge to guide our overall game plan and moment-to-moment decisions.

Sophia: Aha! That's insightful and powerful at the same time.

Alex: And just like in chess, the key is to use all these types of intelligence together to form a comprehensive defense strategy.

Sophia: Speaking of chess, how else would you compare threat intelligence to chess strategy?

Alex: Hm, threat intelligence in cybersecurity is very much like studying your opponents in chess. Just as a grandmaster would analyze their opponent's past games, preferred openings, and typical endgame strategies, we use threat intelligence to understand our adversaries' typical attack patterns, preferred malware, and common targets.

Sophia: So, I suppose, like in chess, this intelligence helps us anticipate and counter our opponent's moves?

Alex: Correct. In chess, if you know your opponent often uses a particular gambit, you can prepare a strong defense against it. Similarly, if our threat intelligence tells us that a certain group of attackers often uses a specific type of malware to breach systems, we can prepare our defenses against that particular threat.

Sophia: Interesting approach. Seems like we need a fundamental shift in how we approach cybersecurity. Am I right?

Alex: You've hit the nail on the head. Traditional cybersecurity often focuses on protecting assets – which is like fortifying each chess piece individually. But with threat intelligence, we shift to a more proactive, threat-informed approach. It's like studying your opponent so well that you can anticipate and counter their moves before they even make them.

Sophia: So how do we make this shift in our approach and elevate our strategy to incorporate CTEM and CRI?

Alex: Traditionally, many organizations have taken an asset-driven approach to cybersecurity or compliance-driven. But with the power of threat intelligence, we can shift to a more effective, threat-intel driven approach and enhance a CTEM program. Although not necessary, but CTEM serves as a good starting point. In fact, that's exactly what I wanted to discuss next, but are you ready?

From Compliance Driven to Threat-Intel Driven

Sophia: You got me hanging here. So, how exactly does this shift work? If a shift is needed, I must say. I mean... oftentimes I hear a paradigm shift is needed, but I am not entirely convinced that is a game changer.

Alex: Look, many organizations have taken what we call an asset-driven approach to cybersecurity. It's like trying to protect every piece on your chessboard equally, without considering which ones your opponent is most likely to target. As such, you are spreading resources evenly, instead of strategically placing your defenses where they are needed the most.

Sophia: That does not sound very efficient. But on the other hand, it provides some peace of mind once completed, right?

Alex: But will it be ever completed? Isn't cybersecurity something constantly changing and evolving? Assets are being added or removed all the time. In an asset-driven approach, organizations typically start by inventorying all their digital assets – hardware, software, data, etc. Then they try to identify vulnerabilities in each asset and protect them all. It's a bit like setting up an equal defense around every square on the chessboard, whether or not those squares are actually under threat.

Sophia: Yes, okay, such approach might spread resources thin indeed. How is that threat-intel driven approach better?

Alex: Instead of starting with our assets, we start with the threats. We ask, "Who's likely to attack us, how, and why?" It's like studying your chess opponent's favorite tactics or signature moves before deciding how to position your pieces, so you can prepare for the most likely attacks.

Sophia: Can you give me a concrete example?

Alex: Sure. Let's say we're a financial services company. In an asset-driven approach, we might spend equal resources securing our customer databases, our website, and our endpoints. But with a threat-intel driven approach, we might learn that attackers targeting our industry are mainly after customer financial data. We would then prioritize securing our customer database and the systems connected to it while still maintaining reasonable defenses elsewhere.

Sophia: I can see the value in that, but don't we risk leaving some assets vulnerable?

Alex: We're not neglecting other assets, but we're allocating resources based on the current threat landscape. It's like in chess – you don't leave your king unprotected, but you might devote more resources to defending the pieces your opponent is most likely to attack.

Sophia: Got it. How does this change our day-to-day operations?

Alex: It changes them quite significantly. In an asset-driven approach, we might have a routine patching schedule for all systems. In a threat-intel driven approach, we prioritize patching based on which vulnerabilities are being actively exploited by threat actors targeting our industry. Think of it as two-lane road. The right lane will be used for business-as-usual activities and therefore regular patching; the left lane will be the fast lane, corresponding to imminent threats.

Sophia: That sounds more responsive to actual threats. Are there any statistics on how much more effective this approach is?

Alex: Indeed, it is, and yes there are. A study by the SANS Institute recently found that organizations using a threat-intel driven approach detected security incidents 33% faster and reduced the impact of these incidents by 23%.

Sophia: Those are impressive numbers. But I imagine this shift comes with its own challenges?

Alex: With great power comes great responsibility... and great challenges! One of the biggest challenges is that it requires a more dynamic, flexible approach. We need to be able to quickly shift our focus as the threat landscape changes. It's like needing to adjust your chess strategy in the middle of the game when you notice your opponent switching to a surprising move. You need flexibility to shift defenses as new threats emerge.

Sophia: That sounds demanding. How do we manage that kind of flexibility?

Alex: It requires a combination of the right tools, processes, and people. We need threat intelligence tools and platforms that can quickly ingest and analyze new threat data, processes that allow for rapid reprioritization, and, most importantly, teams that are trained to think in this threat-centric way. In short, we need to create a seamless, interoperable cyber threat value chain of capabilities.

Sophia: Right, and how does this approach handle unknown threats? Wouldn't focusing on known threats leave us vulnerable to new ones?

Alex: Excellent point. While we do focus on known threats, a good threat-intel driven approach also looks for patterns and trends that might indicate new, emerging threats. It's like in chess, where you might not know exactly what move your opponent will make, but you can anticipate new strategies based on patterns in their play.

Sophia: That makes sense. How does this approach tie into the concept of cyber resilience we discussed earlier?

Alex: The threat-intel driven approach is a key component of building cyber resilience. By focusing our efforts on the most likely and impactful threats, we're better prepared to prevent, detect, and respond to attacks. It's not just about building higher walls, but about building the right defenses in the right places.

Sophia: Okay, I can see how this would make us more resilient. But doesn't it require a significant cultural shift in the organization?

Alex: Indeed, and that's often one of the biggest challenges. It requires everyone, from the executive board to senior and mid-leadership to the IT and security staff, to start thinking in terms of threats rather than just assets. It's a shift from a "protect everything equally" mindset to a "focus on what matters most" approach, as dictated by our threat intelligence.

Sophia: How do we manage that cultural shift?

Alex: It starts with education. Everyone needs to understand why this approach is more effective. It also requires strong leadership support. And importantly, it needs to be reflected in how we measure and report on our cybersecurity efforts.

Sophia: What do you mean by that last point?

Alex: Well, in an asset-driven approach, we might report on metrics like "percentage of systems patched." In a threat-intel driven approach, we would focus more on metrics like "percentage of high-risk vulnerabilities addressed" or "time to mitigate critical threats" or even more specifically, "time to increase our MITRE ATT&CK coverage against Lockbit's TTPs." It's about measuring what matters most in terms of actual risk and attack surface reduction.

Sophia: Right, this all sounds very powerful, but also complex. How do organizations typically start making this shift?

Alex: Most organizations start with a hybrid approach. They begin incorporating threat intelligence into their existing asset-driven processes, gradually shifting the balance over time. It's like slowly changing your chess strategy game by game, rather than all at once.

Sophia: So, the shift to a threat-intel driven approach is really about being more strategic and focused on our collaborative cybersecurity efforts.

Alex: Exactly, it's about working smarter, not just harder. By focusing on the threats that matter most to us, we can make more effective use of our resources and significantly improve our overall security posture.

Sophia: Now that you said it's not about working harder, you know firsthand how hard we are working every day to meet and comply with standards, rules, regulations, directives, and others like ISO 27000 series, NIST CSF, NIS2, DORA, EU AI Act. Now you telling me this isn't the right approach?! I certainly can't convey that to the executive board! Not to mention that some of these are regulations, so we must adhere to.

Alex: Compliance is certainly important, but it's only part of the picture. We can't afford to only focus on compliance or, simply put, being led by compliance efforts.

Sophia: Why not? What are we missing by focusing on compliance or assets?

Alex: Think of compliance like learning and applying the basic rules of chess. It's essential, but it doesn't make you an excellent player, let alone a grandmaster. Just like following rules doesn't guarantee victory, meeting compliance doesn't ensure complete security.

Sophia: That is thought-provoking. Please elaborate on that.

Alex: Compliance standards like ISO 27000 series, NIST CSF, CIS controls, and others provide a baseline for cybersecurity. They're the fundamental hygiene practices every organization should follow. It's like knowing that controlling the center in chess is generally a good strategy or that you shouldn't move the same piece twice in the opening.

Sophia: But if we are compliant, aren't we secure as well?

Alex: That's a common misconception. Compliance is necessary, but not sufficient for true security. It's like knowing the rules of chess doesn't automatically make you a strong player.

Sophia: Then what is missing to be secure and provide that peace of mind to both the board and us?

Alex: What's missing is the proactive, threat-informed approach. Compliance standards often use vague or high-level language and are open to interpretation. They tell you what to do, but not always how to do it effectively and efficiently in the face of real-world threats.

Sophia: And that's where threat intelligence comes in?

Alex: Exactly! A threat-intel driven approach goes beyond compliance. It's like studying your opponents' strategies in chess, not just knowing the rules of the game.

Sophia: But we are already swamped with compliance requirements. NIS2, DORA, and others are keeping us busy. How can we add another approach on top of that?

Alex: I understand your concern, but here's the interesting part. A threat-intel driven approach can help us comply with these regulations.

Sophia: Really? How so?

Alex: Because many of these regulations require us to implement appropriate security measures based on risk. By using threat intelligence, you can better understand and prioritize your risks, making it easier to justify and implement the right security measures.

Sophia: That's intriguing. Can you give me an example?

Alex: Let's say a regulation requires us to implement "appropriate access controls." That's pretty vague, right? But if, for instance, your threat intelligence tells us that attackers in our industry are primarily using stolen credentials to gain initial access, you know to prioritize multifactor authentication and privileged access management.

Sophia: I see. So, we're not just checking boxes, we're implementing security measures that address real threats.

Alex: Precisely! It's like in chess – instead of just memorizing opening moves, you're understanding why those moves are effective and when to use them, and that is a game changer.

Sophia: Right, so how do we start making this shift?

Alex: The best way is to start with a hybrid approach, as we discussed before. First things first, a strong compliance baseline is imperative – that basic cyber hygiene we talked about. Then they start incorporating threat intelligence to guide their security decisions and investments.

Sophia: Can you give me a concrete example of how this might work in practice?

Alex: Let's say we're compliant with a standard that requires regular vulnerability scanning. In a purely compliance-driven approach, we might scan everything quarterly and patch whatever we find.

Sophia: And in a threat-intel driven approach?

Alex: We would still do those scans to maintain our baseline, but we would also use threat intelligence to prioritize. If we know that threat actors are actively exploiting a particular vulnerability in our industry, we'd prioritize finding and patching that vulnerability immediately, rather than waiting for our next scheduled scan.

Sophia: Okay, makes sense and sounds efficient and effective.

Alex: Indeed, this approach can help across the board. It can inform our employee training, our incident response planning, our technology investments – everything.

Sophia: That's a holistic approach to increasing cyber resilience indeed and sounds very powerful, but also like a big change. How do we start?

Alex: A good place to start is by looking at frameworks and knowledge basis that support this approach, like MITRE ATT&CK and D3FEND, for instance. These provide a common language for describing threat behavior and defensive techniques.

Sophia: I am casually hearing these terms lately from peers in the industry. Tell me briefly please, what are these about?

Alex: MITRE ATT&CK is like a comprehensive playbook of the tactics and techniques that attackers use. D3FEND, on the other hand, maps out defensive techniques. Together, they help you understand both the threat landscape and your defensive options.

Sophia: So, it's like having a guidebook for both your opponent's strategies and your own in chess?

Alex: That's a great analogy, and just like in chess, the key is not just knowing these strategies, but understanding how to apply them in your specific situation.

Sophia: Fascinating!

Alex: Indeed! So, combining a strong compliance baseline with a threat-intel driven approach, we can create a cybersecurity strategy that is robust, proactive, and even adaptive. It's like mastering both the fundamental rules of chess and the advanced strategies that win games.

61

Sophia: Exciting indeed and well framed so far. What's the next step in implementing this approach?

Alex: Now that we have established a common terminology and also understand the power of a threat-intel driven approach, the next step is to look at a specific methodology that can help us put this into practice. That's where TIBSA comes in.

Sophia: TIPSY...? Well, although I don't drink alcohol, given our nice dialogue I could make an exception and have a beer to hear more about this cyber resilience index. I want us to master the threat-informed defense!

Alex: Hmm... I said TIBSA, not TIPSY! It stands for threat intelligence–based security assessment.

Sophia: Oh, yes, of course, threat intelligence–based security assessment, TIBSA (eyeroll)! Let's get another coffee, shall we?

Overview of the TIBSA Methodology

Alex: The threat intelligence–based security assessment (TIBSA) is a structured approach designed to integrate actionable threat intelligence into our security assessments, helping us align our defenses with the evolving threat landscape. It sounds simple, but it's a strategic shift that requires precision.

Sophia: Not sure if it's easy, but it sounds interesting approach. How does it work?

Alex: TIBSA expects actionable cyber threat intelligence as input, to guide our security assessments and decisions. It's like using intelligence about your opponent's favorite strategies to inform how you set up your chess pieces.

Sophia: Interesting, so it ties back to our discussion being threat intelligence driven. Can you explain this further?

Alex: Yes, indeed. TIBSA consists of several key steps. First, we start by understanding the cyber threat landscape specific to our organization.

Sophia: How do we do that?

Alex: We use threat intelligence to identify the most relevant threats to our industry and our specific organization. This might include information about active threat actors, their typical tactics, techniques and procedures, the kinds of assets they usually target, and their ultimate motives and goals.

Sophia: Okay, so, primarily, we are focusing on the threats that are most likely to affect us, right? That's step 1, what then?

Alex: Correct. The next step is to identify the assets that are most likely to be targeted based on the received threat intelligence. This is where TIBSA differs from traditional asset-driven approaches.

Sophia: How so?

Alex: Instead of trying to protect everything equally, we are prioritizing based on what the threat intelligence tells us is most at risk. It's like reinforcing the parts of your chess defense that your opponent is most likely to attack.

Sophia: Sounds reasonable, and what happens after we've identified these potentially impacted assets?

Alex: Then we move on to identifying the specific tactics, techniques, and procedures (TTPs) that threat actors are likely to use against these assets. This is where frameworks like MITRE ATT&CK come in handy.

Sophia: Right, and how do we use this information?

Alex: This is where it gets interesting... We then use this information to assess our current security controls that correspond to the mentioned TTPs. We're not just checking if controls exist, but whether they're effective against the specific threats we are likely to face.

Sophia: That sounds more targeted and more effective than our usual assessments. More... hands-on I would dare to admit. But how do we measure effectiveness?

Alex: TIBSA introduces a scoring model to quantify the effectiveness of our controls against these identified TTPs. It's not just a yes/no question of whether a control exists type of questionnaire that a product owner needs to fill in an excel sheet with answers. It is about figuring out how well our controls stand up against real-world threats.

Sophia: I like the sound of that. It seems indeed more hands-on and actionable.

Alex: Exactly! And that leads us to the next step. Using this assessment to identify gaps in our defenses and prioritize improvements.

Sophia: Ehm, you know me, I am a practical person, and this all sounds great in theory, but how does it work in practice?

Alex: Let me give you a concrete example. Say our threat intelligence tells us that financial services companies like ours are being targeted by a group that typically uses spear phishing to gain initial access and, from there, deploy ransomware, okay?

Sophia: Okay, I am following.

Alex: Using TIBSA, we would first study the threat actor's profile provided by our intel to identify the assets most likely to be targeted or participate in one or another way.

Alex: In this spear phishing and ransomware example, probably our email system will play a role delivering that phishing email to the end user, then a user's endpoint would be impacted or at least participate in the attack chain, then probably file servers or mounted drives and shared storage, then our proxy server to exfiltrate data, and so forth.

Sophia: But wait, I understand the email gateway and the user's endpoint would have a role to play, but why the file servers or shared storages and mounted drives are added in scope for assessment?

Alex: It all starts with cyber threat intelligence and the threat actor's TTPs, remember? Their goal is to deploy ransomware. So, ransomware not only encrypts the local user's endpoint files but also all the mounted drives or shared storage that is found through that endpoint! Moreover, some ransomware strains are exfiltrating data; therefore, we add the outbound proxy in scope of assessment.

Sophia: Aha! Now it all makes sense. We are following the TTPs of the actor and mapping it throughout our assets and the applicable controls, right?

Alex: You got it! As you nicely described, then we would look at our controls related to email security, endpoint security, user awareness training, file server/storage security, outgoing connections through proxy, and so forth. So, ultimately, we match the TTPs with our corresponding security controls.

Sophia: And then we would score the effectiveness of the security controls?

Alex: Exactly. We'd assess how effective our current email filters, anti-phishing training, endpoint protection, backup/recovery, and other relevant controls are against these specific TTPs. If we find gaps, those become our top priorities for improvement.

Sophia: Fascinating! Although… it sounds like it requires a lot of ongoing work.

Alex: You're right; it does. But that's one of the strengths of TIBSA. It's not a one-time assessment, but an ongoing process. As the threat landscape changes, our assessments and priorities change with it.

Sophia: Indeed, it makes sense to be dynamic, similarly to the threat landscape, right?

Alex: Yes, correct. There's one more crucial element. TIBSA highlights the importance of validating the effectiveness of our controls. It's not enough to just have controls in place; we need to regularly test them against realistic threat scenarios.

Sophia: Like penetration testing?

Alex: Penetration testing can be part of it, but TIBSA goes further. It dictates purple team exercises, where our defensive team (blue team) and offensive team (red team) work together to test our defenses against specific threat scenarios.

Sophia: This all sounds very comprehensive. How does it tie back to our earlier discussion about compliance?

Alex: TIBSA doesn't replace compliance efforts; it complements them. While we're meeting our compliance requirements, TIBSA adds the extra layer of security that we're also effectively defending against real-world threats.

Sophia: Right, it's like the difference between knowing the rules of chess and actually being good at playing the game?

Alex: That's an excellent analogy! Compliance gives us the rules of the game, but TIBSA helps us play the game effectively.

Sophia: Hmm... very good. But implementing something like this isn't easy, I presume. What are some of the challenges organizations face?

Alex: One of the biggest is the need for good-quality, relevant threat intelligence. Without that, the whole process falls apart.

Sophia: And I suppose keeping up with the changing threat landscape is another challenge?

Alex: Absolutely. It requires a commitment to continuous learning and adaptation. But that's also one of its strengths – it keeps us agile and responsive to new threats.

Alex: Another challenge is the shift in mindset required by our risk assessors. Having experience in IT audits, ISO 27000 series audits, or typical risk assessments is not sufficient. Organizations need to invest into their people to become technically savvy and think like attackers, rather than checking boxes or filling in checklists.

Sophia: This is a lot to take in. Do you have any visual representations that might help me understand TIBSA better?

Alex: Yes, I do. Here is an overview diagram of TIBSA that might help.

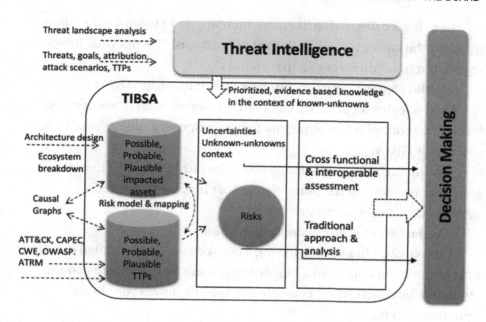

Alex: Let me walk you through briefly. Think of it as our strategic chessboard for cybersecurity. We start with threat intelligence – that's our study of the opponent's tactics. This feeds into TIBSA, where we contextualize these threats for our specific environment. We categorize potential impacts and tactics as possible, probable, or plausible – it's like anticipating different chess moves. We use various inputs like architecture design and frameworks to inform this analysis. Then, we combine this threat-informed view with traditional security approaches for a comprehensive assessment. All of this feeds into our decision-making process, allowing us to make strategic moves that are both reactive to immediate threats and proactive for long-term resilience. It's a holistic approach that helps us stay several moves ahead in the cybersecurity game.

Sophia: This visual really helps to put things into perspective. I can see how all the pieces fit together now. So, what's our next step in understanding how to implement TIBSA?

Alex: Before discussing the implementation of TIBSA, I remembered a quote by the ancient Greek philosopher Epictetus: "It's not what happens to you, but how you react to it that matters."

Sophia: I agree in general, but how does it relate to TIBSA?

Alex: In cybersecurity, we can't always control what threats emerge, but we can control how we prepare for and respond to them. That's the essence of TIBSA.

Sophia: Right, it's about being proactive rather than reactive.

Alex: Yes! You got the point! Remember how we compared cybersecurity to chess earlier?

Sophia: Yes, I found that analogy helpful.

Alex: Great. TIBSA is like having a chess coach who's studied hundreds of your potential opponents. This coach doesn't just teach you generic strategies, but helps you prepare for the specific moves your likely opponents prefer.

Sophia: Interesting, but you mentioned MITRE ATT&CK earlier. Is TIBSA utilizing that knowledge base? And if yes, do you think that is a limitation or an advantage?

Alex: TIBSA isn't limited to any single framework or knowledge base. While MITRE ATT&CK is incredibly useful, TIBSA can incorporate any relevant knowledge base or framework depending on the assets we're protecting.

Sophia: Can you give me an example?

Alex: Let's say we are concerned about potential attacks against our artificial intelligence (AI) powered systems. In that case, we might use MITRE ATLAS, which is specifically designed for AI security. Or if we're focusing on our Azure cloud environment, we might combine the Azure components from MITRE ATT&CK with the Azure Threat Research Matrix directly by Microsoft.

Sophia: Right, so TIBSA is flexible and can adapt to different types of assets and threats.

Alex: Precisely. It's a matter of finding the most applicable knowledge base and utilizing it accordingly. Think of this like a chess player who can adapt their strategy based on whether they're playing classical chess, where you have a lot of time to make decisions; speed chess, where the time is extremely limited and the pressure is high; or even a variant like Chess960, where the pieces have been randomly shuffled on each player's back rank.

Alex: So, depending on the type of game you are playing, you won't be using the same strategies and tactics to defend, right? Same applies here.

Sophia: It makes sense. That flexibility sounds valuable. But how does TIBSA compare to other methodologies we've used, like TIBER, the threat intelligence–based ethical red teaming? I know we had extensive TIBER exercises done in the past.

Alex: That's a great question. TIBER and TIBSA are both valuable, but they serve different purposes. A "fun fact" is that TIBSA's name was inspired originally by TIBER, but let me use an analogy to explain.

Alex: Think of TIBER as a high-precision rifle. It's designed to find the quickest path to a specific target – like capturing a flag in a capture-the-flag exercise. It might find a critical weakness, like a domain admin password left in a desktop notepad, and the exercise ends there.

Sophia: Okay, I follow. And how about TIBSA?

Alex: TIBSA is more like a shotgun. It covers a wider area, examining all possible, probable, and plausible TTPs and their corresponding controls for effectiveness. It's not just looking for the easiest way in but evaluating our overall defense posture.

Sophia: I see. So, TIBER might find a critical weakness quickly, while TIBSA gives us a more comprehensive view?

Alex: Exactly. And here's the key. TIBSA can incorporate TIBER where needed. If we need more precision in a specific area, we can use TIBER-like exercises as part of our TIBSA assessment.

Sophia: That's fascinating. It's like having both a sniper and a squad in our army.

Alex: That's a great way to put it. Now, let me share another quote, this time from the psychologist Alfred Adler: "The greatest danger in life is not to take the adventure."

Sophia: And how does that apply here?

Alex: In cybersecurity, the greatest danger is not in facing threats, but in failing to prepare for them. TIBSA encourages us to "take the adventure" of exploring our vulnerabilities proactively, rather than waiting for an attack to expose them.

Sophia: I like that perspective. It turns threat assessment into a positive, proactive activity. Can we instill this into our teams perhaps?

Alex: Exactly, and yes, we can. After all, we fight for a common cause, right? Our people, our capabilities, and security professionals in the field overall share the same cause, namely, keep our organizations secure against threats. Therefore, we must instill this mentality not only to our people but in the cybersecurity community overall. That's how we can all collectively rise to higher maturity levels.

Alex: Now, TIBSA brings one more critical concept we need to discuss. The concept of possible, probable, and plausible. Understanding this is key to prioritizing our efforts effectively.

Sophia: Sounds important... and confusing at the same time.

Alex: Indeed, but before we do, let me ask you the following. In chess, do you prepare equally for all possible moves your opponent might make?

Sophia: No, I suppose not. One would focus more on the moves they are likely to make, based on the current board position and what you know about their style, right?

Alex: Precisely. And that's exactly what we do in TIBSA when we distinguish between possible, probable, and plausible TTPs, or PPP TTPs.

The Concept of Possible, Probable, Plausible

Sophia: You have mentioned these possible, probable, and plausible TTPs, or "PPP TTPs" a couple of times. Can you explain this further to me?

Alex: Yes, indeed; PPP stands for possible, probable, and plausible, and TTPs are tactics, techniques, and procedures. This concept is crucial in TIBSA because it helps us prioritize our efforts and resources.

Sophia: Right, so how do we distinguish between these three categories?

Alex: Well, think of it like planning a chess strategy. Possible moves are any legal moves your opponent could make. Probable moves are the ones they're likely to make based on common strategies. Plausible moves are the ones that make sense given the current board state and what you know about your opponent's style.

Sophia: Hm, that makes sense in chess, but how does it apply to cybersecurity?

Alex: It is literally the same! Chess is very much like cybersecurity. In cybersecurity, possible TTPs are those that could theoretically happen. They're capable of existing or being true, without contradicting any known facts or circumstances.

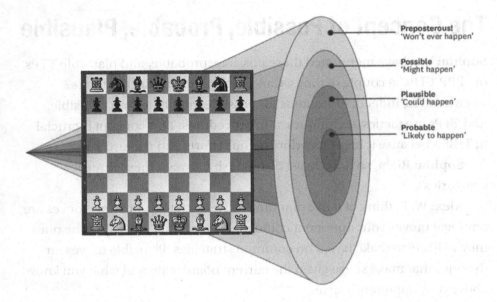

Alex: Probable TTPs are those likely to occur, based on what we know about threat actors and their common tactics.

Alex: Plausible TTPs are those that seem valid given the bounds of uncertainty; they might not be common, but they fit with what we know about the threat landscape and our specific situation.

Sophia: Wow, that requires some thinking. Please help me understand this better; give me a concrete example.

Alex: Let's consider a financially motivated threat group like FIN7. We know they often use ransomware to extort money from victims. Our intel tells us that one of their common TTPs is using phishing campaigns with malicious email attachments to compromise endpoints.

Sophia: Okay, so that would be a probable TTP?

Alex: Exactly. Now, a possible TTP might be them using an exploit directly against a vulnerability in a popular Internet-facing service. It's not their usual method as per our intel, but it's certainly possible.

Alex: And finally, a plausible TTP might be them customizing their ransomware to target specific systems in our infrastructure. Remember, adversaries will adapt to the uncertainties found within a specific IT landscape to achieve their goal.

Sophia: I see. But how do we account for uncertainty ourselves then? Threats are always evolving, and they seem to account for uncertainties they face within the IT landscapes they are breaking into, right? Do you mean we must do the same?

Alex: Exactly, and that's where the real power of this approach comes in. Traditional methods often fail to account for uncertainty. They might assume that if we're not using a specific technology that a threat actor has targeted before, we're safe. But that's not always true.

Sophia: Because the threat actor might adapt their tactics?

Alex: Precisely. Let's say our intel tells us that FIN7 has been targeting ESXi servers with a custom ransomware. If we're using the Citrix Hypervisor instead, we might be tempted to think we're safe. But that would be a mistake.

Sophia: Because they could adapt their ransomware to target our systems?

Alex: Exactly. That's the uncertainty we need to account for. FIN7 might react to the limitations they encounter and devise new TTPs to achieve their goals. That's why in TIBSA, we consider not just what's probable based on past behavior, but what's possible and plausible given our specific IT landscape.

Sophia: This sounds comprehensive, but also potentially overwhelming. How do we avoid getting lost in all the possibilities?

Alex: That's a great question. It's all about balance. We start by considering what's possible, but we focus our efforts on what's probable and plausible. It's like in chess; we are aware of all possible moves, but we spend most of our energy preparing for the ones our opponent is likely to make.

Sophia: Right, and I suppose this approach helps us avoid "analysis paralysis" or falling victims of an endless "cat and mouse" chase?

Alex: Exactly. By focusing on probable and plausible TTPs, we can prioritize our efforts without overengineering every theoretical possibility.

Sophia: Aha! But how does this translate into our actual security measures?

Alex: That is the next step. Once we have identified our PPP TTPs, we use that information to guide our selection of security controls. We end up with a set of PPP security controls; existing operational controls in production environments that address our possible, probable, and plausible threats.

Sophia: So, we are not just implementing every possible security measure, but focusing on the ones most relevant to our threat landscape?

Alex: Precisely. It is about being smart and strategic with our resources. Just like in chess, where we position our pieces to defend against our opponent's most likely and dangerous moves, not every theoretical possibility, but also not a static, high-level, generic questionnaire.

Sophia: Got it. Seems like there is potential for improvement here as opposed to how we approach the topic currently.

Alex: Yes, there certainly is. Considering PPP TTPs, we can create a more nuanced, adaptable, and effective security posture. We are not just reacting to known threats but preparing for how those threats might evolve, given the specific IT landscape that an attack is happening.

Sophia: I can see why this is so important in TIBSA, and I find it reasonable. Is there anything else we need to understand about this concept? It was not as complicated as I initially thought!

Alex: Happy to hear that. Here is one last thing to remember. This is not a one-time assessment. The landscape of possible, probable, and plausible TTPs is always shifting. We need to continually reassess and adjust our understanding.

Sophia: Similarly to a chess game, the probable and plausible moves change as the game progresses, right?

Alex: Right! You are really getting the essence of this! That ongoing reassessment is key to staying ahead of threats.

Alex: To add to that, in chess, a grandmaster doesn't just look at the current board state. They're always thinking several moves ahead, considering not just what's immediately possible, but what could become possible as the game progresses.

Sophia: And how does this relate to our PPP TTPs?

Alex: Likewise in cybersecurity, we need to think like a grandmaster. We're not just looking at current threats but anticipating how they might evolve. A TTP that seems merely possible today could become probable tomorrow as threat actors adapt and innovate.

Sophia: So, we're always trying to stay a few moves ahead?

Alex: Exactly, and moreover, in chess, certain moves might seem improbable early in the game, but become highly plausible in the endgame. The same is true for cyber threats. If the adversaries are innovating, the same goes for us, cyber defenders; thereby, cyber defense innovation becomes key.

Sophia: You lost me now; what do you mean?

Alex: Capture this; early in our security journey, a sophisticated AI-driven attack might seem like a mere possibility. But as our defenses mature and simple attacks become less effective, such advanced techniques become more plausible.

Sophia: So, our own security measures can influence what becomes plausible?

Alex: Precisely! It's like in chess where your defensive moves can sometimes open new attack vectors for your opponent. We need to be aware of how our security landscape shifts the threat landscape.

Sophia: This is a fascinating concept. It seems like there's a real art to this, not just science.

Alex: You're absolutely right. It's a blend of analytical thinking and creative cyber-foresight. We're not just reacting to known threats, we're anticipating potential futures; thus, we can provide early warnings.

Sophia: But how do we balance this forward-thinking approach with addressing immediate, known threats?

Alex: That's where the "probable" part of PPP comes in. We prioritize based on what's most likely right now, but we keep an eye on what's possible and plausible to ensure we're prepared for shifts in the threat landscape.

Sophia: It feels like playing chess, while the rules of the game are slowly changing. This doesn't sound fair!

Alex: That's an excellent analogy nonetheless! In fact, let's extend that a bit. Imagine you're playing chess, but every few moves, a new type of piece could be introduced to the board. That's similar to how new technologies can introduce new vulnerabilities and attack vectors, which, by the way, happens all the time and our engineers already facing such events with success.

Sophia: That would certainly keep you and the teams on your toes!

Alex: Exactly. And that's why the PPP approach is so crucial. It helps us stay adaptable and forward-thinking in a constantly evolving threat landscape.

Sophia: This all sounds incredibly dynamic. How do we keep track of all these possible, probable, and plausible TTPs?

Alex: Using causal graphs.

Sophia: What kind of graphs? You really like to throw unknown terms at me!

Alex: Causal graphs. They are a powerful tool for mapping out these complex relationships and possibilities. But before we discuss that, any more questions about PPP TTPs?

Sophia: Just one. How do we communicate this concept to the rest of the organization? It seems complex.

Alex: It's about framing it in terms of risk and preparedness. We're not just defending against what's happening now, but what could happen. It's like having a fire extinguisher – you hope you never need it, but you're glad it's there if you do.

Sophia: That makes sense. Let's go back to these... causal graphs now.

Alex: On another note, we could explain all of these to our people by hosting a chess day fun event!

Sophia: Nice idea, which would promote or even elevate the strategic thinking on one hand. On the other hand, I am curious to see how all these pieces fit together, but first, causal graphs.

The Role of Causal Graphs in Threat Analysis

Sophia: Causal graph sounds... mathematical. Are we about to discuss complex mathematical formulas?

Alex: No, don't worry. We won't be solving any differential equations today. Think of causal graphs more like a chess player's mental map of possible moves and their consequences.

Alex: They are a powerful tool in our TIBSA methodology, helping us map out the complex relationships between threats, assets, and controls.

Sophia: Okay, that sounds less daunting. But what exactly is a causal graph?

Alex: It is essentially a visual representation of cause-and-effect relationships. In our context, it shows how different elements in our cybersecurity ecosystem interact and influence each other.

Sophia: So, it's like a flowchart?

Alex: It's similar, but more sophisticated. Imagine a chess player thinking, "If I move my knight here, it threatens their bishop, which might force them to move their queen, opening up their king's defense." That chain of potential events is what a causal graph helps us visualize in cybersecurity.

Sophia: And how does this apply to our threat analysis?

Alex: Aristotle said, "We do not have knowledge of a thing until we have grasped its why, that is to say, its cause." I think this quote captures the essence of why causal graphs are so powerful.

Sophia: Hmm. So causal graphs help us understand the "why" behind the potential moves of threat actors?

Alex: Exactly! They help us map out not just what could happen, but why it could happen and what effects it might have. It's like tracing the ripple effects of a single move in a chess game.

Sophia: Very interesting. Can you give me a concrete example of how we would use a causal graph in our threat analysis?

Alex: Let's say we are analyzing the potential threat of a ransomware attack. Our causal graph might start with an initial threat vector, like a phishing email which is very common.

Sophia: Right, that's often how many ransomware attacks begin.

Alex: Correct. From there, we'd map out the potential chain of events. The phishing email leads to a user clicking a malicious link, which downloads malware, which then spreads through the network, encrypting files and so on and so forth.

Sophia: And eventually leading to the ransom demand?

Alex: Yes, but here's where it gets interesting. Our causal graph wouldn't just show this linear path. It would also include branching possibilities, defensive measures, and potential outcomes.

Sophia: What do you mean with that?

Alex: For instance, we might include nodes for our email filtering system, user training programs, endpoint protection software, network segmentation... Each of these represents a point where we could potentially break the chain of events.

Sophia: Aha! So, it's not just about mapping the threat but also our defenses?

Alex: Precisely! It's like in chess, where you're not just thinking about your opponent's potential attacks but also how your pieces are positioned to defend against them.

Sophia: This is fascinating, but at the same time I imagine these graphs getting very complex, very quickly.

Alex: (Laughs) You're not wrong there! It can indeed get quite complex. But that complexity is also what makes causal graphs so powerful. They help us see connections and vulnerabilities we might otherwise miss.

Sophia: But how do we manage all this complexity without getting overwhelmed?

Alex: This is where technology plays an important role. We use MITRE's attack flow to create and analyze these graphs. It's like having a chess computer that can analyze millions of potential move combinations. There are other custom-made tools we use as well, and recently we have started our own efforts to automate all this process with the help of artificial intelligence. So, worry not! Soon we will be able to delegate this to an AI, hehe!!

Sophia: Sounds futuristic and intriguing. Doesn't relying on software and specifically AI remove the human element from our analysis?

Alex: Not at all. The software is a tool, but the interpretation and decision-making still require human expertise. It's like how chess grandmasters use computers for training but still rely on their intuition and experience during actual games.

Sophia: Right, so the causal graphs inform our decisions, but don't make them for us?

Alex: Exactly! They are a powerful tool in our TIBSA toolkit, helping us make more informed, strategic decisions about our cybersecurity posture.

Sophia: Superb. Now please explain to me how this fits into our business-as-usual operations. Can you give me a practical example of how we might use causal graphs?

Alex: Let's consider a real-world scenario we've faced recently. Remember the Log4j vulnerability that had us all working overtime?

Sophia: How could I forget? That was a nightmare.

Alex: Indeed, it was. But imagine if we had a causal graph mapping out the potential impacts of a zero-day vulnerability in a widely used library like Log4j.

Alex: Our graph would start with the vulnerability itself, then branch out to show all the systems in our organization that use that library. From there, it would map potential attack vectors, the types of data that could be compromised, the business processes that could be disrupted...

Sophia: And our potential mitigations?

Alex: Exactly! We would include nodes for our patching processes, our network segmentation, our monitoring systems... Everything that could help us detect, prevent, and recover or mitigate an attack exploiting that vulnerability.

Sophia: I can see the value in this, but wouldn't creating such a comprehensive graph take a lot of time? Do you have any visual perhaps?

Alex: It does require an initial investment of time and effort, yes. But once the basic structure is in place, updating it becomes much easier. Plus, the insights we gain are unique.

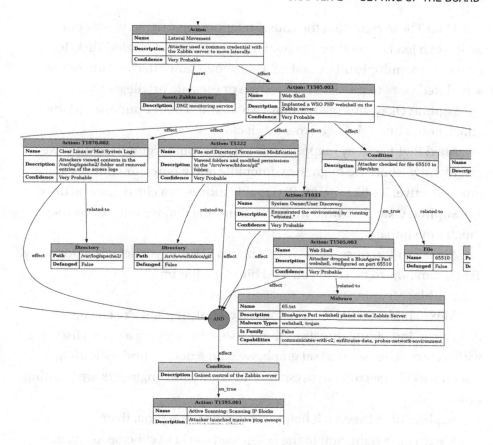

Alex: Here's an actual example visualizing the FIN13 campaign. This graph shows how different elements of a cyber-attack are connected.

Sophia: Wow, that looks complex. Can you briefly tell me what we see here?

Alex: At the top, we see the initial access vectors – usually this starts with a phishing email and a patient zero endpoint or exploiting public-facing applications. These lead to various steps the attackers might take, like credential access or lateral movement within the network.

Sophia: I see. And all those lines connecting everything?

Alex: Those represent the causal relationships, namely, how one action can lead to another. For instance, see how "Scheduled Task/Job" connects to multiple other nodes? That shows how attackers might use scheduled tasks to persist in the system or escalate privileges.

Sophia: Okay, this really helps visualize and better understand the attack flow, although I need to study it closer.

Alex: Right, and by mapping our defenses onto a graph like this, we can identify where we might be vulnerable and where our controls are most effective. It's like seeing all possible moves in a chess game at once.

Sophia: Okay, but what makes it so unique that we must devote so much time into it?

Alex: Lao Tzu once said: "Give a man a fish and you feed him for a day. Teach him how to fish and you feed him for a lifetime."

Sophia: Meaning?

Alex: Think of it like this. Without a causal graph, we're constantly reacting to individual threats as they arise – that's giving a man a fish. But with a comprehensive causal graph, we gain a deeper understanding of our entire cybersecurity ecosystem. Our teams and engineers are learning how to fish.

Sophia: Aha! I see, so it helps us become more proactive?

Alex: That's right, and in the fast-paced world of cybersecurity, being proactive is key. It's like in chess; the player who can think several moves ahead usually has the advantage.

Sophia: This all sounds promising, but I must ask, how does this tie into our cyber resilience index?

Alex: The causal graphs are a key component in calculating our resilience index. They help us understand the complex interrelationships between our threats, assets, and controls, which is essential for accurately assessing our overall resilience.

Alex: They also help us build confidence in our security controls, each time we assess our security control effectiveness against threat actors.

Sophia: What do you mean?

Alex: I mean that many threat actors utilize the same set of TTPs, perhaps with slight variations. This is very common. So, the first time we create a causal graph, indeed, might take some time. However, as we validate our security control effectiveness, we assign confidence scores within the causal graphs. Thus, the next time we face another threat actor using the same TTP, we will already have established a baseline and confidence in our security control effectiveness. Meaning, we are becoming faster and faster each time, therefore reducing the time to produce the graphs and responding to threats.

Sophia: Interesting. So, we are becoming more efficient over time, while the causal graphs feed into the resilience index calculation?

Alex: They do indeed. But that's a topic that deserves its own discussion. What do you say we take a quick break, grab some coffee, perhaps play a quick ten-minute chess game, and then discuss how causal graphs and the resilience index work together?

Sophia: Sounds good! I could use a caffeine boost before we tackle more complex topics!

Alex: I couldn't agree more. Chess and cybersecurity, they both require a sharp mind and a good cup of coffee!

From Attack Trees to Causal Graphs: A Paradigm Shift

Sophia: I understood that causal graphs represent a significant change to threat modeling. I am wondering though; what are we shifting from? What's the actual change and why do we need it?

Alex: Traditionally, many organizations have used what we call "attack trees" for threat modeling. These are hierarchical structures that show different ways an attacker might compromise a system.

Sophia: And why do we need to move away from that?

Alex: We should not move away. But we should evolve our approach. Attack trees are useful, but they have limitations. Think of it like chess openings. They're great for understanding common attack patterns, but they don't capture the full complexity of a real game.

Sophia: And how are causal graphs different?

Alex: Causal graphs allow us to represent more complex relationships between different elements of our cybersecurity landscape. They're not just about showing a linear path to an attack. They show how different factors interact and influence each other.

Sophia: Can you give me an example?

Alex: Yes, imagine we are modeling a potential ransomware attack. An attack tree might show a linear progression such as phishing email to ➤ malware download to ➤ encryption of files. But a causal graph could show how factors like user training, email filtering, payload emulation, endpoint detection and response, backup systems all interact to influence the likelihood and impact of the attack. It captures the cause-and-effect relationships between all the elements.

Sophia: That indeed does sound more comprehensive, but at the same time I presume it will increase complexity, right?

Alex: And you are right; it is more complex. But as Aristotle said, "The whole is greater than the sum of its parts." When we capture these complex relationships, we gain insights that we might miss with simpler models.

Sophia: I get that, but how does this help us in practical terms?

Alex: One of the key advantages is that causal graphs allow us to account for uncertainty and adaptation. In the real world, attackers don't follow a preset script. They adapt to the environment they find themselves in. In other words, the IT landscape they are attacking.

Sophia: I see... like a chess player adapting their strategy based on their opponent's moves...

Alex: Exactly! Despite not being a very strong chess player, you can easily grasp all these chess analogies! Impressive! (Both laugh.) Causal graphs help us think more like how attackers think, in terms of goals and adaptable paths to those goals, rather than fixed sequences of actions.

Sophia: Doesn't this make our job as defenders more challenging?

Alex: In some ways, yes. But it also makes our defenses more robust. Understanding these complex relationships means we can make more informed decisions about where to focus our efforts.

Sophia: So instead of just trying to block specific attack paths, we're looking at the whole system?

Alex: Yes, correct. It's about understanding the cause-and-effect relationships in our cybersecurity ecosystem. This allows us to make better decisions, even in the face of uncertainty.

Sophia: This all sounds powerful, but also quite abstract. How do we implement this in our day-to-day operations?

Alex: That's where tools and methodologies like TIBSA play a major role. They help us translate these complex models into actionable insights.

Alex: Here's another important point. The structure of attack trees is purely hierarchical, namely, each node has only one parent, except for the root. Look at this attack tree-based analysis of the Lapsus$ threat actor:

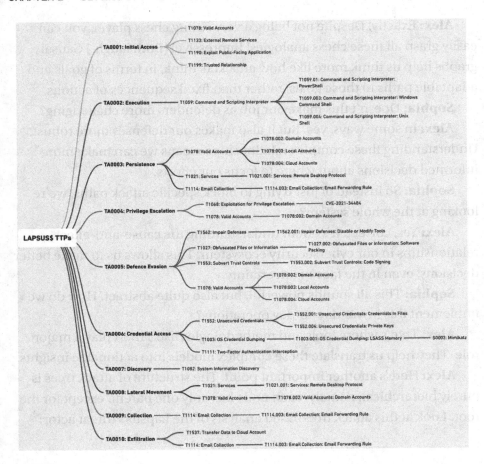

Alex: Causal graphs, on the other hand, allow for much more complex relationships.

Sophia: How so?

Alex: In a causal graph, a node can have multiple connections, both incoming and outgoing. This allows us to represent more realistic scenarios where multiple factors influence an outcome or where a single factor can have multiple effects. Now observe the difference in this figure.

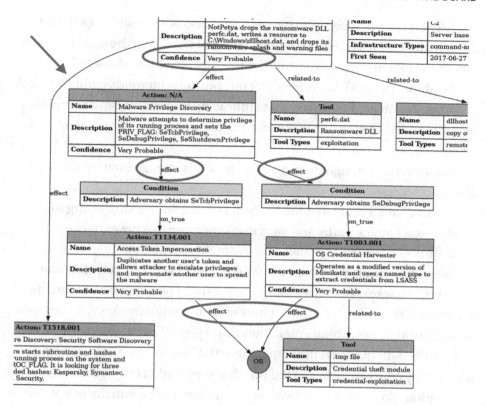

Description	NotPetya drops the ransomware DLL perfc.dat, writes a resource to C:\Windows\dllhost.dat, and drops its ransomware splash and warning files
Confidence	Very Probable

Name	C2
Description	Server base
Infrastructure Types	command-an
First Seen	2017-06-27

effect   *related-to*   *related-to*

Action: N/A

Name	Malware Privilege Discovery
Description	Malware attempts to determine privilege of its running process and sets the PRIV_FLAG: SeTcbPrivilege, SeDebugPrivilege, SeShutdownPrivilege
Confidence	Very Probable

Tool

Name	perfc.dat
Description	Ransomware DLL
Tool Types	exploitation

Name	dllhost
Description	copy o
Tool Types	remote

effect   *effect*

Condition

Description	Adversary obtains SeTcbPrivilege

Condition

Description	Adversary obtains SeDebugPrivilege

on_true   *on_true*

Action: T1134.001

Name	Access Token Impersonation
Description	Duplicates another user's token and allows attacker to escalate privileges and impersonate another user to spread the malware
Confidence	Very Probable

Action: T1003.001

Name	OS Credential Harvester
Description	Operates as a modified version of Mimikatz and uses a named pipe to extract credentials from LSASS
Confidence	Very Probable

effect   *effect*   *related-to*

Action: T1518.001

re Discovery: Security Software Discovery

re starts subroutine and hashes running process on the system and OC_FLAG. It is looking for three ed hashes: Kaspersky, Symantec, Security.

OR

Tool

Name	.tmp file
Description	Credential theft module
Tool Types	credential-exploitation

Sophia: I see. It seems like causal graphs give us a more nuanced view of the attack surface, right?

Alex: Exactly. And there's another key point: probability. Causal graphs allow us to represent probabilistic relationships between different elements.

Sophia: Probability? That sounds mathematical. How does that work in practice?

Alex: Think of it this way. In the real world, nothing is certain. A phishing email doesn't guarantee a successful attack, it just increases the probability. Causal graphs let us model these uncertainties.

Sophia: But doesn't this make our analysis more complicated?

Alex: It does add complexity, yes, but it also adds realism. Bertrand Russell once said, "The fundamental cause of trouble in the world today is that the stupid are cocksure while the intelligent are full of doubt."

Sophia: (Laughs) Are you calling our previous methods stupid?

Alex: Not at all! I'm saying that embracing uncertainty and complexity in our models is a sign of a more mature, nuanced understanding of cybersecurity.

Sophia: Fair enough then. So how does this change how we think about attackers?

Alex: That's a crucial point. With causal graphs, we stop trying to predict exact attack paths and start thinking more like how attackers actually think, in terms of goals and adaptable strategies.

Sophia: Sounds we are on something good here; can you elaborate?

Alex: Attackers don't follow a preset script. They have goals, and they adapt their tactics based on what they encounter. For instance, if they gain access through a phishing email, they don't just follow a predetermined sequential path like ttp1, then ttp2, then ttp3, and so on. They explore, they adapt, they course-correct based on what they find in our network.

Sophia: So, what you are saying is... we need to be equally adaptable in our defenses.

Alex: Spot on. As the military strategist Sun Tzu said, "Water shapes its course according to the nature of the ground over which it flows." Our defenses need to be similarly fluid and adaptive.

Sophia: This sounds, yet again I admit, fascinating. But I'm wondering, how does this affect our security teams practically? Do they need new skills?

Alex: Great question. It does require a shift in mindset. Our teams need to start thinking more holistically, understanding how different parts of our system interact. They need to become comfortable with probabilities and uncertainty.

Sophia: That sounds like a significant change. How do we manage that transition?

Alex: It's definitely a journey. We start by introducing these concepts gradually, providing training, and, most importantly, showing how this approach leads to better outcomes. It's like teaching a chess player to think beyond just the next move, to consider the entire game strategy.

Sophia: I can see how this could dramatically improve our threat analysis. But I'm curious; how does this tie into our overall cybersecurity strategy?

Alex: That's where it gets even better. This approach doesn't just improve our threat analysis, it transforms how we approach cybersecurity. Utilizing TIBSA and causal graphs, we can enhance our ability to understand and respond to adversary movements. Therefore, we can be more proactive, more strategic in our resource allocation, and ultimately more resilient.

Sophia: I follow... but please explain it a bit more. Sounds like you are making a practical conclusion.

Alex: Let me put it in simple words. Attack trees, as we discussed, are purely hierarchical structures. Think of it as a tree that grows branches and leaves, but those branches and leaves cannot and do not ever touch each other.

Sophia: Okay, I can visualize that. So, the branches and leaves represent different aspects of the attack?

Alex: Yes, and the branches represent tactics, while the leaves represent techniques. But here's the crucial part. This hierarchical structure often leads us, as defenders, to adopt a checklist mentality.

Sophia: A checklist mentality? What do you mean by that?

Alex: We tend to think linearly, checking off items as we go. "Okay, we've secured against this tactic, now onto the next." But that's not how attackers think.

Sophia: No?? How do they think then?

Alex: Attackers think in graphs. They are hunting for their goal relentlessly, and they will jump from branch to branch and from leaf to leaf if they must to achieve their goal.

Sophia: That sounds... unpredictable.

Alex: Exactly! And that's why the shift to causal graphs is so important. It allows us to follow the attackers' thought process more closely.

Sophia: How so?

Alex: With causal graphs, we can model these jumps, from branch to branch, from branch to leaf, even from leaf to leaf. This enables us to apply mitigating measures faster because we're thinking more like the attacker.

Sophia: I see. So, we're not just defending against a linear attack path, but preparing for a more dynamic, adaptive threat?

Alex: Precisely! And, to add to that, causal graphs allow us to assign probabilities based on cause-and-effect relations. This is imperative for two reasons.

Sophia: Tell me.

Alex: First, it allows us to prioritize our work better. We can focus our efforts on the most likely and impactful attack vectors. Second, and this is really exciting, it allows us to predict their next move with greater accuracy.

Sophia: Predict their next move? Like in chess?

Alex: Exactly like in chess! By understanding the relationships between different actions and their probabilities, we can anticipate where the attacker is likely to go next.

Sophia: Aha! And this happens through TIBSA, right?

Alex: Yes, TIBSA provides the framework, the methodology if you will, to apply these concepts in a systematic way. But hold on for a second, let's take a moment to reflect. How do you think this shift in perspective might change our approach to security control implementation?

Sophia: Hmm… I presume we would be looking at how different controls interact, rather than just implementing them in isolation?

Alex: Yes! That's exactly the point. And that holistic view is crucial for building true cyber resilience. How do you think this shift in perspective might change our overall approach to cybersecurity?

Sophia: (Pauses thoughtfully) It seems like we would need to be much more dynamic and adaptive in our defenses… We can't just set up static barriers and hope they hold.

Alex: Excellent insights! This approach pushes us toward a more fluid, responsive cybersecurity posture. We can't just build walls, but rather understand and anticipate the flow of the battle.

Sophia: It's fascinating, but I must admit, it also sounds challenging. I am skeptical on how do we prepare our teams for this kind of thinking?

Alex: I get your concern. For now, however, it is important that we set solid groundwork, understand, and then act. Next, we can discuss how we can operationalize these concepts and build a more resilient cybersecurity posture step by step.

Alex: Before that, how about we take a quick break? I think we both could use a moment to digest all of this.

Sophia: (Laughs) You're right about that. My brain feels like it's been through a chess tournament and a cybersecurity bootcamp all at once!

Alex: That's not a bad analogy! In many ways, that's exactly what we're preparing for, a complex, strategic game where the stakes are high, and the opponent is always adapting. But with the right approach, it's a game we can win.

Asset Identification and Risk Scoring in Threat-Intel Context

Alex: Now that we've covered causal graphs, let's talk about how we approach asset identification and risk scoring in the threat intelligence-driven context.

Sophia: Alright, I'm curious. How does this differ from our traditional approach?

Alex: Well, it's quite a shift, but we also touched upon the subject briefly before. Traditionally, we might start with a comprehensive inventory of all our assets and then try to assess risks for each one. But in a threat-intel context, we do it the other way around!

Sophia: How so?

Alex: Instead of starting with assets, we start with the threat intelligence input. It's like in chess; instead of inventorying all our pieces first, we begin by studying our opponent's most likely strategies.

Sophia: That sounds more focused. But how do we identify which assets to prioritize?

Alex: That's a great question. See how it all fits together now. We use what TIBSA calls "Identify Possible-Probable-Plausible TTPs and corresponding PPP Impacted Assets." It's a two-step process guided by our threat intelligence.

Sophia: I remember, the PPP concept. So, it's not only PPP TTPs, but also the same applies, and we get... PPP impacted assets? Please explain it to me now practically.

Alex: Yes, that's correct. First, we follow the threat research provided by our cyber threat intelligence team. This helps us identify assets that are likely targets based on the threat actor's goals, attack scenarios, and TTPs. However, the goal leads the way.

Alex: Remember we discussed the attackers will relentlessly hunt within our network to achieve their goal? Meaning, if we understand their why, and research enough their modus operandi and TTPs, then we take the upper hand as we know what they want and how they usually try to get it.

Sophia: Yes, I remember. That's why causal graphs are also so important, right? Because we can follow the attackers as they jump or move from branch to branch or from branch to leaf, where branches are tactics and leaves are techniques and procedures. But, how about the second step?

Alex: Superb! The second step is where it gets really interesting. We draw tailored scenarios based on our specific IT landscape and technology stack. This helps us refine our list of potentially impacted assets.

Sophia: So, we're not just looking at their generic modus operandi and TTPs, but how they might specifically apply to our environment?

Alex: Exactly! As Heraclitus said, "No man ever steps in the same river twice, for it's not the same river and he's not the same man." Similarly, no two organizations have the exact same IT landscape because their IT and security ecosystems are unique.

Sophia: You and your philosophy quotes! But I get it, in a simple sentence what you are saying is that we're tailoring our approach to our specific situation.

Alex: Precisely. And this approach helps us avoid a common pitfall in cybersecurity, the "checklist mentality."

Sophia: Checklist mentality? I recall we discussed this before, right? Can you please remind me?

Alex: Yes, it's the trap of thinking we're secure just because we've ticked off all the boxes on a standard compliance checklist. But attackers don't follow checklists, they adapt to what they find in our specific environment.

Sophia: That makes a lot of sense. But how do we score the risks once we've identified these assets?

Alex: That's where TIBSA's scoring model comes in. It's a semi-quantitative approach that helps us prioritize our efforts. Nonetheless, this is what we do specifically right now. Other organizations follow a fully quantitative approach and customized scoring models. So, TIBSA is flexible in that sense, and organizations must adapt the models according to their maturity.

Sophia: Aha! That's very good, meaning TIBSA is flexible and customizable. But tell me about what we do now; you mentioned semi-quantitative? Can you elaborate?

Alex: Yes, of course. The model uses a range of factors and criteria, each scored on a scale. For example, we might score the likelihood of a threat, the potential impact, and the effectiveness of our current controls.

Sophia: That sounds complex. How do we manage all that data?

Alex: It can be complex, which is why TIBSA recommends implementing this in an automated system with a user-friendly interface. Think of it like a chess computer that can analyze millions of potential moves but presents the results in a way that's easy for us to understand and act on.

Sophia: But doesn't this approach require a lot of expertise and resources?

Alex: It does require expertise, indeed, but that's where the collaborative nature of TIBSA comes in to form the cyber value chain. It brings together insights from various teams, such as threat intelligence, red team, IT architects, threat hunting, detection engineering, monitoring, supply chain security, network security, and others. It's like having a team of grandmasters advising you on your chess strategy.

Sophia: This all sounds very thorough, but how does it help us make better decisions?

Alex: The key is that this approach gives us a much more nuanced and context-specific understanding of our risks. We're not just looking at generic vulnerabilities, but at how real threats might actually play out in our environment.

Sophia: Okay, sounds very promising. Now please tell me how on earth this works in practice please!

Alex: Let's walk through a concrete example using our comprehensive scoring model. Imagine our threat intelligence team has just alerted us to a new campaign by the FIN7 group, known for their sophisticated attacks in the financial services sector. They are a financially motivated group, while their end payload is ransomware.

Sophia: Okay, I'm with you. Short clarification, by payload you mean the piece of malware that FIN7 delivers to the victim, right?

Alex: Yes, correct. Here is the sequence; first, we don't start with a full asset inventory. Instead, we begin by researching at the goal and motives of the adversaries. At the same time, we analyze the modus operandi and specific TTPs that FIN7 is known to use.

Alex: For instance, they often start with spear-phishing attacks targeting finance department employees, using DHL as a subject, PDF or ISO files as attachments, containing auto-opening links to destinations for the payload to be downloaded onto the victim's workstation.

Sophia: So, we would focus on assets related to our finance department's email systems?

Alex: Exactly. But we don't stop there. Knowing their goal, we would also focus on how they could steal money assuming a victim clicked on that email, the payload was successfully executed, and a command and control channel is established. Namely, we assume a "patient zero" workstation being under remote control by the attackers.

Sophia: Okay, so we've identified that "patient zero" workstation, which means the workstation of the user clicked on that malicious email, and now the attackers are controlling it remotely. What follows next?

Alex: We would also follow the potential attack path. After initial access, FIN7 typically moves laterally to gain access to financial systems.

Sophia: I see. So, we'd also look at our internal network structure, privileged access management systems, software or systems where financial transactions can be altered or money can be extracted?

Alex: Precisely. We're essentially mapping out the potential attack surface specific to this threat actor's modus operandi, rather than trying to assess every asset we own. A clear chain of assets that would participate in the subject chain of attack is being revealed to us step by step.

Sophia: Aha! But how do we...

Alex: Wait, there is more! We said that the adversary's goal leads the way, but now that we know the payload is ransomware, that adds more context and data. So, if previously we had the possible and probable assets and TTPs, we can also draw plausible ones.

Alex: Meaning, we would add file servers into our impacted assets, network shares, and other assets that the ransomware would try to encrypt after being dropped into patient zero workstation. We would also add other impacted assets following this attack chain to map out the entire threat surface. And that is how we would end up into our causal graph having the PPP TTPs and PPP impacted assets altogether.

Sophia: Right! Now it all makes sense indeed. It is about more effective and efficient attack surface management then; got it. I was about to ask though; how do we actually score all that?

Alex: This is where it gets even more interesting. We use a comprehensive scoring model that considers multiple factors.

Alex: Let me briefly describe the simplified version of it. For each TTP, we evaluate factors like

- Evidence of the TTP in adversary knowledge bases
- Skill level required to apply the TTP
- The TTP's applicability to our systems
- Positioning effect of the TTP
- Recovery time
- Estimated cost impact
- Detectability
- Prevent/deter ability
- Monitoring and coverage
- Confidence level in our security control effectiveness based on our causal graph analysis

Each factor is scored on a scale of 1 to 5 for simplicity, with specific criteria for each level.

Sophia: That's quite detailed. How do we manage all this information?

Alex: It can be complex, which is why many organizations are moving toward automated systems. Some, including us, are even experimenting with AI to help with the scoring process.

Sophia: Yes! I heard this project from the head of digital transformation. What do we do with AI on the topic? How does that work briefly?

Alex: AI can help in a few ways. It can quickly process large amounts of threat intelligence to provide initial scores. It can also learn from past assessments to improve consistency and flag unusual patterns for human review.

Sophia: That sounds promising. Is it removing the human element though?

Alex: Not at all. AI is a tool to augment our decision-making, not replace it. It's like how chess players use computers for training but still rely on human intuition during actual games.

Sophia: Sounds good, but back to the current topic of discussion. How would we apply this scoring to our email gateway example?

Alex: Let's walk through it. For the spear-phishing TTP targeting our email gateway, I recall we scored it as such:

- Evidence: 5 – This was confirmed evidence plus widespread use reported

- Skills Required: 3 – Some skills on the targeted assets

- Applicability: 4 – A system of systems

- Positioning Effect: 3 – General segment with Internet access

- Recovery Time: 2 – (8–16 hours)

- Estimated Cost: 3 – 50k €

- Detectability: 3 – Detection likely with simple refinements of detection methods

- Prevent/Deter: 2 – Verified; we do not block such attachments, nor we run them in a sandbox beforehand at this point due to the exception list

- Confidence Level: 4 – Large certainty on our existing controls

Sophia: And then what? Do we just add up the scores?

Alex: Not quite. We use a weighted formula based on certain factors. The exact weights might vary based on our organization's priorities and the specific threat actor and its corresponding TTPs we're assessing.

Sophia: This is much more focused than our old method of trying to assess everything equally.

Alex: Indeed. Ready for another quote? Sun Tzu said, "He will win who knows when to fight and when not to fight." In our case, we're choosing where to focus our defensive efforts based on actual threats.

Sophia: Both you and Sun Tzu are spot on I must say! I like this approach. But how often do we need to reassess?

Alex: That's a crucial question and a valid point. I see your potential concern regarding resource management, right?

Alex: Unlike traditional asset-based approaches, this is a dynamic process. We reassess whenever we get new threat intelligence, when we make significant changes to our infrastructure, or on a regular schedule, usually quarterly at minimum. But remember, we are not skipping the asset-based approach. So, there are no gaps here; we utilize both methods as they complement each other. The key is that we are threat-intel driven, not the other way around.

Sophia: Yes, got it. It's a synergy and both approaches are required. The cyber threat intelligence updates though sound like they could be quite frequent, which leads me to believe they will generate lots of work.

Alex: It can be, yes. But remember, we're not reassessing everything each time, only the assets relevant to the specific threats we're tracking and only the additional TTPs or specific tools and changes in their modus operandi. It's like a chess player constantly reevaluating the most important pieces on the board as the game progresses.

Sophia: Right, this really does tie back to our earlier discussions about being more adaptive in our approach. Let me challenge you a bit more here; how do we make sure we are not creating a complex system just for its own sake?

Alex: That's a very valid and crucial point. The goal isn't complexity, it's actionable insight. We continually refine our model to ensure it provides valuable, decision-driving information. It's about finding the right balance between thoroughness and practicality.

Sophia: And how does this tie into our overall cyber resilience index?

Alex: This scoring model is a key input for our CRI. It helps us understand where we're most vulnerable, where our controls are most effective, and where we need to focus our resources. It's not just about having the most pieces on the board, but about having the right pieces in the right places.

Sophia: Got it, and I can see how this approach would give us a much clearer picture of our actual risks. However, how does TIBSA integrates or influences the cyber resilience index?

Integrating TIBSA with CRI

Alex: Think of the cyber resilience index as the equivalent of a financial index, but for cyber resilience. Just as the S&P 500, for instance, gives you a quick snapshot of the stock market's health, our resilience index gives us a holistic and comprehensive view of our cyber resilience.

Sophia: Okay, I can see that analogy, and that's also a nice explanation that will help me articulate our cybersecurity message overall to the executive board and other stakeholders within our organization. On a second thought... even outside of our organization! But please continue; how do TIBSA scores feed into this?

Alex: TIBSA scores directly contribute to our overall resilience index. Each assessment we perform using TIBSA results in a score, and these scores are weighted and aggregated to influence the index.

Sophia: Can you give me a concrete example?

Alex: Let's say our TIBSA assessment reveals that by refining our detection rules against a specific set of TTPs, we could increase our resilience index score by 150 points.

Sophia: (Leaning forward, interested) And how does that translate to our overall index?

Alex: Well, that 150-point increase in our TIBSA score might translate to a 2% increase in our overall resilience index, depending on how all the other elements come together. It's not a one-to-one relationship because the index takes into account many factors, but it's a significant impact.

Sophia: Interesting. And how does this help with decision-making?

Alex: Here's where it gets really powerful. Let's say we're also considering purchasing a new security tool. Our analysis shows that this tool could potentially increase our cyber resilience index score by 200 points, which might translate to a 2.5% increase in our index.

Sophia: Wait that is super interesting, so we can directly compare the impact of different actions?

Alex: Exactly! Now we have a quantifiable way to compare the effectiveness of refining our existing processes versus investing in new technology. We can weigh the 150-point increase from refining detection rules against the 200-point increase from investing in a new tool that might cost a million euros. So, we can calculate the return on investment (ROI) by comparing the potential resilience increase of 150 points versus 200 points against the cost of each action, showing exactly where your money goes further.

Sophia: And I assume we'd also factor in the costs of each option?

Alex: Absolutely. This is where it becomes much like a financial decision, as I talked about before. We can calculate the return on investment for each option. For instance, if refining our detection rules costs significantly less than purchasing the new tool, it might be the more efficient choice, even though it offers a slightly lower point increase. In terms of cost versus benefit, or value realization, the decisions are becoming clear and thereby easily articulated to the board.

Sophia: This seems like it would make our budget discussions much more straightforward.

Alex: That's one of the big benefits. We can go to the board with concrete numbers. Instead of just saying, for instance, "we need to improve our cybersecurity," we can say "this specific investment will increase our cyber resilience index by X%, giving us Y return on investment."

Sophia: Wow, that's powerful. But if I am going to discuss this with the board, I'm provoked to ask, how do we ensure the accuracy of these scores? How can you provide me with that confidence?

Alex: Great question. We regularly validate our scoring model against real-world outcomes. Our team of experts throughout the cyber value chain is there continually refining the model based on new threat intelligence and changes in the cybersecurity landscape, against the impact on our specific IT landscape.

Sophia: This all sounds very data driven. Does that also change your team's decision-making process?

Alex: Absolutely, it made our process much more objective. We're no longer relying on gut feelings or the loudest voice in the room. Every decision is backed by data and clear metrics. Of course, there is some room for subjectivity in some points in the process, and that is normalized again through a panel of experts and multiple opinions.

Sophia: You bring up another interesting point. I would like to hear more about that expert panel and the normalization of biases. But what you mention indeed sounds particularly useful when we are dealing with limited resources.

Alex: Exactly. In a world of unlimited budgets, we might do everything. But in reality, we need to prioritize. This system helps us do that in a systematic, defensible way. That's how we are being pragmatic rather than trying to solve every problem at any time.

Sophia: I'm starting to see why you're so excited about threat intel–based defense and the formulation of the cyber resilience index. It really does provide a comprehensive view of our cybersecurity efforts.

Alex: Agreed, it does. And the best part is, it's not static. As new threats emerge or our infrastructure changes, our TIBSA assessments update, which in turn updates our index. We're always working with current, relevant data.

Sophia: You mean as we continuously analyze the threat landscape, right? Can you walk me through a specific scenario perhaps?

Alex: Imagine our intel tells us about a new threat actor targeting cloud-based financial systems. It's using a novel exploit that our current controls might miss; that is our initial assessment.

Sophia: Okay, I'm following. How would that feed into our resilience index?

Alex: First, it would immediately impact our index. The score would drop, and a dip in the trendline would be directly noticeable.

Sophia: Okay... Go on...

Alex: Then, using TIBSA, we verify our initial assessment, and the score would likely decrease because we've identified gaps. For instance, our incident response readiness might also take a hit if we don't have a specific playbook for this type of attack. Or, if we do not have coverage (e.g., prevent-detect-respond) against the TTPs given by our intel team when looking at our MITRE ATT&CK board, the cyber resilience index score would drop.

Sophia: I see. So, the security control effectiveness against multiple TTPs would either increase or decrease the CRI accordingly. And that is because of a single piece of threat intelligence?

Alex: Exactly. And here's where it gets better. Our automated system would immediately recalculate our overall resilience index based on these changes.

Sophia: Sounds great and responsive. How would that improve our strategic decision-making?

Alex: Great question. Because our resilience index has updated in real time, we can immediately see the potential impact of this new threat on our overall cyber resilience. This allows us to make rapid, informed decisions about where to allocate resources and what to work on next.

Sophia: Can you give me an example of such a decision?

Alex: For example, we might decide to fast-track the hiring of people to reinforce our security operations center (SOC) or change our quarterly objectives and key results (OKRs) focus. The cyber resilience index helps us quantify the potential improvement these actions could bring and thereby steer our defenses better.

Sophia: Okay, I got the helicopter view of how CRI helps decision-making through all technical, tactical, and strategic levels. How does this approach compare to industry standards like the NIST Cybersecurity Framework? You can imagine that would be a question coming from risk management or even audit. So, please prepare me in advance.

Alex: Frameworks like NIST CSF provide a solid foundation, similar to what we discussed with the compliance-driven approaches. Our threat-informed defense with the cyber resilience index brings dynamism and specificity to our organization's security effectiveness and efficiency.

Sophia: Does this approach require a significant investment in technology up front or maintaining a large-scale technological infrastructure? What role does automation play in all this?

Alex: No, simply because this is a way of working. It does not depend on tools or technologies, although the security and IT telemetry would certainly help in scaling and automating. An example on automation is the use of AI-driven systems to process the exceptionally large amounts of threat data, update our TIBSA assessments, and recalculate our cyber resilience index in real time. Without automation, the volume of data would be a lot, but not unmanageable still.

Sophia: So primarily it is about proper people and technology streamlining, right? That's how I interpret it.

Alex: Yes, correct; it's about forming that seamless and interoperable cyber value chain. A fusion of people and technologies united against cyber threats.

Sophia: Speaking about people and a way of working, what kind of training do our teams need to cope up with this approach effectively?

Alex: It does require some specialized skills. We've implemented a comprehensive training program that covers threat intelligence analysis, risk quantification, and the technical aspects of MITRE ATT&CK, threat analysis, and others.

Sophia: Okay, good to hear. How do we know if it's improving our cybersecurity posture and cyber resilience?

Alex: That's where our success metrics come in. We track things like time to assess end to end a threat actor campaign, coverage of TTPs against MITRE ATT&CK, time for each capability to provide input, scoring on prevent-detect-respond verticals, the accuracy of our risk predictions, and the overall trend of our cyber resilience index over time, among others.

Sophia: Interesting metrics I hear, and how has this affected our budgeting and resource allocation so far; what is your observation?

Alex: It's had a significant impact. The resilience index helps us to more accurately predict where we'll get the most value for money in terms of security investments. We can show concrete, data-driven justifications for our budget requests.

Sophia: Sounds great. So, on the next quarterly update, bring up the cyber resilience index to discuss the budget request I received from you!

Alex: Nice! We can do a pilot together and then see how that stands up to the executive board level.

Sophia: Sounds like a plan. Although, I was just messing with you a bit. Please tell me, what are the main challenges in integrating TIBSA and the cyber resilience index? Have you come across any so far, or do you anticipate some?

Alex: The biggest challenges are usually organizational rather than technical. It requires breaking down silos between different security functions. And it demands a shift in thinking, from static, periodic assessments to a continuous, dynamic threat intel–driven model.

Sophia: How do we overcome this challenge?

Alex: It starts with leadership buy-in, which is why I'm glad we're having this conversation. Then it's about education, clear communication of the benefits, and gradual implementation. We don't have to do everything at once.

Sophia: All right, I get the message. It's clear that this is as much about people and processes as it is about technology. I am curious to hear the implementation details equally for the resilience index and the value chain way of working next. But first, I am looking forward to the weekend. It is a nice opportunity to "digest" all this information.

Alex: I understand. Please do come back when you are ready; operationalization is the best part. You know where to find me!

Your Move: Threat Intelligence Exercise – Operation Conti Counteract

It's your move now, dear cyber defender and reader! Here is your mission for this chapter, if you dare to accept it... Protect CrossBorderPayment Inc. from the notorious Conti ransomware group. This simulation will test your ability to apply the basics of TIBSA methodology in a high-stakes scenario. Are you ready to start mastering the threat-informed defense?

Mission Briefing: CrossBorderPayments Inc., a cutting-edge fintech company, has received intelligence that they're potentially on Conti's target list. As the lead in this case, you must help fortify the company's defenses. If you need help from colleagues, please feel free to do this as a team exercise!

Phase 1: Actionable CTI

Your first task is to analyze the Conti ransomware attack flow:

1. Go to the following link (or scan the QR code) where you will find the Conti ransomware attack flow diagram: `https://center-for-threat-informed-defense.github.io/attack-flow/ui/?src=..%2fcorpus%2fConti%20Ransomware.afb`.

SCAN ME

2. Study the diagram carefully. As you do, imagine you're piecing together intercepted communications from Conti operators. What's their game plan? How do they move through a network? Try to find reports and threat profiles that would complement the existing attack flow. Discuss it with your fellow CTI peers.

3. In your threat intelligence notebook (use a real notebook for immersion!), note down

    - Key tactics you observe

    - Techniques that seem particularly dangerous for your own IT landscape

    - Any patterns in their attack methodology

Phase 2: Creating the Causal Graph

If you managed to produce actionable and meaningful cyber threat intelligence on top of the provided information, congratulations! This was the very first step toward a successful exercise. Now, it's time to create your causal graph:

1. Having the Conti attack flow on the screen(s), try to expand this universe by adding

    - a) PPP (possible, probable, plausible) impacted assets. Think: What in your infrastructure could be hit based on Conti's modus operandi?

1. Extra step for advanced users: Label each asset with P, PP, or PPP based on likelihood.

- b) Additional PPP TTPs. Think: How might Conti adapt their tactics based on your own specific tech as they hunt for their goal or as they follow their modus operandi?

- c) Security controls. What defenses do you have in place? Add these as "shield" icons on your map or tag them separately for better visibility.

- Use different colors, shapes, or symbols to make your causal graph visually engaging. The more creative, the better!

Phase 3: Building the Defense Matrix

Next

1. Visit the MITRE ATT&CK Matrix web page (or scan the QR code): https://attack.mitre.org/matrices/enterprise/.

SCAN ME

2. Assemble a team of experts from different verticals such as "prevent," "detect," "respond." For instance, one expert from the CTI team, threat hunting, monitoring, detection, endpoint protection, supply chain security, network security, and so forth.

3. Create your own mini version of this matrix, and for each technique used by Conti (from your causal graph), color-code your matrix to create a heatmap, based on what you think will protect you against the identified PPP TTPs:

    • Green: Strong defense

    • Yellow: Partial defense

    • Red: Weak or no defense

As you color, verbalize your reasoning as if you're briefing your management team. Why is each area strong or weak? Try to do this as a team exercise.

Important Note   This is not your validated security control effectiveness; this is your existing heatmap based on what you believe there is in place to protect you, based on data gathering that you will do during the expert panel meeting.

The validated cyber resilience formation will be covered in the next chapter; however, this is the first part toward CRI; hence, the exercise is designed in an iterative manner.

Phase 4: The Counter-Conti Strategy

Based on your cosmic map and defense matrix, it's time to create an action plan:

1. Identify the top 3 red TTPs in your heatmap. Mark these with alarming red exclamation points on your causal graph.

2. Discuss specific improvement actions you could take to lower the red marked TTPs to, at least, yellow. Write each on a separate "Action Card" in the causal graph.

3. Prioritize your Action Cards. If you only had resources for three, which would you choose and why?

Phase 5: Quantification (Bonus Phase for Advanced Players Only)

For those ready to push further:

1. Develop a quantitative model to assess control effectiveness and overall risk, or feel free to use our given semi-quantitative example.

2. Create a formula that combines these factors into a single "Risk Quotient."

3. Apply your model to the top 3 TTPs you identified. Does it change your prioritization?

Phase 6: Community Engagement – Share Your Insights

Now that you've completed this in-depth exercise, it's time to engage with the wider cybersecurity community and share your insights:

1. Reflect on your experience with the basics of TIBSA methodology and this Conti ransomware exercise. Consider

    •   What was the most valuable insight you gained?

- Did this exercise change your approach to threat analysis? If yes, how so?

- What challenges did you face, and how did you overcome them?

Bonus: We would love to see LinkedIn posts about your experience with this exercise or this book overall. Sharing insights and learning from each other is important, and remember to

- Keep it professional and engaging

- Focus on the process and your learnings, not specific results

- Avoid sharing any confidential information or specific vulnerabilities, assets, TTPs.

- Use relevant hashtags to increase visibility, such as #CyberSecurity #ThreatIntelligence #TIBSA #ContinuousLearning

- Engage with others who comment on your post. This is an opportunity to learn from peers and expand your professional network.

Remember, the cybersecurity community is all about shared knowledge and experiences. Your insights could help fellow professionals enhance their own practices, and you might gain valuable feedback in return.

With this bonus phase, we encourage readers to

- Solidify their learning through reflection and articulation

- Engage with the broader cybersecurity community

- Practice professional communication about complex topics

- Contribute to the collective knowledge in the field

Mission Debriefing

Congratulations, cyber defender and fellow learner-reader! You've completed Operation Conti Counteract. It's time to reflect on your experience:

- What was the most surprising insight you gained?

- How did creating the causal graph change your perspective on the threat?

- If you were to brief your organization's board or management team on your findings, what would be your main message?

- Remember, in the world of cybersecurity, the learning never stops. Keep sharpening your skills.

- This expanded exercise maintains the core elements of the TIBSA application while adding narrative elements and creative tasks to make it more engaging and fun. It encourages readers to think critically and creatively while applying the concepts they've learned.

CHAPTER 3

Playing the Game Differently

Prerequisites for the Cyber Resilience Index Implementation

Sophia walked into Alex's office having a determined look on her face. She had spent the weekend thinking their previous discussions about the cyber resilience index and was eager to figure out the practical aspects. If the resilience index was the tool that could help have better conversations with her peers and the executive board, that would be a game changer.

Sophia: I've been thinking about everything we've discussed regarding the cyber resilience index. It's a fascinating concept, but I need more details on how to fully implement this in our organization. So, the burning question now is, how do we move from theory to practice?

Alex: Aristotle once said, "For the things we have to learn before we can do them, we learn by doing them." Implementing the cyber resilience index is no different. With that, I am glad to see you back!

Sophia: That's spot on, now where do we start?

Alex: It is a significant endeavor, but like any complex task, the key is to break it down into manageable steps. Think of it like setting up a chessboard for a grand tournament. We need to ensure all the pieces are in the right place before we can start playing.

© Lampis Alevizos 2025
L. Alevizos, *Cyber Resilience Index*, https://doi.org/10.1007/979-8-8688-1122-7_3

Sophia: Okay, so, what's our first move?

Alex: Our first move is to understand and set up the prerequisites. We need to form what we call the "cyber value chain." Essentially, a collaborative network of cybersecurity capabilities of different expertise within our organization.

Sophia: A cyber value chain? You mentioned that before; it sounds intriguing. I believe it's time to elaborate on this concept.

Alex: Imagine our cybersecurity strategy as a complex chess game. In chess, each piece has its unique strengths and moves. Similarly, in our cyber value chain, we need to bring together experts from various cybersecurity domains, such as threat intelligence, vulnerability management, incident response, threat hunting, security monitoring, and so on. Each brings a unique perspective and skill set to our overall strategy.

Sophia: So, it's about bringing together the right expertise, regardless of our capabilities, departments, or the seemingly walled formation. But what exactly does this team need to do?

Alex: Correct, but we are not forming a team, a virtual team, or any other new team. Different people from different teams will be contributing to the cyber value chain. We streamline the way of working in a way that our existing capabilities and expertise form a seamless and interoperable cyber value chain. This chain will gather and process various inputs to feed into our cyber resilience index.

Alex: These inputs include threat intelligence feeds, vulnerability scan results, incident reports, threat hunters, security operations center experts, security architecture, validation of our security control effectiveness, and others. It's like gathering intelligence from different fronts before planning our next move in a complex chess game.

Sophia: How do we ensure all these different experts work together effectively? In my experience, different teams often end up working in silos.

Alex: You're right; that is why we talk about a paradigm shift, which starts with a change in our way of thinking and thereby way of working. Imagine our current cybersecurity setup as a chess game where each piece moves independently, focused solely on its own objectives. What we're proposing with the cyber value chain is more like a masterfully orchestrated game where every move is part of a greater strategy.

Sophia: That's an intriguing analogy. Tell me more, how does this work in practice?

Alex: In practice, it means we still have our "business-as-usual" services and capabilities –threat intelligence, incident response, vulnerability management, and others – working in silos with their own targets and OKRs. However, this will be until we are fully able to bring them together to work as one cohesive unit, much like how, in chess, the coordination between different pieces often determines the outcome of the game.

Sophia: I can see the potential, but also the challenges. How do we ensure this collaboration happens smoothly and realistically?

Alex: It starts with a fundamental mindset shift. We need to create an overarching set of priorities that transcend individual team goals. This means every team and team member needs to understand that the work of the value chain takes precedence. It's like in chess, where sometimes you need to sacrifice a pawn to protect your queen or to gain a positional advantage.

Sophia: I see you smiling, and I feel we are thinking the same thing here. We both know what is coming...

Alex: Yes... resistance to change!

Sophia: Exactly! So, how do we manage the potential resistance to this change?

Alex: It is indeed a crucial point that we will most likely face. Change is never easy, especially when it involves shifting long-established ways of working. As the philosopher Heraclitus said, "The only constant in life is change." We need to help our teams embrace this change by clearly communicating its benefits and involving them in the process. To facilitate this cultural change, we start by conducting workshops that focus on cross-team collaboration. Additionally, creating common goals with team-wide performance metrics encourages this unified approach.

Sophia: I see, and I assume strong leadership is crucial here?

Alex: Correct, we need a senior leader assigned to oversee this initiative, report on progress, and solve the inevitable roadblocks and problems that will arise. The leader needs to be someone with the authority to make decisions and the respect of all involved teams. Think of this as the chess player, coordinating all the pieces on the board.

Sophia: Agreed, do you think support from the top is necessary?

Alex: Executive sponsorship and support are crucial. This can't be seen as just another IT or security project. It needs to be a strategic priority for the entire organization. The steering committee and, of course, yourself as the CISO need to understand and champion this approach. It's like having the backing of the chess federation when you're implementing a new training regimen. That is the most powerful way to assemble the expert panel and continue from there.

Sophia: Understood, but before you secure my buy-in, what is this "expert panel" you mentioned? Is that the next step? Can you elaborate on that?

Alex: The expert panel is a critical component of our cyber value chain. We bring together one expert from each key capability area such as cyber threat intelligence, threat hunting, security monitoring, supply chain security, risk assessment, red teaming, and others. It's like assembling a team of grandmasters, each with their own specialty, to analyze our cybersecurity position.

Sophia: That's quite a diverse group. What exactly is their role?

Alex: They serve multiple crucial functions. First, they act as a collective filter and gatekeeper for the work to be done. They assess and prioritize the work packages to be distributed to the teams.

Alex: Bringing together diverse expertise, we can normalize subjectivity and make more informed decisions. It's like having a team of grandmasters analyzing a chess position. Each brings a unique perspective, leading to a more comprehensive strategy. Thus, minimizing bias potentially coming from a single grandmaster specialized in offensive play with the knights, for instance.

Sophia: Aha! That's powerful. Tell me more on how this panel operates in practice please.

Alex: They're responsible for work package distribution to the teams. They also play a crucial role in assessing our security controls. They compare "what we think we have in place to protect us" versus "what actually protects us"; that's how the work packages are generated. Ultimately, evaluating the real-world effectiveness of our security measures.

Sophia: That sounds like a significant responsibility. How do they manage all that?

Alex: And indeed, it is. They use their collective expertise to evaluate each security control against real-world threats and attack scenarios. This forms the basis of our two trendlines in the cyber resilience index. One trendline based on initial assessments of our security posture (what we think we have in place to protect us), and another trendline based on validated effectiveness (what actually protects us).

Alex: The gap between these lines shows us where we need to focus our efforts. It's like analyzing the difference between a player's perceived skill level and their actual performance in high-stakes tournaments. Somewhat like the difference between performing well in casual practice versus the actual go-time tournament performance.

Sophia: Aha! You are using "my language" speaking with graphs and trendlines... I like that. I can already see how the resilience index helps us articulate ourselves better not only toward the executive board but also throughout all decision-making layers.

Alex: Indeed! In the meantime, let me find a diagram of the cyber resilience index to visualize the trendlines I mentioned.

Sophia: Okay, but burning question now is the following. What exactly acts as input for this expert panel to start their work? Right now, we have business-as-usual inputs per capability, so what changes with the value chain? What serves as an input for the value chain?

Alex: The first input is identifying our top 5 threats and the top 10 threat actors for each threat. This helps us focus on the most pressing risks to our organization eventually. Think of this like identifying the top players you're likely to face in a chess tournament and studying their favorite openings and strategies. Easy?

Sophia: Kind of, why these specific numbers?

Alex: It's about balancing comprehensiveness with practicality. By focusing on these top threats and actors, we're addressing the most likely and impactful scenarios while keeping the scope manageable. In chess terms, it's like focusing on controlling the center and key squares rather than trying to dominate the entire board at once.

Alex: This, however, will change as we continuously shift from business as usual to fully fledged value chain. But let's stick to the basics for now; how does that sound?

Sophia: Sounds like a good and pragmatic plan. Are there more inputs to the cyber value chain?

Alex: Yes, the second input is focusing on the top 30 TTPs from the MITRE ATT&CK framework that are most relevant to our sector and industry. This gives us a baseline of coverage against the most common attack techniques. It's like mastering the most common and effective chess tactics and strategies.

Sophia: I see. This provokes me to think that we're trying to combine a top-down and bottom-up approach, right?

Alex: That's exactly what we aim for. Starting with both the top threats on one hand and the most common TTPs regardless of threats or threat actors, we're building comprehensive coverage while also prioritizing our most pressing risks. It's a bit like studying both general chess principles and specific game scenarios simultaneously.

Sophia: Okay, it makes sense. What about the third input?

Alex: The third input is day-to-day cyber threat intelligence relevant to our attack surface. For example, if we learn that a threat actor is scanning for the OpenSSH service running usually on port 22 or the remote desktop protocol (RDP), which runs by default on port 3389, and we know we have exposure on those ports, that becomes a priority for us to address. It's like getting real-time intelligence about your opponent's moves in an ongoing chess match.

Sophia: So, we're constantly ingesting and adjusting based on current threat intelligence?

Alex: Precisely. The day-to-day threat intelligence is our opportunity to narrow down the attack surface based on what is going on in the cyber threat landscape. At the same time, this is passed on to the cyber resilience index for scoring, so eventually the positive or negative fluctuations will be reflected there, ultimately forming a very realistic, accurate, and near real-time metric for cyber resilience.

Sophia: Sounds great, indeed. Is there another input?

Alex: Yes, the fourth input is ad hoc exercises or events that impact our security posture. This could be findings from a red team exercise or discovered misconfigurations that could be exploited. These need to be evaluated by the expert panel and factored into our resilience index scoring. It's similar to running practice matches or analyzing your own games to identify weaknesses in your chess strategy.

Sophia: Aha! So, all our activities, even practice activities, influence the cyber resilience index?

Alex: Yes, correct. Practice activities like red team exercises or ad hoc audit findings and risk assessments provide us with gaps to fix. So, initially this is reflected as a negative trend in the resilience index, but when we eventually fix them, they will add points to the resilience index and therefore we would expect a positive trend to return.

Alex: That's also a significant differentiation from the typical qualitative risk matrixes. We don't rely on those with the cyber resilience index. If they do exist to support a typical risk register in organizations, as we used to have in the past, we integrate and influence the cyber resilience index. Therefore, every issue that is solved throughout our risk register will improve or worsen the trendlines and the resilience score.

Sophia: Okay, looks like we will need to have that discussion with our risk management colleagues, but before that, is there a fifth input or that is all?

Alex: There is a fifth and last input. This is our quarterly planning. As our organization plans ahead each quarter, we need to align our cybersecurity efforts with broader organizational goals. Meaning, adjusting priorities or setting new OKRs based on cyber foresight and insights from our cyber defense innovation capability.

Alex: It's like adjusting your chess training regimen based on upcoming tournaments and your long-term career goals. This also helps us form unified, bird's-eye view OKRs for the entire chain and not only per team.

Sophia: Very good. I am happy to hear that planning ahead and overall alignment is being considered. This is incredibly comprehensive, nonetheless. How do we ensure all these inputs are properly considered and integrated?

Alex: That's the work of our expert panel, alongside the right tooling for tracking. They evaluate each input, score its importance and potential impact, and determine how it should influence our cyber resilience index and overall security strategy.

Alex: It's a dynamic, ongoing process that keeps our security posture aligned with both current threats and organizational goals. Think of it as a chess player constantly analyzing the board state, considering past moves, anticipating future possibilities, and adjusting their strategy accordingly.

Sophia: Okay, I understand how this approach gives us a much more dynamic and responsive security posture. But it also seems like a significant change from how we currently operate and that is a concern I still have.

Alex: You're absolutely right, it is a big change, and that's why these prerequisites are so crucial. We're not just implementing a new tool or process. We are fundamentally changing our way of working. It requires buy-in at all levels, from the entire CISO leadership team to the security operations center. As the philosopher Socrates said, "The secret of change is to focus all of your energy, not on fighting the old, but on building the new."

Sophia: Agreed. What do you think is our biggest challenge in setting this up?

Alex: The biggest challenge is likely to be the cultural shift. We're asking teams that have historically operated independently to now work as part of a larger, integrated system. It requires a new level of collaboration and shared responsibility that many might find uncomfortable at first. It's like asking individual chess players to suddenly start playing as part of a team in a simultaneous exhibition.

Sophia: And how do we address that cultural challenge?

Alex: I believe we should start with clear communication about why we're making this change and how it benefits not just the organization, but each individual team and team member. We need to show how the threat-informed approach makes their work more impactful and meaningful, as opposed to the traditional approaches.

Alex: It's also crucial that we lead by example, demonstrating the collaborative approach we're advocating for. As Aristotle said, "We are what we repeatedly do. Excellence, then, is not an act, but a habit." We need to make this collaborative approach a habit.

Sophia: Can't agree more with that! So, tell me, how do we measure the success of this new approach?

Alex: Great question. We will be using our cyber resilience index as our primary metric. The index will give us a quantifiable measure of our cybersecurity posture, allowing us to track improvements over time. We'll be able to see how our collaborative efforts are impacting our overall resilience. It's like tracking your Elo rating in chess; it gives you a clear indicator of your performance and progress.

Sophia: I see. And how does this tie into our broader organizational goals?

Alex: The resilience index isn't just an internal metric. It's something we can use to demonstrate value to the executive board and align with broader business objectives. Showcasing how our improved cybersecurity posture enables the organization to pursue new opportunities or enter new markets more securely, for instance, we're directly contributing to the bottom line. It's like showing how a strong chess team can enhance a country's international prestige and open new diplomatic channels, in a sense, isn't it?

Sophia: Alright, yes, it is certainly something that demonstrates value. What's our first concrete step in putting these prerequisites in place?

Alex: Our first step is to secure that executive sponsorship we talked about. We need to present this to you and your leadership team and get their buy-in. Once we have that, we can start assembling our expert panel and begin the process of forming our cyber value chain. It's a journey, but one that will significantly enhance our cybersecurity posture and resilience.

Sophia: It's certainly a bold move. But I can see the potential. Let's start working on that executive presentation and get this ball rolling, shall we?

Alex: Excellent, and remember, as Sun Tzu said, "The opportunity of defeating the enemy is provided by the enemy himself." Implementing this cyber value chain, we're positioning ourselves to seize those opportunities more effectively than ever before. We're not just playing defense anymore, we're setting up a dynamic, responsive system that can adapt to threats in real time and turn them into opportunities for improvement.

Sophia: I like that perspective, I believe it is also future proof, but that is for later discussion. I feel like there is potential to change the game here.

Alex: Certainly, and just like in chess, the key to victory often lies not in individual brilliant moves, but in the overall strategy and how well all the pieces work together. That's exactly what we're aiming for with this cyber value chain.

Value Chain Formation

Alex: Here is a diagram to discuss the value chain formation.

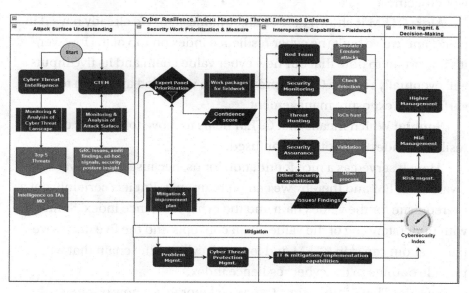

Sophia: That's a lot; what do we see here?

Alex: This is the cyber value chain swim lane. Think of it as our cybersecurity chessboard, if you will. What are your thoughts?

Sophia: To begin with, it's certainly comprehensive. Can you walk me through it?

Alex: Firstly, think of this diagram as our grand strategy for a chess tournament. Each lane represents a key aspect of our cybersecurity posture, all working together toward a common goal.

Sophia: Okay, I can see that. But let's start from the beginning. What's happening in this first lane from the left to right?

Alex: That's our attack surface understanding lane. It's where we gather intelligence about the cyber threat landscape and our own vulnerabilities. It's like studying our opponent's past games and our own weaknesses before a big tournament.

Sophia: (Pointing to the diagram) I see cyber threat intelligence (CTI) and continuous threat exposure management (CTEM) there. How do they work together?

Alex: CTEM is shown here as an optional step. We already have it in place, and we've built the cyber resilience index on top of it. However, it's important to note that our new cyber value chain and its five inputs will eventually replace CTEM, providing an upgraded approach to threat surface and exposure management.

Sophia: Which means that CTEM helps to move toward the cyber resilience index? Or not? I'm confused.

Alex: It served as a nice foundation for us, because people were aware of CTEM and thereby we can build upon it. But it is certainly not a prerequisite for the value chain and the cyber resilience index. Someone with understanding of the value chain concepts and the five inputs we talked about can skip CTEM and form the cyber value chain that will provide outputs to the cyber resilience index.

Sophia: That's interesting. Can you elaborate on how our new approach improves upon CTEM?

Alex: Our cyber value chain, with its five key inputs, offers a more comprehensive and dynamic way to understand and manage our threat surface. It integrates threat intelligence, vulnerability management, and risk assessment in a more cohesive manner. Think of it as evolving from a standard chess opening to a more adaptive, responsive playstyle.

Alex: Nonetheless, they can be complementary processes, for now. CTI gives us insights into the external threat landscape, while CTEM helps us understand our own attack surface. Together, they provide a comprehensive view of our risk exposure. It's the combination of threat-informed and asset-driven approaches.

Sophia: Okay, that sounds good in theory, but how do we ensure the information flow between these components is effective?

Alex: Excellent question. The key is in the close collaboration between the CTEM program and the expert panel. Information flows not just linearly, but cyclically. For instance, the findings from our CTEM process feed back into our threat intelligence, helping us refine our understanding of which threats are most relevant to us.

Sophia: Got it. How about this "Expert Panel Prioritization"? Is that the next step?

Alex: Exactly. Think of the expert panel as our team of grandmasters. They take all the intelligence we've gathered and use it to prioritize our efforts. They're the ones who decide which "moves" we should make next. What will eventually become a work package and therefore advance further in the flow to be distributed into the teams.

Sophia: That's a lot of responsibility for one group. How do we ensure they're making the right decisions?

Alex: It's not just about one group making decisions in isolation. The expert panel draws on input from across the organization. Remember Aristotle's quote? "The whole is greater than the sum of its parts." Bringing together diverse perspectives, we can make more informed decisions.

Sophia: Okay, I can see the value in that. But what about these "work packages for fieldwork"? What exactly are those?

Alex: Those are the actionable tasks that come out of the expert panel's prioritization. Think of them as the specific moves we're going to make in our chess game. They could be anything from implementing a new security control to conducting a targeted vulnerability assessment, to emulating adversaries' TTPs, to initiate a TIBSA, a targeted red team, validating security control effectiveness and so forth.

Sophia: Right, and what about this box labeled "confidence score"? We haven't discussed that yet.

Alex: Excellent observation. The confidence score is a crucial metric; it's essentially our baseline. We've put a lot of work into gathering historical data to inform this score.

Sophia: What kind of data are we talking about?

Alex: Briefly, we've looked at things like how many times we've suffered a breach from spear phishing, how often it was a malicious PDF or DOCX file, the number of confirmed breaches in the past five years, and so on. We've also assessed our existing coverage against the MITRE ATT&CK framework to enhance that baseline.

Sophia: That sounds like a lot of work already. But how does this baseline actually help us in practice?

Alex: This baseline helps our expert panel form opinions on which work packages should advance to the distribution phase for our interoperable capabilities. It's like having a detailed history of past chess games to inform our strategy.

Sophia: I think I see where you're going with this. It helps us avoid redundant efforts?

Alex: Exactly. If our baseline shows we already have strong coverage in certain areas, we can avoid wasting resources on redundant measures or redoing work of little to no value. Instead, we can focus our efforts where they will have the most impact.

Sophia: (Smiling) So it's not just about doing more, it's about working smarter.

Alex: Precisely! Remember Aristotle's quote about excellence? "We are what we repeatedly do. Excellence, then, is not an act, but a habit." This confidence score helps us build habits of efficient and effective cybersecurity practices.

Sophia: I have to admit, that's pretty clever. It adds a layer of smart decision-making that could really sharpen our planning and resource allocation.

Alex: That's exactly right. And, in chess terms, it's like having a strong understanding of the board before making our moves. The confidence score ensures we're not just reacting, but making informed, strategic decisions.

Sophia: Alright, I'm impressed. This is starting to sound less like bureaucratic overhead and more like a real game changer.

Alex: I'm glad you see it that way. Remember, in cybersecurity as in chess, the goal isn't to make the most moves, it's to make the right moves. The confidence score helps us achieve exactly just that.

Sophia: Right, and then we move into the lane of "Interoperable Capabilities." That looks... crowded.

Alex: It can seem that way at first glance. But think of it as our different chess pieces working together. We have our red team of ethical hackers, our "knights" if you will, probing our defenses. Our security monitoring team acts as our "rooks," watching over the entire board. Threat hunting is like our "bishops," moving diagonally across the board to uncover hidden threats.

Sophia: You really love these chess analogies, don't you?

Alex: They do help make complex concepts more digestible, don't they?

Sophia: If you say so. But I'm more interested in how these teams work together. As I mentioned before and in my experience, different security teams often end up working in silos.

Alex: I understand and indeed it is a common problem in many organizations. Although mind you, we're not just putting these teams in the same diagram, we're creating processes for them to work together seamlessly.

Sophia: That's easier said than done.

Alex: You're right; it's not easy, but it's necessary. Blast from the past again, as Heraclitus said, "The only constant in life is change." We need to be willing to change our ways of working to stay ahead of the threats we face.

Sophia: Fair point. So how do we make this collaboration happen, as you claim, seamless?

Alex: It starts with shared goals and clear communication channels. For instance, when our red team simulates or emulates an attack, the findings don't just go into a report. They're immediately shared with the security monitoring team to improve detection capabilities and with the threat hunting team to inform their search patterns.

Alex: And all activities and steps and outcomes are recorded in one shared collaborative platform. The capability representatives in the expert panel assign the work packages to expert team members that work together, despite those experts belonging in different teams as per the organization chart.

Sophia: I can see how that would be powerful. But it also sounds like it could generate a lot of noise. How do we make sure we're focusing on what's important?

Alex: That's where our "Risk Management and Decision-Making Lane" comes in. Think of it as our chess clock, keeping us focused and on track. The findings and insights generated by our interoperable capabilities feed into our risk management process, which in turn informs our cyber resilience index.

Sophia: Like the clock in a chess game... I like that. And how about this "Orchestrate-Steer-Oversee Mitigation" part?

Alex: That's our execution phase. Once we've identified and prioritized risks and decided on a course of action, this is where we put those plans into action. It's like the endgame in chess, where all our previous moves come together.

Sophia: This is certainly comprehensive. But I must ask, how do we measure success? How do we know if the outcomes of this entire value chain are improving our security posture?

Alex: Excellent question. That's where our cyber resilience index comes in. It's not just a final output, it's a dynamic measure that's constantly updated based on the activities across our value chain. Think of it like our Elo rating in chess, giving us a quantifiable measure of our performance.

Alex: The Elo rating system is a method for calculating the relative skill levels of players in zero-sum games like chess. The difference in the ratings between two players serves as a predictor of the outcome of a match. For instance, a player whose rating is 100 points greater than their opponent's is expected to score 64%; if the difference is 200 points, then the expected score for the stronger player is 76% and so on.

Alex: So, there will certainly be dips on the cyber resilience index trend, as new threats arise, or threat actors evolve their TTPs. But as long as we keep on improving our security posture and step ahead of them, our trendline will turn positive, and that's what we should be looking. The overall long-term trend. Much like the S&P500 index or an Exchange-Traded Fund (ETF) that tracks the US technology sector.

Sophia: That's a lot, but I can certainly see the potential.

Alex: You're right. It's not going to be easy. Seneca said, "It is not because things are difficult that we do not dare; it is because we do not dare that things are difficult." The value chain gives us the framework to dare greatly in our approach to cybersecurity.

Sophia: Always with the quotes, Alex. But I take your point. So, what's our first move in implementing this?

Alex: Our first move is to start small but think big. We begin by identifying the key players for our expert panel. From there, we can start implementing the attack surface understanding lane. It's like developing our opening repertoire in chess. We start with the basics and build from there.

Sophia: Alright. You've convinced me it's worth a shot. Let's start putting together the expert panel. But fair warning, I'll be watching closely to make sure this doesn't turn into a bureaucratic nightmare.

Alex: I wouldn't expect anything less from you. Your critical eye will be crucial in making this successful. After all, in chess as in cybersecurity, the best moves often come from constructive challenge and collaboration.

Sophia: One last thing, how do we ensure the value chain remains flexible? The threat landscape is always changing.

Alex: The value chain isn't a static structure. It's designed to evolve. We'll have regular review points to assess its effectiveness and adjust. It's like analyzing our chess games after a tournament – we learn, we adapt, and we improve.

Sophia: Alright. Let's make it happen.

Alex: Remember, in chess and in cybersecurity, the goal isn't just to react to your opponent's moves, it's to control the board. That's what the value chain allows us to do.

Information Flow Within the Cyber Value Chain

Sophia: Alright, I'm ready to see this cyber value chain in action. Show me how the information flows, explain a bit about the expert panel which seems to be crucial in the flow.

Alex: Excellent. Let's use the Lockbit ransomware group as our example. Imagine our cyber chessboard, with Lockbit as our opponent. Our cyber threat intelligence team has just provided us with an updated causal graph of Lockbit's latest strategies; here is part of it:

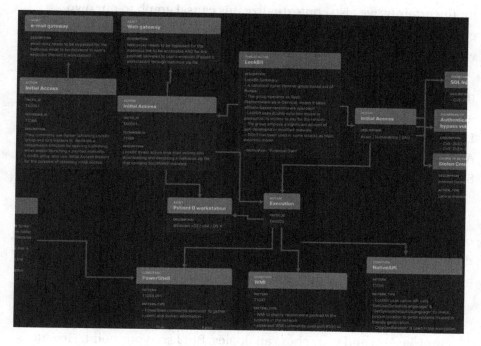

Sophia: (Looking at the graph) This looks like a very complex opening move. How do we even begin to counter this?

Alex: It is rather simple, however. The opening moves are potentially three in this case. They are marked with blue boxes and the tactic is "Initial Access." These are the three most successful opening moves of Lockbit according to our intel. Now, remember Sun Tzu? "If you know the enemy and know yourself, you need not fear the result of a hundred battles." This causal graph is our way of knowing the enemy. Our expert panel will analyze not only the opening moves but also the continuation of their "game," as well as our own measures and countermeasures in place, to know ourselves better.

Alex: So, what we see in this graph is not only their opening move alone, but this is also all their most successful moves they are playing in their "tournaments." In other words, their most successful moves are their most probable ones we are considering. But because we are accounting for uncertainty, we also contextualize this causal graph to our own environment and therefore figuring out how would they alter their "game" within our own IT landscape to achieve their goals.

Sophia: Oh wow... these are great notions, fascinating. Okay, walk me through it. What's our first move now?

Alex: Let's start with their initial access tactics. The graph shows Lockbit often uses phishing emails with malicious attachments. In MITRE ATT&CK terms, we're looking at techniques like T1566.001 – Phishing: Spearphishing Attachment.

Sophia: So how do our "pieces" defend against this?

Alex: Our email filtering systems act like pawns, forming our first line of defense. Our user awareness training programs are like bishops, moving diagonally across departments to educate our people. And how about our endpoint detection and protection measures? What do you think?

Sophia: Ehm...

Alex: They're our rooks, providing strong, linear defense.

Sophia: You and your chess analogies. But I see your point. How does the expert panel use this information?

Alex: The expert panel identifies, firstly, if indeed we have rooks, bishops, pawns in place. Namely, what kind of security measures and potentially even countermeasures we have in place to detect, prevent, and recover if needed. Then they evaluate each of these "pieces" against Lockbit's known tactics.

Alex: For instance, they might ask: "How effective is our email filtering at detecting the specific file types Lockbit is using? Are our users trained to spot the current phishing lures? Is our endpoint protection capable to detect and block the specific malware payloads? What if the adversaries slightly change their payload or one of their TTPs to match our IT landscape?"

Sophia: That sounds like a lot of questions to answer.

Alex: Indeed. But as Socrates said, "I know that I know nothing." Our expert panel starts from this humble position, forming hypothesis and then questioning everything. They are trying to validate or invalidate the hypothesis. But we don't have unlimited resources to address every single question. Hence, they also make use of our baseline. The confidence scoring, remember?

Sophia: That's an interesting way to approach it. Seems like we are applying scientific methods to our cybersecurity strategy. We form hypotheses about our vulnerabilities and defenses, then test them rigorously. But as you said, we can't experiment endlessly; we have budgets and deadlines to meet.

Sophia: On the other hand, I like how you've balanced this scientific approach with practical business needs through the confidence scoring. It reminds me of what management guru Peter Drucker once said: "What gets measured, gets managed." Quantifying our confidence in our defenses means we are not just theorizing, rather we are creating actionable insights.

Alex: You are spot on! And to add to that because I some time ago mentioned "it's simple," I still believe that it is indeed simple.

Sophia: How so?!

Alex: Because all these activities happen only the first time we run these exercises. Once our confidence score reaches up to par, specifically, when we start building coverage against our top 5 threats and their respective threat actors, then it will be a matter of reassessing only the new TTPs or tooling of the relevant threat actors. Thus, significantly speeding up the entire value chain, maximizing its outputs, and minimizing the time to respond to threats. As Plato said, "the beginning is the most important part of the work."

Sophia: Aha! Now I get it... then indeed if we put the hard work in the beginning to build our confidence score, then it's a matter of following up on the developments of the threat landscape and keep on improving our cyber resilience.

Sophia: On a lighter note... it reminds me of my fitness journey, as every new beginning it was tough, but once I reached a solid fitness level, then it's not hard anymore and it becomes a matter of maintenance in a sense.

Alex: Well... Yes, okay! Hehe!

Sophia: Okay, back to work packages, how do we prioritize them?

Alex: This is where our Partially Observable Markov Decision Process, or POMDP, comes into play.

Sophia: The POMDP what? You lost me here! What is that? Can you explain it in layman's terms?

Alex: Heh, sure... Think of POMDP as our specialized chess engine for cybersecurity. It helps us make decisions in situations where we have incomplete information, which is almost always the case in our field.

Sophia: Okay, but how does it work exactly?

Alex: POMDP considers our current state, the possible actions we can take, and the potential outcomes of those actions. But here's the key; it also factors in the uncertainty of our observations. We might think we know what's happening on our network, but we can never be 100% sure.

Sophia: That sounds a lot like playing chess with some of the pieces hidden, right?

Alex: Exactly! In chess, you can see all the pieces on the board. But in cybersecurity, it's like playing with some of your opponent's pieces, and even some of your own, hidden from view, which is exactly the case, for instance, remember that our CMDB is not to be trusted 100% due to our inability to map the entire Internet-exposed application list? POMDP helps us make the best decisions possible given this partial observability.

Sophia: So how does the expert panel use this to prioritize work packages?

Alex: The expert panel inputs various factors into the POMDP model. These include our current security controls, the potential actions we could take, like implementing new controls or improving existing ones, and the likelihood and impact of different attack scenarios based on the Lockbit causal graph.

Sophia: And the model helps decide which actions to take?

Alex: Yes, but it's not just about picking the single best action. POMDP helps us develop a policy. A set of actions to take over time that maximizes our expected long-term reward, which in our case is improved cybersecurity posture and cyber resilience.

Sophia: Can you give me a concrete example?

Alex: Let's say we are considering whether to prioritize improving our email filtering or enhancing our network segmentation. The POMDP model might suggest that while email filtering provides an immediate benefit, enhancing network segmentation brings better long-term protection against Lockbit's lateral movement techniques.

Sophia: I see. So, it's not just about the immediate payoff, but the long-term strategy.

Alex: Precisely. As the philosopher Seneca said, "If one does not know to which port one is sailing, no wind is favorable." POMDP helps us chart our course in the uncertain seas of cybersecurity.

Alex: However, it is important to remember that through POMDP we gain these insights, but the decision is our own at the end. We might consciously choose to address the "low-hanging fruits" over the long-term wins sometimes. And that is visible in the resilience index; it is reflected in the point system. And that's one of the significant advantages of the cyber resilience index. Making informed decisions based on facts and data, rather than assumptions, gut feelings, or rough estimations between high-low-medium boundaries.

Sophia: Why do you say that?

Alex: Because sometimes, we take actions that can take out fires immediately and then think of the longer run. While in other cases we might choose to aim for the long-run benefits directly. It's all about prioritization versus effort versus cost versus benefit.

Sophia: This is fascinating and indeed spot on. I assume this model might have many parameters, nonetheless. And potentially introduce complexity, right? If that's the case, how does the expert panel handle the complexity of this model?

Alex: It's a collaborative effort. Our data scientists and analytics team help set up and run the model, but the expert panel provides the crucial domain knowledge to interpret the results. They use their experience and expertise to contextualize the POMDP outputs and make final decisions on work package prioritization.

Sophia: It sounds like we're really leveraging both human expertise and advanced analytics here.

Alex: Yes, you got it. In chess and in cybersecurity, the combination of human intuition and computational power is oftentimes the winning strategy.

Sophia: And how about these confidence scores? How do they fit in?

Alex: Our confidence scores are like our evaluation of our chess position. They represent our baseline understanding of how effective we think our current controls are. The expert panel combines these with the POMDP model outputs to prioritize our efforts.

Sophia: What would be an example in this case?

Alex: Let's say our POMDP model indicates that Lockbit's use of PowerShell scripts for execution (T1059.001) has a high probability of success in our environment, given our current state and observable information. Our confidence score for detecting malicious PowerShell activity is 22%. This combination would make improving our PowerShell monitoring a high priority.

Sophia: Aha! Now I am getting the full operational picture as well. So, we're not just reacting to the last attack, we're anticipating the next one.

Alex: Exactly. As Gretzky said, "I skate to where the puck is going to be, not where it has been."

Sophia: I thought we were sticking to chess.

Alex: Just keeping you on your toes! Now, once we've prioritized based on the POMDP insights, the expert panel creates work packages. These are like our planned moves in response to Lockbit's strategy.

Sophia: And how are these work packages distributed?

Alex: They're assigned to the relevant teams based on their expertise. Our red team might be tasked with simulating Lockbit's PowerShell techniques. Our SOC could be asked to verify coverage on detection or an improvement work package, namely, introduce tailor detection rules for these activities. Our IT team might need to implement stricter PowerShell controls and so forth.

Sophia: How do we ensure all these teams are working together effectively?

Alex: That's the beauty of our cyber value chain. It's like a well-coordinated chess team, where each player understands not just their own move, but how it fits into the overall strategy. Our red team findings immediately inform SOC improvements. SOC detection insights guide IT control implementations. It's a continuous circle, constantly updating our POMDP model. A way of working very well streamlined, empowered with the right technology, people, and processes to achieve that.

Sophia: And how do we validate that all of this is improving our defenses?

Alex: Our red team and security assurance teams play a crucial role here. They essentially play the role of Lockbit, testing our defenses using the TTPs from our causal graph. They might attempt to use PowerShell Empire for post-exploitation activities or try to use BITSAdmin for persistence.

Sophia: Sounds intense. What happens with the results?

Alex: The results feed back to our expert panel and into our POMDP model. If our new PowerShell controls successfully block the red team's attempts, it updates our model's understanding of our current state and the effectiveness of our actions. This in turn increases our confidence score for that control and against that specific TTP. If they find a way around it, that also informs our model, helping us refine our strategy.

Sophia: And all of this impacts our cyber resilience index?

Alex: Precisely. The resilience index is like our chess rating. It goes up when our POMDP-guided actions successfully improve our defenses, and it might dip temporarily when we discover new vulnerabilities. But the goal is continuous improvement of cyber resilience over time.

Sophia: Okay, got it, but do you have any visual I could take with me to reflect on the entire information flow later?

Alex: Yes. The entire information flow can be captured within seven steps on a high level, as shown in this figure.

01	02	03	04	05	06	07
Threat landscape analysis	Identify PPP impacted assets	Identify PPP TTPs	Apply scoring model	Identify security controls	Assess control effectiveness	Reporting
· Information to intelligence · Balanced strategic - operational - tactical	· Goal-led AND · Tailored	· Connect the WHY and HOW · Create blueprint	· Customized · Weighted · Validated · Consistent · Updated	· Prevent · Detect · Deter · Deceive · Recover	· Silobreaking · Collaboration · Data-backed validation	· Concise · Reasonable · Actionable · Indexed

Sophia: Perfect. I see during the last step, the report must be concise, reasonable, actionable, and indexed. Assuming "indexed" means to be integrated eventually within the cyber resilience index, right?

Alex: Yes, exactly.

Sophia: But what does "indexed" practically means? How do we translate this into a language the board will understand?

Alex: Great question, and that I believe is a topic on its own. Briefly, we frame it in terms of business impact. We might say, "Our improvements have reduced our vulnerability to ransomware attacks by 20%, avoiding €X million in ransom demands and operational disruptions."

Sophia: Excellent, that's the kind of language that gets attention in the boardroom.

Alex: Very glad to hear. As Cicero said, "If you wish to persuade me, you must think my thoughts, feel my feelings, and speak my words." We're translating our technical chess game into the business language our executives understand. But here is where we need your input as the CISO. We must tailor the language accordingly. Each organization and each executive board may be slightly different.

Sophia: Alex, I have to say, this is impressive. It's like we're not just playing defense anymore, we're controlling the whole board. And on top of that, we are figuring out a way to articulate ourselves best all the way up to the executive board.

Alex: That's exactly right. In chess, the best players don't just react to their opponent's moves, they control the flow of the game. That's what our cyber value chain allows us to do, but in the cybersecurity domain.

Sophia: Superb. I would like to hear more about the cyber resilience index interpretation and how to read it. How it could be used to drive our decision-making throughout all managerial and leadership layers.

Reading the Cyber Resilience Index

Sophia: So, how do we read the cyber resilience index? And how do other leaders and managers read it or utilize it? Can you walk me through it, especially from an executive perspective? I recall you promised me a figure of the cyber resilience index; did you find that?

Alex: Oh, you are right, indeed! Yes, I got it. Let's start with how executives and managers can interpret the cyber resilience index. Imagine our cybersecurity posture as a complex chess game. The resilience index is like a grandmaster's evaluation of the position, a single number that captures the overall state of play.

Sophia: But how does this look? Can you show me?

Alex: Yes, I got the figure handy now. This is our cyber resilience index. Notice the main graph, the orange line, that's our cyber resilience trendline over time.

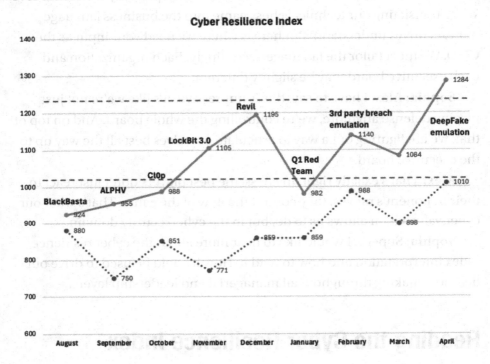

Cyber Resilience Index

Sophia: Aha! This looks interesting. And what is the blue dotted line?

Alex: This is our initial assessment from the expert panel. Remember? We first measure "what we think we have in place to protect us" versus "what f-actually we have in place to protect us." In simple words, the orange trendline is our validated security control effectiveness, while the blue trendline is our initial assessment.

Sophia: Excellent. And why do we notice these dips only in the blue trendline, while the orange trendline is steadily going upward?

Alex: Look from left to right. When BlackBasta threat profile was created by our intel team, we thought we are quite well protected. However, as we discussed, this is not a paper exercise, nor a compliance

140

or excel sheet-based exercise. When we emulated BlackBasta's TTPs and incorporated uncertainty arising from their own moves and our own IT landscape, we discovered that we overrated our protection. Hence the dip in the blue trendline.

Sophia: Aha! Very interesting findings. And what happened next?

Alex: Next, the expert panel alongside the interoperable value chain discussed the mitigating measures. They quantified all, and it's fed into the resilience index. We then decided which ones to implement, and that is how the orange trendline is formed.

Sophia: I see. It seems very well thought out and effective. And, I must admit, much cleaner than the maze of charts we usually get bombarded with.

Alex: Exactly. Many organizations fall into the trap of creating numerous Power BI dashboards with countless metrics. It's like trying to play chess by simultaneously watching a hundred different boards. Our cyber resilience index serves as that single, powerful metric – the "lighthouse" that guides our cybersecurity strategy.

Sophia: But we also need more detailed information.

Alex: Absolutely. Just like a car's dashboard has a prominent speedometer along with other gauges, our resilience index dashboard includes sub-metrics. These are like the oil pressure, tire pressure, and engine Revolutions Per Minute (RPM) gauges. They provide detailed insights, but the cyber resilience index trendline remains our primary focus.

Sophia: Fair view, okay. And I see these green dotted lines on the graph as well. What do they represent?

Alex: Good catch. The lower dotted line represents our minimum acceptable cyber resilience score based on our risk tolerance. The upper dotted line is our target resilience score, aligned with our risk appetite. Staying between these lines is our goal. That's how we can have a solid decision-making and avoid over- or underspending. Over- or underestimate our security controls and so forth.

Sophia: So, how do executives interpret this?

Alex: Think of it like a chess rating. If our resilience index is trending upward, it means our overall cybersecurity posture is improving. A downward trend indicates emerging threats or areas needing attention. Sudden dips represent newly discovered vulnerabilities or evolving attack techniques, hence attention to work on very specific things.

Sophia: And how does this tie into decision-making?

Alex: That's where it gets interesting. The resilience index doesn't just show us where we are; it guides where we should go. For instance, if we're consistently below our risk tolerance line, it might be time for significant investment in our cybersecurity program.

Sophia: I see. Now, how do we use this to drive our objectives and key results (OKRs)?

Alex: Great question. The resilience index becomes the north star for our OKRs. For example, an objective might be "Enhance our ransomware resilience," with a key result of "Increase our index score for ransomware defense by 3% this quarter, or by X amount of points this quarter." Therefore, overarching OKRs for the entire value chain can be formed, which also help in prioritizing work throughout our teams.

Sophia: How does that differ from our KPIs?

Alex: KPIs are more granular, day-to-day operational metrics. They're the individual moves in our chess game, while OKRs are more like our overall game strategy. A KPI might be "Percentage of endpoints with up-to-date anti-malware software," which contributes to our broader OKR of improving ransomware resilience. One is measuring direction; the other measures performance.

Sophia: So, we use both?

Alex: Exactly. KPIs help us manage daily operations, while OKRs, driven by the resilience index, help us achieve strategic goals. It's like a chess player tracking their move accuracy (KPI) while working toward improving their overall rating (OKR).

Sophia: Excellent, I got it. How do we use the index to steer our value chain work? You mentioned it can be used for prioritization.

Alex: It helps us make data-driven decisions about resource allocation. Let me give you an example.

Sophia: Please do.

Alex: Let's say we're considering two options: implementing a new network detection and response (NDR) system that would cost us around €1 million and could increase our CRI by 80 points or enhancing our existing security awareness training program for €100,000 that could increase our CRI by 60 points.

Sophia: The training seems like the better investment.

Alex: Exactly. It's like choosing between buying an expensive new chess engine or investing in targeted training with a grandmaster. The latter often yields better results per euro spent. The CRI helps us quantify and compare these options. Of course, always considering the risk tolerance and appetite boundaries.

Sophia: But how do we know these point values are accurate?

Alex: That's where our expert panel and POMDP model comes in. They assess each option based on our current state, the threat landscape, and potential outcomes. It's not only the accurate, raw point increase, but how those points contribute to our overall resilience.

Sophia: Can you give me another example of how this steers our work then?

Alex: Let's say our threat intelligence suggests a rise in supply chain attacks. We might see that improving our third-party risk management could increase our resilience index by 200 points, while further enhancing our already strong perimeter defenses might only yield a 20-point increase. This insight would steer us toward prioritizing supply chain security initiatives.

Sophia: Oh wow, that's powerful. I see how this could really focus our efforts and resources.

Alex: Precisely. Remember Seneca's saying? "If one does not know to which port one is sailing, no wind is favorable." The index gives us that clear destination, allowing us to steer our cybersecurity ship more effectively.

Sophia: Okay... Let me challenge you a bit again, being suspicious... Is there a threat to validity here that we miss? For instance, how do we avoid misinterpreting or misusing the cyber resilience index?

Alex: Excellent point! And yes, there are threats to validity. One common pitfall is focusing too much on short-term gains. It's like a chess player sacrificing too many pieces for a temporary advantage. We need to balance short-term improvements with long-term resilience.

Sophia: Looks like you have given a thought on this as well, which is good, but what other pitfalls should we watch out for?

Alex: Another is neglecting the sub-metrics in favor of just the overall cyber resilience score. It's like only looking at our chess rating without analyzing our game performance. We need to dig into the details to truly understand our security posture.

Sophia: Okay, so, overall, how do we ensure the cyber resilience index's validity?

Alex: We regularly audit our index calculations and assumptions. We also compare our index trends with actual security incidents to ensure it is accurately reflecting our resilience. It's like analyzing our chess games to ensure our rating truly reflects our skill.

Sophia: Speaking of comparisons, can we use the resilience index to benchmark against other organizations? You know we are committed to excellence, but how exactly do we define excellence? Perhaps the cyber resilience index could be used as such?

Alex: That's a nice idea. Although we need to be cautious. It's like comparing chess ratings across different leagues. We can use the resilience index to benchmark against industry standards, and if other organizations use a similar framework, we can compare our trends. But the most valuable comparison is against our own historical performance.

Sophia: How does the CRI help with both short-term and long-term decision-making?

Alex: Think of it like chess time control. In blitz chess (commonly known as speed chess), you make quick decisions based on immediate threats; that's our short-term tactical use of the cyber resilience index. In classical chess, where each player has a significant amount of time to make decisions and moves, you plan several moves ahead; that's our long-term strategic use.

Sophia: Help me understand this better; what would be an example here?

Alex: In the short term, a sudden dip in our resilience index due to a new vulnerability might prompt immediate patching efforts. Long term, a consistently low resilience index in a particular area might drive us to completely overhaul that aspect of our security architecture.

Sophia: Understood. How do we align the index with our broader business strategy?

Alex: The resilience index should support our business objectives. For example, if we're planning to launch a new digital product, we should see our cyber resilience index improving in areas related to application security and data protection. It's like adjusting your chess strategy based on the tournament you're preparing for.

Sophia: That makes sense. But how do we communicate these insights effectively to different stakeholders?

Alex: That's where the art of translation comes in. For the executive board, we may want to focus on how trends relate to risk and potential financial impact. For the C-suite, we could emphasize how the cyber resilience index supports business initiatives. For technical teams, we would dive into the specific sub-metrics and how their work impacts the overall cyber resilience index.

Sophia: So, we follow the need for different "languages" on different audiences. Sounds like a good plan.

Alex: Exactly. As Wittgenstein said, "The limits of my language mean the limits of my world." We need to adapt our language to expand the understanding of cybersecurity across our organization.

Sophia: Nicely said. But I have to ask, how do we ensure we're continually improving the index itself and it does not remain a static thing?

Alex: The index isn't static. We regularly review and refine our CRI model based on new threats, technologies, and lessons learned. It's like how chess engines are continually updated with new strategies and data.

Sophia: So, it's a living, breathing metric?

Alex: Correct. As the Roman emperor Marcus Aurelius observed, "The universe is change; our life is what our thoughts make it." Our threat landscape is always evolving, and our resilience index must adapt with it, guiding our response to these constant changes.

Alex: And another very relevant one, Confucius said, "The man who moves a mountain begins by carrying away small stones." Which practically means for us that we start gradually. First, we ensure our leadership understands and buys into the CRI concept. Then we align our OKRs with the cyber resilience index improvement. We train our teams on how to interpret and act on the index data. And lastly, we continuously refine our approach.

Sophia: It sounds like a journey...

Alex: It is. But as Lao Tzu said, "The journey of a thousand miles begins with one step." And in this case, that step is understanding and leveraging our cyber resilience index.

Sophia: You have a quote for everything?

Alex: Well, I did consider getting "Cybersecurity Philosopher" added to my job title, but HR wasn't too keen on the idea.

Sophia: (Laughing) I can imagine. But I must admit, your quotes do help put things in perspective.

Alex: That's the goal!

Sophia: But maybe ease up on the quotations for the next few minutes?

Alex: I'll do my best, but no promises. After all, as someone once said... (stops himself and smiles).

Sophia: Alright, I think I'm starting to see the full picture. The cyber resilience index isn't just a metric. It's a new way of thinking about and managing our cybersecurity.

Alex: Exactly. It's like moving from playing individual chess games to managing a grandmaster's entire chess career. We're not just defending against individual attacks; we're trying to build long-term cyber resilience. And remember, in chess and in cybersecurity, the key to victory is not just in the moves you make, but in the strategy that guides them.

Sophia: (Smiling) Ah... we got into chess analogies now! Anyway, they do help get the message across, so it's all fine. For now, I find this... somewhat fascinating.

Alex: ...somewhat?

Sophia: It's already late for today; will see you tomorrow!

Interoperability: Breaking Down Silos

Sophia: (Walking into Alex's office) Alex, I'm back again. I've been thinking about the value chain and the interoperability part you keep talking about.

Alex: (Looks up from his computer, intrigued) Oh? What's on your mind?

Sophia: Well, I realized my teenagers at home are the perfect example of a lack of interoperability. They each have their own language, their own tools, and they certainly don't share information willingly!

Alex: Ah, the classic "silo-ed teenager" problem, right?! A challenge that's stumped even the best IT architects for generations.

Sophia: Exactly! So, I was thinking, if we can solve interoperability in our cybersecurity teams, maybe you could help me with my home interoperability issues next?

Alex: I appreciate your faith in our capabilities, but I think we should tackle one impossible task at a time. Let's start with our cybersecurity interoperability, and if we succeed there, we can consider expanding into the treacherous world of teenage communication.

Sophia: (Laughing) Fair enough. So, where do we begin with breaking down our professional silos? And please tell me it doesn't involve TikTok dances or cryptic text messages.

Alex: Well, now that you mention it... (pauses for effect). No, I'm just kidding. Let's start with something a bit more traditional, shall we?

Sophia: Yes, I'm still trying to understand how we make all our different teams and tools work together effectively.

Alex: That's where our concept of cross-divisional value chains comes in. We call them "parachains" or "cross-chains."

Sophia: Parachains? That's a new term for me.

Alex: Think of it as an extension of our main cyber value chain. When we identify a specific threat actor or attack pattern, we form a specialized team that cuts across traditional department boundaries.

Sophia: Can you give me an example?

Alex: Consider a sophisticated supply chain attack, similar to the SolarWinds one. Our main cyber value chain might not have all the expertise we need to address this comprehensively.

Sophia: So, what do we do?

Alex: We form a parachain. We would bring in experts from our supply chain security department for their specialized knowledge. We would also include key business leaders who know exactly where our crown jewels related to supply chain operations are located and IT or data architects with that specific know-how.

Sophia: I see. So, we're creating a custom team for each major threat?

Alex: Not exactly. The foundation remains the same, our value chain with the standard capabilities and the expert panel but have some buffer to allow for extra expertise to join when necessary. It's like forming a special task force in chess, where we bring together experts in different aspects of the game to tackle a particularly tricky opponent.

Alex: Think of it as creating a flexible, modular structure for our interoperability efforts. Instead of building rigid connections between our tools and teams, we design systems that can be quickly reconfigured as needed. You could also imagine the parachains as a set of building blocks, like Lego pieces. Each block represents a specific tool, process, or team capability. We can quickly assemble these blocks in different configurations to respond to new threats or organizational changes; however, the foundation is already in place and works well.

Sophia: That makes sense. But how do we manage all the tools and technologies across these parachains?

Alex: That's a critical point, Sophia. Over the years, we've accumulated a vast array of security tools and telemetry sources. Many organizations try to make sense of it all by consolidating outputs into Power BI dashboards.

Sophia: I've seen those. They can be overwhelming. I believe we are also victims of this approach.

Alex: Precisely. It's like trying to play chess while simultaneously monitoring a hundred different games. It's ineffective and often counterproductive. I will refrain from saying... even misleading sometimes... but let's move on, you got the point.

Sophia: I get it, so what's the alternative?

Alex: We need to focus on true tooling interoperability. Some organizations are exploring data mesh architectures or trying to connect everything through APIs.

Sophia: Is that the solution?

Alex: It's a step in the right direction, but I believe we need to go further. We need to start what I call "decomplexifying" both our security tooling and our security controls.

149

Sophia: Decomplexifying? Is that even a word!?

Alex: (Smiling) It is now! And it's crucial. Our IT landscape is already incredibly complex. Security shouldn't add another layer of complexity on top. Instead, it should simplify and streamline.

Sophia: How do we achieve that?

Alex: First, we need to standardize our data formats and taxonomies across all tools and teams. This creates a common language for our entire security ecosystem.

Sophia: Okay, that makes sense.

Alex: Then, we look at automation and orchestration. We want to create seamless information flow and coordinated action across different teams and tools. Imagine if in chess, each piece could automatically adjust its position based on the moves of others, all working in perfect harmony.

Sophia: That would be powerful. But how does this tie back to our parachains?

Alex: When we form a parachain to address a specific threat, like our supply chain attack example, this interoperable tooling allows us to quickly aggregate relevant data from across the organization, thus helping our expert panel become even more efficient while improving the accuracy of our POMDP models.

Sophia: So, the supply chain security experts could immediately access relevant data from our main security operations?

Alex: Exactly. And not just access but integrate it with their specialized tools and knowledge. Meanwhile, the business leaders in the parachain can instantly see how the threat relates to our crown jewels, all using the same standardized data and interfaces.

Sophia: This sounds powerful, but also a bit worrying to set the right boundaries, both from access control and privacy perspectives.

Alex: Indeed. The American poet Walt Whitman once said, "Be curious, not judgmental." In our effort toward interoperability, we need to approach each team's processes and tools with curiosity rather than judgment. We need to understand how we can work together, rather than criticizing how we've worked apart. Ultimately, we need to dare to simplify and integrate our security approach.

Sophia: Okay, sounds good. Where is the cyber resilience index in this?

Alex: The "blue line" of the resilience index becomes our north star. Remember the blue line? The initial assumed resilience, the "what we think we have in place to protect us." So, this trendline would guide which integrations and simplifications will have the most impact on our overall cyber resilience. It helps us prioritize our de-complexification efforts.

Sophia: How so?

Alex: Because the expert panel performs the first, initial assessments based on historical data and using our current baseline supercharged by the POMDP models. So, imagine if we could see that our coverage against MITRE ATT&CK is constantly leading our experts to believe that we are effective against lateral movement. By the third or fourth threat actor that we would notice on this trend, we would clearly have a priority to fix that. Thus, correcting our initial beliefs.

Sophia: Very interesting notion. That would transform our cybersecurity operations and improve our baseline. I think it would also boost our confidence score and improve our efficiency as we keep on assessing our resilience over and over against threat actors, right?

Alex: That's exactly the goal; you are spot on. By breaking down silos, forming agile parachains, and creating a truly interoperable way of working and technology ecosystem, we're not just improving our defenses. We're improving our effectiveness and efficiency constantly, ultimately revolutionizing how we approach cybersecurity.

Sophia: Very good. Where does that interoperability journey starts?

Alex: We start by bringing together our key technology leaders and process owners. We need to create a road map for this interoperability journey. It won't happen overnight, but each step will make us more resilient.

Sophia: I must admit that with all this data sharing and interoperability, I'm concerned about privacy and ethical implications. How do we ensure we're not overstepping boundaries? I hinted about this before, but now I am directly saying it. It is a concern, don't you think?

Alex: That's an excellent point, and I agree. In our drive for interoperability, we must never lose sight of our ethical obligations and privacy concerns.

Sophia: How do we balance that with our security needs?

Alex: It's not easy to find balance. We need to implement strong data governance policies across our parachains. This includes data minimization principles and reasonable assurance that we only collect and share what's necessary.

Sophia: Additionally, we must be transparent about how we're using this data.

Alex: Agreed, transparency is key. We should also implement strong access controls and audit trails. Every data access within our interoperable system should be logged and justifiable.

Sophia: What about regulatory compliance? Do you foresee any issues from that angle?

Alex: That's crucial. Our interoperability efforts need to be designed with regulations like GDPR, CCPA, and industry-specific requirements in mind. It's not just about sharing data efficiently but doing so responsibly and legally.

Sophia: This adds more work to the entire project.

Alex: It does, but it's necessary. As the philosopher Immanuel Kant said, "Science is organized knowledge. Wisdom is organized life." In our case, we need to organize our knowledge in a way that respects individual privacy and supports ethical standards. However, we are aiming for smart work prioritization, remember? We can worry on how to cross this bridge when the right time comes. For now, we can focus on forming and operationalizing the primary value chain. The standard Lego pieces that will always be the working foundation.

Sophia: Indeed, I got a bit carried away. Perhaps I am also getting excited about this project! Since we are discussing tools and processes, what about the human element in all this. How do we ensure our people are as interoperable as our systems?

Alex: People are indeed the linchpin in our interoperability efforts. That's the primary essence of the cyber value chain.

Sophia: Then how do we approach this?

Alex: We need to focus on what I call "cognitive interoperability." We need to ensure our teams not only have the technical skills but also a shared mental model of our cybersecurity landscape.

Sophia: Cognitive interoperability? What do you mean? What's the analogy here?

Alex: Imagine a chess team where each player not only knows their role but understands the strategies of every other player. That's what we're aiming for in our security teams.

Sophia: I see, but how do we make this happen?

Alex: First, we implement cross-functional training programs. Everyone in our value chain, and even the parachains onward, needs to understand not just their part, but how it fits into the bigger picture.

Sophia: Good, what else?

Alex: We also need to create a common language. Too often, different teams use different terminologies, leading to miscommunication. We need a standardized cybersecurity lexicon across all teams.

Sophia: Very well! That makes sense and I can see how that would help. Reminds me of our previous discussion that established a common terminology for risk, threat, threat actor, impact, likelihood, intelligence versus information, and others. Any other aspects to this cognitive interoperability?

Alex: Yes, we need to foster a culture of collaborative problem-solving. We could host, for instance, regular cross-team workshops, simulations, or even cybersecurity war games.

Sophia: War games? That sounds intense.

Alex: It can be, but it's also incredibly effective. These exercises force teams to work together, sharing knowledge and resources in real time. It's like a chess simultaneous exhibition, but for cybersecurity.

Sophia: Although it sounds great in theory, is there also a way to measure if it's working?

Alex: That's where our resilience index comes in again. We can track how quickly and effectively our parachains respond to simulated threats. Improvements in these metrics over time would indicate growing cognitive interoperability, while a negative trendline would indicate otherwise. It can also be done through our sub-metrics.

Sophia: What sub-metrics?

Alex: The cyber resilience index is the main and north star type of metric, but we also measure other things to calibrate interoperability. For instance, the time to process a threat actor profile through the entire value chain. The time for each capability in the value chain to deliver their part. These are some of the small indicators that can be used to measure success overall, as well as interoperability.

Sophia: I see. So, we have the resilience index as our main indicator, and then we are building a dashboard of cybersecurity gauges relevant to the index and the entire value chain, which ultimately means we're not aiming to simply connect our tools and processes, but our people's minds as well. And while we are doing so, we establish meaningful metrics throughout to help us steer and calibrate whenever pain points seem to arise. Am I getting this right?

Alex: Excellent. And as the psychologist Mihaly Csikszentmihalyi once said, "A joyful life is an individual creation that cannot be copied from a recipe." Similarly, true cognitive interoperability isn't about forcing everyone to think the same way, but about creating an environment where diverse minds can seamlessly connect and collaborate, each bringing their unique perspective to the value chain. Fostering cognitive interoperability, we're creating a cybersecurity workforce that's far more effective than just a collection of individual experts.

Sophia: Fascinating. It seems like achieving true interoperability is as much about psychology as it is about technology.

Alex: Exactly! In the end, our most powerful security tool is the collective intelligence of our people. Everything else is just there to support and amplify that.

Sophia: It sounds like we're not just going to break down silos, but we will make our entire security structure more fluid.

Alex: Indeed. And soon entirely automated! The military strategist John Boyd said, "The enemy's time-cycle is getting shorter. So, if we cannot break into it, we are going to find ourselves increasingly disadvantaged." Capture that for a moment. Is that where things are headed to? Fully automated defensive versus offensive cyber value chains, fighting with each other?

Alex: Well, maybe I got carried away this time... anyhow, one thing is certain, the value chain interoperable way of working allows us to shorten our own time cycles.

Sophia: Fascinating forward thinking, but let's focus on the task at hand for now. Perhaps we can come up with a simpler term than "decomplexifying" before we present to the board?

Alex: (Laughing) Fair enough. How about we just call it "smart simplification"?

Sophia: Much better. Now, let's get to work on building the value chain and simplifying our security landscape.

Alex: Agreed. Remember, in chess as in cybersecurity, the key to victory often lies in how well all the pieces work together.

Integrating the Cyber Resilience Index into Risk Management

Sophia: I've been thinking about our risk management and operational security teams. Sometimes, I feel like they're playing different games entirely.

Alex: Let me guess, risk management is playing chess while ops security is in the middle of a game of whack-a-mole?

Sophia: (Laughing) That's not far off. Risk management is all about careful strategy and long-term planning, while ops security is constantly putting out fires.

Alex: Well, maybe it's time we got them playing on the same board. Speaking of which, I've been thinking that the cyber resilience index can help both functions play in the same board eventually. In other words, the resilience index can help integrate ops security with our existing risk management framework.

Sophia: That's very close to what I wanted to discuss. I've been thinking about how we can integrate our cyber resilience index and the threat intel–based approach with our existing risk management framework as well. We're currently using NIST CSF as you already know, and I'm concerned about potential conflicts or redundancies.

Alex: Integrating the resilience index with NIST CSF is key. The same applies for any other established risk management framework, like ISO 27000 series or others; integration becomes imperative for its long-term success and adoption.

Sophia: Exactly. How do you propose we approach this?

Alex: I believe we need to view the cyber resilience index not as a replacement for our current framework, but as an enhancement. Think of it as adding a new dimension to our risk management approach.

Sophia: Can you elaborate on that? How exactly does the resilience index enhance our existing risk management framework?

Alex: Think of it as adding a dynamic, threat-informed layer to each NIST function. It's like upgrading from a standard chess set to a 3D chessboard. We're not changing the rules, just adding new dimensions to our strategy.

Sophia: What do you mean?

Alex: For instance, in the "Identify" function of NIST, the index helps us prioritize assets based on current threat landscapes. It's like knowing which pieces your opponent is most likely to target. In the "Protect" function, it guides resource allocation to the most critical areas – like reinforcing the squares on the board where the action is most intense.

Alex: Likewise, for "Detect," "Respond," and "Recover," the cyber resilience index provides context-aware metrics. Instead of just counting incidents, we measure our effectiveness against the most relevant threats. It's like measuring not just how many pieces we've lost, but how well we're defending against the opponent's specific strategy.

Sophia: That's quite a shift in perspective.

Alex: Indeed, but as the philosopher Nassim Nicholas Taleb said, "You find peace by coming to terms with what you don't know, not by resting in the comfort of your own interpretation." The cyber resilience index helps us embrace the uncertainties in our threat landscape while enhancing our understanding of our capabilities.

Sophia: Okay, good. You know that risk management is used to produce and show those... red-yellow-green heat maps, right? What's the relationship with that element and the resilience index?

Alex: The cyber resilience index brings a multidimensional view of risk. Imagine a 3D holographic chessboard, where each piece represents a key asset or process. Its height shows the current risk level, color indicates the trend, and size represents potential impact.

Sophia: Sounds... complex. How do we make it digestible for risk management team members and even nontechnical board members?

Alex: By placing it in an interactive dashboard. At the highest level, we show the overall cyber resilience index trends – like the overall state of the chess game. Users can then drill down into specific areas of concern, getting as granular as analyzing individual piece positions.

Sophia: How do we ensure this doesn't become information overload?

Alex: Leonardo da Vinci said, "Simplicity is the ultimate sophistication." We start with a simple view and offer an "expert mode" for those who want more detail. It's about providing the right information at the right time.

Sophia: Superb then. Sounds like we will show the standard cyber resilience index you've shown me before with the basic trendlines and risk tolerance/appetite boundaries, but there will be an interactive drill down to more detailed metrics, correct?

Alex: Yes, that's correct.

Sophia: And how about the quarterly risk assessments and reporting they are doing already? How does the cyber resilience index change this? Unless it does not affect that cadence at all.

Alex: The index enables near real-time risk assessment. It's like transitioning from correspondence chess, where moves are made over days or weeks, to a live chess match where the state of play is constantly evolving.

Sophia: But then how do we act on this continuous stream of data without becoming overwhelmed?

Alex: We set thresholds for significant changes. When crossed, it triggers reassessment and potential action. It's about being responsive without causing alert fatigue. Think of it as a chess clock – it's always running, but you only make moves at strategic moments.

Sophia: This sounds like a significant shift in how we approach risk.

Alex: Exactly. As Alfred North Whitehead once said, "The art of progress is to preserve order amid change and to preserve change amid order." The cyber resilience index allows us to maintain a structured risk management framework while adapting to the cybersecurity landscape.

Sophia: Some aspects of cybersecurity risk seem impossible to quantify. My peers at risk management as well as other leaders from that division mentioned it quite a few times. How does the resilience index handle this? Does it bring any change there?

Alex: The index embraces uncertainty. We use calibrated estimation techniques, where experts provide confidence ranges rather than point estimates. It's like a chess player assessing possible moves – they don't know exactly what will happen, but they can give a range of likely outcomes.

Sophia: How do we ensure these estimates are reliable?

Alex: We conduct regular calibration training for our experts, improving their ability to provide accurate probability ranges over time. It's like chess players reviewing their games to improve their judgment.

Sophia: This sounds more nuanced than our current approach.

Alex: It is. Aristotle said, "It is the mark of an educated mind to rest satisfied with the degree of precision which the nature of the subject admits, and not to seek exactness where only an approximation is possible." That's exactly how we approach this as well during expert panels.

Sophia: Yes, the expert panel calibration. I know this from the theory of economics, the notion of approximation in measurements is well established. How do we ensure the resilience index doesn't just produce numbers though, but rather drives meaningful actions?

Alex: Each of the index component is tied to specific actions. For example, if the index indicates increased risk from new phishing techniques, it automatically suggests updating email filters and conducting targeted training. It's like a chess computer that doesn't just evaluate the position but suggests the best moves. We discussed this before in more detail, where the point system drives actionability.

Sophia: Yes, I recall. We've covered the most important notions about the technical aspects of integrating the index with our risk management. But I'm wondering about the organizational impact. How do we ensure our people and processes are ready for this change?

Alex: That's an excellent point. Peter Drucker said, "Culture eats strategy for breakfast." We need to address the cultural shift required to make the resilience index integration successful.

Sophia: What kind of cultural shift are we talking about?

Alex: We're moving from a periodic, compliance-focused risk management approach to a continuous, threat-informed one. It's like transitioning from playing occasional chess matches to being in a constant state of strategic thinking.

Sophia: Indeed, how do we prepare our teams for this? And how do we start such discussions with risk management colleagues?

Alex: First, we need to foster a culture of continuous learning. Our teams need to be comfortable with constant updates to our risk landscape. We should implement regular training sessions and threat briefings for risk management colleagues to keep everyone informed.

Sophia: Makes sense. What about our decision-making processes?

Alex: We'll need to streamline them. The index will provide us with more frequent, data-driven insights. We need to ensure our leadership is prepared to make quicker, more frequent decisions based on this information.

Sophia: I can see that being a challenge for some of our more traditional managers.

Alex: Absolutely. Machiavelli once noted, "There is nothing more difficult to take in hand, more perilous to conduct, or more uncertain in its success, than to take the lead in the introduction of a new order of things."

Sophia: Nice quote by Machiavelli, but how do we overcome this resistance that we both foresee?

Alex: We start by clearly communicating the benefits. We can show how resilience index–driven decisions lead to more effective risk management and resource allocation. It's about demonstrating value early and often.

Sophia: What about our relationships with other departments?

Alex: The resilience index integration will require closer collaboration between cybersecurity, IT, and business units. We'll need to break down silos and establish new communication channels. It's like coordinating different pieces on a chessboard – they all need to work together for an effective strategy.

Sophia: This sounds like a significant change management effort.

Alex: It is. We should consider appointing "Cyber Resilience Index Champions" in each department – individuals who can advocate for and assist with the integration process.

Sophia: That's a nice idea. How do we ensure this cultural change sticks?

Alex: We need to align our incentives and performance metrics with the value chain approach and the cyber resilience index. For example, we could include resilience index–related goals in performance reviews across the organization.

Sophia: That makes sense and sounds like a good plan. It seems like we have a good chance of bridging the gap between our strategic risk management and our day-to-day operational security.

Alex: That's exactly it. We're creating a more dynamic, responsive system that can adapt to the changing threat landscape while still maintaining the structure our stakeholders expect.

Sophia: (Nodding) And the best part is, we're not throwing out our existing framework. We're enhancing it, making it more relevant and actionable.

Alex: Precisely. As the saying goes, "The best time to plant a tree was 20 years ago. The second-best time is now." We're planting that tree today, setting ourselves up for a more resilient future.

Sophia: (Smiling) Always with the quotes. But you're right. This feels like a significant step forward. We're integrating the cyber resilience index and threat-informed defense with risk management, bridging the gap and ultimately uniting these two worlds.

The Human Element: Leadership in the Cyber Resilience Index Implementation

Sophia: Now, I'm impressed with all the technical aspects of integrating cyber resilience index and ops security into our risk management. However, I can't help wondering about the human element in all of this.

Alex: (Looking slightly uncomfortable) The human element? What do you mean exactly?

Sophia: Listen, implementing such a significant change isn't just about the technology and processes. It's also about managing people, their expectations, and potential resistance to change.

Alex: (Hesitating) Ah, yes… I suppose that is an important factor to consider. We've touched upon this slightly, right? Although I admit, I've been primarily focused on making sure the technical integration is seamless.

Sophia: Yes, indeed, that's understandable, and your work there is crucial. But remember, we're not just implementing a new system; we're changing how people work and think about risks and threats.

Alex: When you put it that way, it does sound more complex. What kind of challenges do you anticipate now that you have a good picture?

Sophia: To begin with, there's the natural resistance to change. People get comfortable with their routines, and the cyber resilience index will disrupt that. We'll need to manage that carefully.

Alex: (Nodding slowly) I see. And I suppose different departments might have different concerns?

Sophia: Exactly. IT might worry about increased workload, finance about costs, and business units about how it affects their operations. We need to address each of these concerns.

Alex: (Looking a bit overwhelmed) That's a lot to consider. How do we even begin to tackle all of that?

Sophia: It starts with strong leadership. We need to communicate the vision clearly, engage stakeholders early and provide robust support throughout the transition.

Alex: Right, managing people's emotions and expectations... that's going to be a challenge.

Sophia: (Smiling reassuringly) That's okay. Nobody's an expert at everything. That's why we work as a team.

Alex: I appreciate that. Can you give me an example of how you've handled something like this before?

Sophia: In my previous role, we implemented a new data privacy framework. Technically, it was straightforward, but we faced significant pushback from various departments.

Alex: How did you handle it?

Sophia: We started by forming a cross-functional team to represent all stakeholders. We held "town halls," meaning open meetings for the audience to explain the changes, created a comprehensive training program, and kept the lines of communication open; we were open to feedback continuously and addressed concerns in near real time.

Alex: That sounds like a lot of work beyond just the technical implementation.

Sophia: It was, but it paid off. The smooth transition made the technical implementation much easier and more effective.

Alex: Okay, I understand how that would be crucial for the technical part of the cyber resilience index to be successful... but it feels overwhelming to convince all these people. Perhaps by the time we convince them, threat actors are already within our network... (pauses).

Alex: Sophia, I think I could learn a lot from you about this aspect of the implementation. Would you be willing to guide me through it?

Sophia: Of course. I'd be happy to mentor you on the leadership and people management aspects of this project. It's just as important as the technical side, if not more so. You did the same for me these days for the technical part, so how about we swap roles now? I might not be a chess grandmaster... but perhaps I could find analogies too!

Alex: (Looking relieved) Heh, thank you. I'm realizing there's a lot more to implementing the cyber resilience index than I initially thought. What do you think should be our first steps?

Sophia: We should start by mapping out our stakeholders and their potential concerns. Then we can develop a communication strategy and a change management plan.

Alex: That makes sense. And I suppose we'll need to think about training programs too?

Sophia: Absolutely. We'll need to ensure everyone understands not just how to use the new system, but why it's important and how it benefits them and the organization.

Alex: I've always focused on the technical side, but I can see how leadership skills are crucial for success. I'm looking forward to learning from you.

Sophia: And I'm looking forward to teaching you. Your technical expertise combined with strong leadership skills will make you an even more effective cybersecurity leader.

Alex: (Smiling) Thank you. I think this is going to be a valuable learning experience for both of us. Shall we set up some time to start planning our people strategy for the cyber resilience index implementation?

Sophia: Yes, let's block out some time tomorrow to begin. We'll start with stakeholder mapping and developing our communication strategy.

Alex: Sounds great. I'll bring my technical implementation plan, and we can align it with the people management aspects.

Sophia: Perfect. Together, we'll ensure that our resilience index integration is a success, both technically and organizationally.

Sophia: But wait, have you heard anything about emotional intelligence?

Alex: Emotional intelligence? I'm not sure I'm familiar with that concept in a professional context.

Sophia: It's about recognizing and managing emotions – both your own and others'. In cybersecurity, where we often deal with high-stress situations, it's particularly important.

Alex: I can see how that would be valuable. How does it apply to the resilience index implementation though?

Sophia: Well, for example, when we're communicating changes, we need to be adjusted to how people are feeling. Are they anxious? Resistant? Excited? Understanding these emotions helps us tailor our approach and message.

Alex: (Nodding thoughtfully) I've never really considered that aspect before. It sounds like another area where I could improve.

Sophia: Perhaps. But don't worry, emotional intelligence can be developed with practice. It's another skill we'll work on together.

Sophia: It can be particularly useful when introducing such changes. For instance, when implementing the resilience index, we will be asking teams to collaborate in new ways. This can sometimes lead to conflicts.

Alex: Conflicts? I thought improving collaboration would reduce conflicts, not create them.

Sophia: In an ideal world, yes. But in reality, when teams start working more closely together, it often exposes differing priorities and work styles.

Alex: Such as?

Sophia: Let's assume our threat intelligence team identifies a new threat event that requires immediate attention. But the IT operations team is in the middle of a critical system upgrade. Whose priority takes precedence?

Alex: That's a tough one. Both seem important.

Sophia: Exactly. And in situations like this, team members might push for their own team's priorities rather than considering the overall goals of our cybersecurity value chain.

Alex: That could definitely cause friction. How do we handle that?

Sophia: It requires a fine balance. We need to create a culture where everyone understands and works toward the overarching goals of our cybersecurity strategy while still respecting individual team needs.

Alex: That sounds challenging. Do you have strategies for achieving that balance?

Sophia: There are some strategies, yes, or principles let's say better – clear communication of shared goals, fostering a collaborative culture, and sometimes conflict resolution. It's about helping teams see beyond their immediate priorities to understand how their work fits into the bigger picture.

Alex: I understand why you highlighted the importance of leadership skills. This goes far beyond technical expertise...

Sophia: It does, but, again, don't worry. We'll work on developing these skills together. We can discuss solid strategies for fostering cross-team collaboration and resolving conflicts in more detail later.

Your Move: Operationalizing the Cyber Value Chain

It's your move now dear reader and cybersecurity strategist! It's time to put your newfound knowledge into action. In this exercise, you'll be forming your own expert panel, leveraging the Conti ransomware causal graph from Chapter 2, and creating a functioning cyber value chain for your organization.

Ready to play the game of cyber chess at a grandmaster level?!

Step 1: Assembling Your Expert Panel

Form a cross-functional team of five to seven colleagues, each representing different cybersecurity capabilities (e.g., threat intelligence, vulnerability management, threat hunting, TIBSA assessors (or risk assessors), incident response, risk management, SOC operations).

Note   If you're doing this alone, create personas for each role.

- **Quick Task:** For each panel member, write a brief strength and a potential bias they might bring to the table. Remember, diversity of thought is key!

Step 2: Baseline Assessment

Retrieve the Conti ransomware causal graph from Chapter 2. Your mission:

- Identify the top 30 TTPs from the MITRE ATT&CK framework that are most relevant to the Conti attack chain.

- Rate your organization's current capability to prevent-detect-respond against each TTP on a scale of 1–5.

- Calculate your baseline cyber resilience index (CRI) score by averaging these ratings.

Fun Challenge: Set a 30–45-minute timer for this task. Chess players think fast – can you?

Step 3: Designing Your Cyber Value Chain

Now, it's time to create your cyber value chain. On a large piece of paper or digital canvas:

- Draw swim lanes for each of your key capabilities.

- Indicate information flows between capabilities.

- Mark decision points where CRI metrics would influence actions. Identify potential parachain formation points.

Creativity Boost: Use different colors for each capability. The more visually appealing, the easier it will be to spot potential gaps or bottlenecks!

Step 4: POMDP in Action

Using your expert panel, create a simple Partially Observable Markov Decision Process (POMDP) model for responding to a Conti ransomware threat:

- Define five possible states of your system (e.g., "Uncompromised," "Initial Access," "Lateral Movement," etc.)

- List five possible actions your team could take.

- Estimate probabilities of transitioning between states given each action.

Brain Teaser: How would uncertainty in your observations affect your decision-making process?

Step 5: Value Chain Simulation

Time to put your value chain to the test! Using the Conti causal graph:

- Walk through each step of a potential Conti attack. For each step, discuss as a panel:
  - Which capabilities are activated?
  - How does information flow through your value chain?
  - Where do you form parachains?
  - How do CRI metrics influence your decisions?
  - What POMDP state are you in, and what action do you take?

Make It Real: Set a five-minute timer max for each attack step. Rapid decision-making is essential.

Step 6: Interoperability Check

After your simulation:

- Identify any bottlenecks in information flow.
- Spot any missed opportunities for collaboration.
- Determine if any capabilities were underutilized or overwhelmed.

Quick Poll: Have each panel member anonymously rate the value chain's performance from 1 to 10. Discuss any significant discrepancies in scores.

Philosophical Moment: As you do this, ponder the quote: "The art of progress is to preserve order amid change and to preserve change amid order." How does this apply to your integration efforts?

Step 7: Refine and Present

Based on your simulation and discussions:

- Refine your cyber value chain design.

- Test your readiness to draw the actual CRI.

- Prepare a ten-minute presentation for your organization's leadership, highlighting

  - Key features of your value chain

  - How it performed against the Conti scenario

  - Anticipated benefits and challenges of implementation

Presentation Tip   Use a chess metaphor to explain your strategy. How has your value chain prepared you to think several moves ahead of cyber adversaries?

Conclusion

If you reached this point, congratulations! You've now designed, tested, and refined a cyber value chain tailored to your organization. You've applied the concepts of CRI, POMDP, and interoperability to create a more resilient cybersecurity posture.

Remember, as in chess, the game is never truly over. Keep refining your strategy, adapting to new threats, and striving for cyber resilience excellence.

Final Reflection: Did this exercise change your perspective on cybersecurity strategy and operations? What's the most valuable insight you've gained?

CHAPTER 4

Check and Countercheck

The Art of Leadership in Cybersecurity

Sophia was reviewing the latest cyber resilience index implementation reports when Alex knocked on her door, looking thoughtful.

Sophia: Alex, come in. You look like you've got something on your mind.

Alex: I've been reflecting on our resilience index rollout and the value chain we've designed. I'm confident in the technical aspects, but I've realized there is a whole other dimension to leading this initiative that I'm not sure I'm fully prepared for.

Sophia: You've been the head of cyber resilience for a few years now, proving yourself both technically and in leading the team. Are there specific areas of leadership that you find challenging when implementing the cyber resilience index?

Alex: It's the scale, I think. Leading my teams is one thing but steering an organization-wide initiative like the cyber resilience index... we are trying to integrate multiple departments into a value chain... It feels like a different game entirely. For instance, I'm struggling with how to get buy-in from departments that don't see cybersecurity as their primary concern.

© Lampis Alevizos 2025

L. Alevizos, *Cyber Resilience Index*, https://doi.org/10.1007/979-8-8688-1122-7_4

Sophia: That's a common challenge when moving from team leadership to organizational leadership, especially with something as comprehensive as the resilience index. You need to transition from tactical to strategic thinking. It's like in chess – you're no longer just moving your own pieces; you're trying to control the entire board. In chess, is the king the most active piece?

Alex: No, the king is usually protected, while other pieces do most of the active work.

Sophia: Exactly. So, when you start implementing the cyber resilience index and form the value chain, your role isn't to do all the work yourself, but to enable each part of the value chain to function effectively and... become the value chain. Your technical expertise is still valuable, but now it's about using that knowledge to guide and empower others.

Sophia: I can see you are still confused; can you give me a specific example of a department you're having trouble integrating into the value chain?

Alex: The security operations center (SOC), for instance. They're focused on increasing their coverage for monitoring crown jewels, the very important applications we have, as well as other topics. When I try to explain how adopting MITRE ATT&CK to prioritize threat coverage aligns with the resilience index's objectives, they lose interest. They see it as an obstruction to their own OKRs or deliverables rather than a necessity for the value chain.

Sophia: This is where balancing technical knowledge with people skills comes into play. You need to translate the cyber resilience index's technical imperatives into a language that aligns with the SOC's goals and challenges.

Alex: I understand that conceptually, but how do I do that effectively?

Sophia: Instead of focusing on the technical details of the index, frame it in terms of enhancing the SOC's effectiveness and efficiency. For the SOC, that's their currency. You might say, "The cyber resilience index and our value chain approach will actually streamline our threat detection process. Prioritizing the analysis of threat actors' modus operandi and aligning with MITRE ATT&CK means we prioritize our monitoring efforts more effectively. Therefore, reducing alert fatigue and increasing our ability to detect sophisticated threats."

Alex: So, it's all about finding the intersection between their priorities and our cyber resilience index objectives?

Sophia: Exactly. Show them how the resilience index can help them achieve their OKRs more efficiently. For instance, explain how building coverage against MITRE ATT&CK isn't just another task, but a way to guarantee they're focusing on the most relevant threats to our crown jewels. It's about making their work more impactful and aligned with the overall security strategy of the organization.

Alex: Okay, it sounds reasonable, but certainly not easy to do in practice.

Sophia: Indeed, but this is part of your transition from being primarily a technical expert to being a leader who can bridge different worlds within our value chain. It's a fine balance, like tuning a guitar. Too tight, and the string snaps. Too loose, and you can't make music. Your technical knowledge on the value chain is like the guitar itself – essential, but without the right tuning across departments, it won't produce harmony.

Alex: Yes, it makes sense. But I worry about losing touch with the technical details of the index if I'm always thinking at this high level.

Sophia: That's a valid concern, and it brings us to the importance of delegation within our value chain. You need to trust your teams with the technical details while you focus on the bigger picture of the implementation. How comfortable are you with delegating technical tasks related to the resilience index?

Alex: Honestly? Not very. I'm used to being hands-on with all the technical aspects. It's hard for me to let go.

Sophia: Many technical leaders struggle with this. Effective delegation doesn't mean offloading work; it means developing your team and freeing yourself to focus on strategic issues within the overall index implementation. Can you think of a recent project related to the index where you could have delegated more?

173

Alex: Well, in our last threat actor processing through the value chain, I found myself getting drowned in the details of their modus operandi, double-checking a monitoring rule against data exfiltration. I probably could have delegated that to my senior analysts.

Sophia: That's a perfect example. Delegating that task means you would have freed yourself to focus on how that threat hunting initiative aligns with the broader index goals or to engage with other departments about its importance in our value chain. Or even optimize the performance and synergies between different parts of the value chain.

Alex: I see your point. But how do I ensure I'm still making informed decisions about the index if I'm not in the trenches?

Sophia: This is where you need to develop a system for staying informed without getting drowned in details. Think of regular briefings related to the index metrics, key performance indicators for each part of the value chain, and strategic check-ins can help. But more importantly, you need to sharpen your ability to ask the right questions about our cyber resilience index implementation.

Alex: Asking the right questions... that sounds like it requires more than just technical knowledge of the index.

Sophia: Exactly. This is where emotional intelligence comes into play, even in cybersecurity leadership. It's about understanding the underlying concerns, reading between the lines, and picking up on nonverbal cues. For instance, when a team member says they're "fine" with handling a work package in a specific way you may ask, but their body language suggests otherwise, that's a clue to dig deeper.

Alex: Emotional intelligence in cybersecurity leadership? That sounds... soft. No offense!

Sophia: (Smiling) None taken. But let me put it this way: Have you ever tried to solve complex implementation problems when you're frustrated or angry?

Alex: Yeah, it's usually a disaster. I end up making more mistakes than I fix.

Sophia: Exactly. Emotions affect performance, whether we're talking about problem-solving, programming, pentesting, the index implementation, or leading the value chain formation. Emotional intelligence means recognizing and managing those emotions – both in yourself and in others.

Alex: I never considered it from that angle before. How do I develop this skill in the context of the cyber resilience index?

Sophia: Start by practicing self-awareness. Reflect on your own emotions and reactions to index-related challenges. Then work on recognizing emotions in others involved in the value chain, as an example. It's like learning to read the board in chess – you need to see not just the pieces, but the tensions and opportunities between them.

Alex: This is a whole new way of thinking about leadership in cybersecurity for me.

Sophia: It is for many technical leaders. But let's focus on something we'll face soon during the value chain formation and the index implementation. Namely, dealing with resistance to change. We're going to encounter this at all levels of the organization as we implement each stage. How have you dealt with resistance in your teams before?

Alex: Usually, I try to explain the technical reasoning behind the change in our security measures. If they understand why something is necessary for the cyber resilience index, they're more likely to get onboard.

Sophia: That's a good start, but at an organizational level, you need to go further. This is where leadership truly differentiates itself from management.

Alex: What do you mean?

Sophia: Peter Drucker said, "Management is doing things right; leadership is doing the right things." Management is about implementing the processes, the tools, the metrics to form the value chain and eventually produce the resilience index. Leadership, on the other hand, is about inspiring and guiding people through those changes. You must paint a vision of why the index matters and how it aligns with our larger goals. Can you articulate why the index matters to the organization as a whole?

Alex: Well, it enhances our security posture, makes us more resilient to threats...

Sophia: Those are good technical reasons. But think bigger. How does the index impact our business goals? Our competitive advantage? Our ability to innovate?

Alex: I see. So, it's not just about the what and how of the index, but the why.

Sophia: Exactly. And this brings us to the importance of developing a leadership philosophy within the context of our cybersecurity initiatives. What do you stand for as a leader implementing the resilience index? What are your guiding principles?

Alex: I'm not sure I've ever articulated that.

Sophia: That's okay. It's something that evolves over time. But starting to think about it now will help guide your decisions and actions as you lead this initiative.

Sophia: And I recall you referred to Lao Tzu a lot; let me be the one to do so now. As you develop your leadership philosophy for the index implementation, remember Lao Tzu said: "A leader is best when people barely know he exists, when his work is done, his aim fulfilled, they will say: we did it ourselves." Let's try an exercise. Think of a leader you admire in the cybersecurity field. What qualities do they represent?

Alex: Well, I've always admired our former CTO. He was technically brilliant, but also had this ability to make complex cybersecurity concepts simple for anyone to understand. And he always seemed to know how to motivate people, solve their problems, and get them excited about new security projects.

Sophia: Those are great observations. How can you incorporate those qualities into your own leadership style as you form the value chain or implement the cyber resilience index?

Alex: I suppose... I could work on my communication skills? Find ways to make our initiatives more accessible and exciting to nontechnical staff. And maybe focus more on the "why" behind our projects, not just the "how" of the technical implementation.

Sophia: Excellent. That's the start of your leadership philosophy for the index right there. But you need to work on it, and polish it, and shape your message according to your audience each time.

Sophia: Now, there's one more thing I want to address. Throughout this conversation about the index, I've noticed you seeming a bit... uncertain, at times. Like you're not quite sure you're up to this challenge of leading such a comprehensive initiative. Am I reading that right?

Alex: Is it that obvious? Sometimes, I feel like I'm in over my head, like someone's going to realize I'm not qualified to lead something as complex as the cyber resilience index implementation.

Sophia: Ah, welcome to the world of imposter syndrome. It is the feeling of doubt in one's abilities or accomplishments and often accompanied by a fear of being exposed as a fraud, despite evidence of success. It's incredibly common, especially among technical experts moving into broader leadership roles. I still feel it sometimes, even after years as a CISO.

Alex: Really?! How do you deal with it, especially when leading major initiatives like the resilience index?

Sophia: Remember that feeling uncertain doesn't mean you're unqualified. It means you're pushing yourself to grow. Embrace it as a sign that you're challenging yourself with the index implementation. I keep a file of positive feedback and achievements related to our cybersecurity initiatives to look back on when I'm doubting myself. And don't be afraid to lean on your team and peers for support throughout the index rollout.

Alex: That's very helpful and good to hear.

Sophia: That's what I'm here for. Leadership in cybersecurity, especially with a project as comprehensive as the cyber resilience index. It is an ongoing journey of growth and learning, and it's okay to not have all the answers, yet. The key is to keep asking questions, keep learning, and stay true to your values throughout the implementation process.

Sophia: And another thing to keep in mind, every great leader was once in your shoes, grappling with these same challenges. Mistakes are inevitable, Alex. The key is to learn from them. Samuel Beckett said, "Ever tried. Ever failed. No matter. Try again. Fail again. Fail better."

Alex: Somehow, I don't think "fail better" is going to go over well in the next board meeting when we're discussing the cyber resilience index trending downward!

Sophia: (Laughing) Maybe not in those words. But the principle stands. Personal resilience and the ability to learn from setbacks are crucial leadership traits, especially in a field as dynamic as cybersecurity and with an initiative as complex as the resilience index. It will take some time to digest all of this, I know, but make sure you commit some time to self-reflect. Then we will be able to discuss some specific strategies for leading the index implementation.

Alex: Sounds great. I'm looking forward to it and thank you very much.

Sophia: It's my pleasure. That's what leadership is all about – helping others grow and succeed, especially in critical initiatives like the one we are planning. Now, go on and start putting some of these ideas into practice. I have a feeling you're going to surprise yourself with how well you can handle this challenge of implementing the index and leading our value chain.

Sophia: Oh wait, one more thing to remember. Before you judge a situation or a person's perspective on the cyber resilience index, try to walk a mile in their shoes. As a leader of this initiative, you'll need to do a lot of metaphorical shoe-trying. Understanding different perspectives within our value chain will do wonders.

Alex: I should have known you were going for one more analogy.

Sophia: (Laughing) Get used to it. Analogies are a leader's secret weapon! They help make complex ideas like the cyber resilience index more relatable. Now, how about we grab some coffee and discuss emotional intelligence in the context of the cyber threat value chain?

Alex: I have a feeling I'm going to need the caffeine for this leadership crash course.

Sophia: The chessboard of cybersecurity leadership is complex, especially when forming a cyber value chain or implementing the cyber resilience index. But with each move, you get closer to becoming a grandmaster of both technical expertise and leadership. Just don't give up.

Effective Communication: A Leader's Most Powerful Tool

Sophia: What do you think is the most powerful tool in the hands of a leader?

Alex: Management support?

Sophia: That's important but think more broadly. How did you manage to get these series of meetings with me, when previously we only saw each other in quarterly briefings?

Alex: Well, I came up with that thought experiment with the red and black balls. I figured it would catch your attention.

Sophia: Exactly! So, you see now one of the most powerful tools for leaders is...

Alex: The ability to communicate ideas effectively?

Sophia: Precisely! You framed your message in a way that resonated with your audience, in that case, me. You used a thought experiment to get my attention, which is a form of storytelling. In leadership, especially when dealing with complex topics like our cyber resilience index, the ability to tell a compelling story is incredibly powerful. Think of it like...

Alex: Wait, let me guess, chess analogy incoming?

Sophia: (Laughing) You know me too well. But think about it – in chess, each piece has its own way of moving, just like each department in our value chain has its own priorities. Your job as a leader is to coordinate all these pieces to achieve a common goal – in our case, process the work packages seamlessly through the value chain and contribute to the cyber resilience index.

Alex: Fair point. I've always prided myself on being precise and concise in my technical communications about the cyber resilience index, but I'm guessing there's more to it when leading this value chain implementation? I can imagine that leading the value chain implementation requires more than just technical accuracy.

Sophia: Exactly. Aristotle said, "The fool tells me his reason; the wise man persuades me with my own." In leadership, communication means more than just conveying information about the resilience index. It's about inspiring, persuading, and bridging gaps between different perspectives within the entire value chain.

Alex: Right, like with the SOC team? I still struggle with how to make them understand the importance of our value chain way of working and how they can contribute to the index without glazing their eyes over with technical jargon regarding quantification.

Sophia: That's a common challenge in our value chain. The key is to bridge the gap between technical complexity and business priorities, regulatory requirements, and operational workflows. Think of it like being a translator for the index.

Alex: But how do I do that effectively?

Sophia: You've already used one of the most powerful techniques – storytelling. So, instead of bombarding them with technical details of the resilience index, threat actors, cyber threat intelligence, threat hunting, and red teaming work packages, try framing our cybersecurity initiatives as stories within our value chain.

Alex: (Sarcastically) Stories? Like "Once upon a time, there was a vulnerable endpoint..."?

Sophia: Not quite so literal. But how about talking around implementing new MITRE ATT&CK–based detection rules? You could tell a story about a company that suffered a major breach because they couldn't detect lateral movement. Then explain how our value chain works, leading into measured results shown in the form of a stock market–like index, the cyber resilience index. This initiative is like giving the SOC team superpowers to spot sneaky intruders, right?

Alex: Hmm, that could be a nice story, yes... So, it's about making the abstract concepts of the resilience index concrete and relatable within our value chain and the parts of the chain.

Sophia: Exactly. Data might speak to us tech folks, but stories speak to everyone. From the operational value chain all the way up to the board. Plus, you need to make the cyber resilience index's data meaningful.

Alex: Okay, I get it, but since you mention that storytelling would be applicable all the way up to the board, what about when I'm communicating with the management team or other executives about the index? Surely, they want hard facts and figures, not stories, right?

Sophia: Good question. This is where tailoring your communication to different audiences in our value chain comes in. With the management team, you might use a mix of high-level storytelling and key index metrics. For instance, you could start with a brief anecdote about a recent cyber threat, then pivot to how our resilience index score has improved and therefore our overall cyber resilience against similar threats.

Alex: I see. So, I need to find the right balance for each audience in the value chain and around it?

Sophia: Precisely. It's like in chess – you wouldn't use the same opening strategy against every opponent, right? You tailor your approach based on who you're playing against.

Alex: How do I know what approach will work best with different audiences in our value chain?

Sophia: By sharpening your active listening. That's another crucial communication skill.

Alex: Active listening? Is that different from... just nodding while thinking about firewall configurations?!

Sophia: (Laughing) Definitely! Active listening means you are fully concentrated on what is being said rather than just passively "hearing" the message. You need to listen with all your senses to understand how each part of the value chain perceives the resilience index, for instance, the work packages, the risk analysis methodology, and what we are trying to achieve here overall.

Alex: Okay, but how does that help me communicate better about the entire initiative?

Sophia: When you truly listen to your audience, you can pick up on their concerns about the resilience index, their priorities within the value chain and the work packages, and even their communication style. These are very important details.

Alex: But, why exactly?

Sophia: Because this allows you to tailor your message more effectively. For instance, if you're actively listening to a risk management leader, you might pick up that they're particularly concerned about how the index affects regulatory compliance. You can then frame your initiatives in terms of how they help meet compliance requirements and address the concerns.

Alex: Ah, so it's not just what I'm saying about the resilience index but also understanding what my stakeholders are truly saying – and not saying – about their part in the value chain? For example, what's their role, how could they contribute to the cyber resilience index perhaps, or how can they benefit from it? Am I getting this right?

Sophia: Exactly right. Remember the emotional intelligence we talked about? This is where it really comes into play in implementing the cyber resilience index. You need to listen to the words, but you also need to observe the body language, tone, and the underlying emotions about the changes, the work packages that our expert panel is distributing, and so on.

Alex: This sounds like it requires a lot of practice. Maybe I should have taken that improvise class instead of the advanced cryptography seminar.

Sophia: (Smiling) It's never too late to start! It's a skill that will serve you well in all aspects of leading our index implementation. Let's try a quick exercise. I'll play the role of a skeptical CFO, and you try to convince me of the importance of increasing our cybersecurity budget for the cyber resilience index. Try to use storytelling, tailor your language to a financial perspective, and practice active listening.

Alex: Okay, I'll give it a shot. Just don't expect me to break out in song about the virtues of multifactor authentication.

Sophia: (Laughing) Maybe save that for the company talent show. Now, let's begin. (In character as CFO) So, you're asking for an additional two million dollars for this cyber resilience index thing. That's a significant amount. Please explain to me in two minutes, why should we allocate funds here instead of other pressing business needs?

Alex: Imagine we're building new corporate headquarters. We wouldn't spare on the security system or use cheap locks, would we? Our digital assets that are protected through the value chain are just as valuable, if not more so, than our physical ones.

Alex: Now, picture this: it's a quiet Sunday night; news are spreading about a group of highly skilled cybercriminals that has breached the perimeter of a company using similar systems to ours. Their target is customers' data, financial records, and eventually the company's reputation.

Alex: In this moment, our cyber resilience index isn't just a line item on a budget sheet – it's our first and best by test line of defense. It's the thickness of our vault walls, the complexity of our lock, the vigilance of our guards. Every dollar we've invested in it is now working overtime to help us defend against a similar attack.

Alex: Without this investment, we'd be scrambling in the dark, potentially losing millions in data, facing hefty regulatory fines, and watching our stock price plummet as news of the breach hits the morning headlines. But because we had the foresight to invest in our cyber resilience index and strengthen our value chain, we turn a potential catastrophe into a footnote in our annual report.

Alex: So, the two-million-dollar investment in the cyber resilience index is like installing a state-of-the-art security system for our digital headquarters. Therefore, it's not just an expense – it's an insurance policy that protects hundreds of millions in assets and preserves the trust our customers place in us. Can we really afford not to make this investment?

Sophia: (Nodding approvingly) Not bad. You used a relatable analogy with a vivid scenario and tied it to business value regarding the value chain. You also painted a clear picture of the potential risks and benefits, very good! How did that feel?

Alex: It felt... different. I had to really think about how to frame the index in a way that would resonate with a financial perspective. I think I prefer designing red team scenarios though.

Sophia: (Encouragingly) That's only the beginning idea. It takes practice, but over time, it'll become second nature. Eventually, effective communication about the index means to build bridges across our value chain stakeholders, between technical and nontechnical, between data and story, between speaker and listener. Master this, and you'll be well on your way to becoming a truly effective leader of the threat-informed defense.

Alex: I can see why you call it a leader's most powerful tool. There's a lot more to communicating about the resilience index than I realized. I might need to upgrade my mental CPU to handle all this.

Sophia: (Smiling) Your mental CPU is more than capable. It just needs some reprogramming. Why don't you spend the next week consciously practicing these techniques with the relevant stakeholders comprising the value chain? Pay attention to how you communicate about the index in different situations, try out some storytelling about our security initiatives, and really focus on active listening to understand each department's perspective on the value chain.

Alex: Sounds like a good plan. I'm looking forward to trying this out. Who knows, maybe by the end of the week, I'll be able to explain the cyber resilience index in interpretive dance!

Bidirectional Understanding in Cybersecurity Leadership

Sophia: Alex, you look like a chess player who's just realized their opponent doesn't know how the pieces move. What's on your mind?

Alex: It's this latest management team meeting... I presented our resilience index improvements and value chain implementation progress to vice presidents (VPs) and senior vice president (SVP), but I could tell most of them were lost. One VP even asked if our "value chain" was some kind of blockchain technology...

Sophia: Well, at least they're trying to use tech terms. But I sense there's more to your frustration.

Alex: There is. I spent hours simplifying my presentation, using analogies, even throwing in a few chess references. But it feels like I'm always the one who must adapt. Shouldn't the leadership teams and even all the way up to the board make some effort to understand our world too?

Sophia: Ahmmm, now I get it. Look, in chess, both players need to understand the rules and basic strategies to have a meaningful game. The same applies to cybersecurity leadership, I believe. Although I understand where you are coming from, and trust me, I face similar issues when talking with board members.

Alex: Exactly! We talk about our value chain approach, but if the top of the chain doesn't understand the basics, how effective can it really be?

Sophia: You're right. What we need is a bidirectional approach to understanding. Just as we learn to communicate in business terms, the board and executives should learn some cybersecurity fundamentals. Or at the very least, have a representative with some understanding on the topic.

Alex: Bidirectional understanding... I like that term. But how do we make it happen? I can't exactly send the board or the senior leadership team back to school for a cybersecurity degree.

Sophia: (Smiling) No, but we can bring the school to them, in a manner of speaking. Think about how we've structured our value chain. Each component builds on the others, right?

Alex: Right, from threat intelligence all the way up to strategic decision-making.

Sophia: So, what if we applied that same principle to building understanding? We could create a learning program that follows our value chain structure.

Alex: Interesting. Can you give me an example?

Sophia: Let's start with threat intelligence. We could create a simplified briefing that shows to the senior leadership team and perhaps a board representative how we gather and analyze threat data. Then, we could run a simulation where they have to make decisions based on that intelligence.

Alex: I see where you're going with this. For the vulnerability management part of our chain, we could have them participate in a high-level penetration testing exercise.

Sophia: Exactly! And for incident response, we could run a tabletop exercise where they play different roles in managing a cyber crisis.

Alex: (Excited) This could actually work. It's like creating a cybersecurity chess academy for the board.

Sophia: Indeed, but be careful; just like in chess, the goal isn't to make them grandmasters, but to give them enough understanding to appreciate the complexity of the game and make informed strategic decisions.

Alex: But what about the time investment? Senior leadership team and especially board members are always pressed for time.

Sophia: That's where we need to be creative. We could integrate these learning experiences into regular board activities. For example, we could start each cybersecurity briefing with a ten-minute "Cyber Concept of the Month."

Alex: Sounds good. How about if we create a "Cybersecurity Mentor" program, pairing senior leadership members and the board representative with field directors for monthly catch-ups?

Sophia: Excellent idea. This approach would not only improve their understanding but also bridge the gap between the board and our middle layer leadership. We know directors can speak tech to power without much technical jargon, so that would be a win-win in theory.

Alex: Indeed! And here how it ties back to the cyber resilience index. If the board better understands our cybersecurity posture, they're more likely to support initiatives that improve our resilience score, right?

Sophia: Absolutely. And it goes both ways. As you learn more about communicating with the board or the senior leadership teams, you'll be able to present the cyber resilience index in ways that resonate with their business perspective...

Alex: I like this bidirectional understanding; it could be a game changer. But I can already anticipate some resistance. Some board members, EVPs, SVPs, or VPs might feel it's not their job to understand the technical details. Speaking of which, we are not even discussing technical details with them, we are only talking high level! But imagine... the know-how sometimes is at that point where our high-level discussion is perceived as "too technical."

Sophia: I understand. That's where your leadership skills play an important role. You'll need to frame this as an essential part of their governance role. In today's digital world, cybersecurity isn't just a technical issue – it's a core business concern.

Alex: You're right. I could use the analogy of financial literacy. We expect board members to understand basic financial concepts to govern effectively. In the digital age, basic cyber literacy is equally crucial.

Sophia: Excellent point. It reminds me of a quote by the management guru Peter Drucker: "The most important thing in communication is hearing what isn't said." So, for us, it's about understanding the unspoken assumptions and concerns on both sides – the technical details we take for granted and the business pressures the board faces.

Alex: That's insightful. So, it's not simply an exchange of information, but really trying to understand each other's perspectives and challenges.

Sophia: Exactly. Now, let's think about how we can measure the success of this approach. Any ideas?

Alex: Hmm... We could track improvements in the quality of board-level or senior leadership discussions about cybersecurity. For example, are they asking more informed questions during our cyber resilience presentations?

Sophia: Good one. We could also look at the speed and quality of cybersecurity-related decision-making. If the board or senior leadership understands the basics, they should be able to make more timely and effective decisions when we need to implement new security measures.

Alex: And from our side, we could measure how well we're able to tie cybersecurity initiatives to business outcomes. The better we understand their perspective, the more effectively we can present our projects in terms of business value.

Sophia: Excellent. These metrics will help us demonstrate the value of this bidirectional approach. How about potential challenges? What obstacles do you foresee?

Alex: Besides the time constraint we mentioned earlier, there might be some ego issues, I believe. Some leadership team members might feel uncomfortable admitting they don't understand something.

Sophia: That's a good point. We'll need to create a safe, judgment-free learning environment. Maybe we could start by sharing our own learning journeys? Showing how we've had to learn about business concepts could make them more comfortable with learning technical concepts.

Alex: I like that idea. We should create a culture of continuous learning throughout the entire value chain actually.

Sophia: Exactly. This isn't just about education, rather building relationships and trust. The more the board understands and trusts our work, the more effective our entire cybersecurity program will be.

Alex: Right. So, this is not simply improving communication – we need to create a more resilient, agile organization, one that pawns, rooks, kings, and queens understand and share a common strategy.

Sophia: Now you're thinking like a true cyber leader.

Alex: Thanks, Sophia. I feel much better about this now. Instead of feeling frustrated, I'm excited about the potential to elevate our entire organization's cyber awareness.

Sophia: Good to hear. In the grand chess game of cybersecurity, every piece on the board needs to understand not just its own move, but the overall strategy to win.

Alex: Well, time to start planning our "Cybersecurity Chess Academy for the Leadership Team." First lesson: Pawns may move slowly, but they're crucial to protecting the king.

Sophia: (Laughing) Just be careful not to call any of the leadership team members pawns in your analogies!

Alex: Noted. Kings and queens, it is, then. After all, in this game, we're all on the same side.

Sophia: Indeed, we are. And with this bidirectional understanding, we'll be better equipped to face whatever cyber challenges come our way.

Alex: Absolutely. I'm looking forward to joining the next senior leadership meeting, or you might be joining a board meeting and share details. It's time to turn this one-way street into a two-way superhighway of cyber understanding!

Sophia: Sounds like a good plan. How about we start drafting that "Cyber Concept of the Month" for the next board meeting? I think "Understanding the Cyber Resilience Index" would be a perfect place to start.

Alex: Agreed. And who knows? Maybe by this time next year, we'll be running full-fledged cyber wargames with the leadership team.

Sophia: (Laughing) One step at a time, Alex. But with your enthusiasm and this new approach, I wouldn't be surprised if we get there sooner than you think.

Navigating Corporate Dynamics and Building Corporate Relationships

Alex: How soon is the question, however. I must admit, I've hit a roadblock that I'm not sure how to handle.

Sophia: What's on your mind?

Alex: Technically speaking, the cyber resilience index and the value chain implementation framework is solid. But I'm finding that the real challenge isn't in the technology – it's how to talk to people about it. For instance, I feel like we could form and operationalize the value chain within a single quarter practically, but I'm constantly navigating office politics, which eventually lead to huge delays. How do you deal with all of this... relationship stuff?

Sophia: (Smiling knowingly) Ah, you've discovered the secret challenge of leadership. Technical skills are crucial, but navigating corporate dynamics, I don't like the work "politics," and building relationships are equally important, especially for a project as far-reaching as the cyber resilience index.

Alex: Hmm, I was afraid you'd say that. I've always tried to stay out of office... politics. It feels... uncomfortable. Like playing games instead of focusing on the real work.

Sophia: I understand that feeling. Many technical leaders feel the same way at first. But let's reframe how we think about this. Let me bring up one of your favorites... the strategist Sun Tzu said, "The supreme art of war is to subdue the enemy without fighting." So, for us that translates to achieving our goals without unnecessary conflicts, right?

Alex: (Looking intrigued) Hmmm... that's an interesting way to look at it. But how does this apply to implementing the cyber resilience index or forming our value chain?

Sophia: Think about it this way. Each component of our value chain doesn't just represent a technical process but also the people managing those processes. To make the index effective, we need buy-in and cooperation from all these individuals. Can you think of a specific challenge you've faced in this area?

Alex: Sure, a lot! I've been having a hard time with the head of security operations. He sees our security measures as obstacles to efficiency. Every time we try to implement something new, he pushes back hard.

Sophia: That's a common challenge in cybersecurity leadership. How have you been dealing with it so far?

Alex: Mostly by trying to overwhelm him with data showing why specific security measures are necessary. But it doesn't seem to be working.

Sophia: I see. It looks like we have a lot to discuss about navigating corporate dynamics and building relationships.

Alex: I want to learn how to handle these situations better.

Sophia: Excellent. Let's start by talking about how to understand different perspectives and find common ground...

Alex: Common ground practically means... playing the "office politics" game better? This is really not my cup of tea. When we enter such games, not only we are being held hostages, we are delaying every project and every deliverable because of endless political discussion, but it also feels... uncomfortable.

Sophia: I understand that discomfort. Many technical leaders feel the same way. Let's try to reframe it. Aristotle said, "Man is by nature a political animal." In the corporate world, "politics" is simply about understanding and navigating human relationships and power structures.

Alex: When you put it that way, it sounds less nefarious. But how does this apply to our cyber resilience index implementation?

Sophia: You designed the value chain; you must know it better than me that there are several people, several process owners that we need buy-in and cooperation from all these individuals, if we want to make the cyber resilience index a success.

Alex: So, what you are saying is that we should not only focus in the technical integration, but also prioritize understanding and navigating human relationships when integrating people and their interests?

Sophia: Exactly. Let's take a concrete example. Remember when we were implementing the threat intelligence component of our value chain?

Alex: Yes, it was challenging to get the different teams to share information effectively; that's where you want to drive the discussion, right?

Sophia: Exactly right. But that wasn't just a technical challenge, was it? It was about breaking down silos, building trust between teams, and aligning different departmental goals.

Alex: In retrospective, that's true. We had to do a lot of relationship building to make that work.

Alex: I see your point, okay. On one hand, I understand that, but on the other hand, couldn't we avoid all this politicking if you, as the CISO, simply mandated the implementation of the value chain from the top down? Wouldn't that get everyone's buy-in and make the process smoother?

Sophia: (Smiling knowingly) Ah, if only it was that simple. Let me ask you this: Have you ever tried to force a chess piece into a position it doesn't want to be in?

Alex: (Looking confused) Well, no. That's not how chess works.

Sophia: Exactly. And that's not how effective organizational change works either. Yes, I could mandate the implementation from the top down, but that approach has several pitfalls.

Alex: Like what?

Sophia: First, it often leads to passive resistance. People might verbally agree but then drag their feet or find ways to work around the new system. Second, we'd miss out on valuable input from those on the front lines who might see potential issues or improvements we haven't considered.

Alex: Okay... I hadn't thought of it that way.

Sophia: Moreover, a top-down mandate doesn't build the kind of buy-in we need for long-term success. We don't just need compliance; we need commitment. We want people to understand and believe in the value of the cyber resilience index and our value chain approach.

Alex: Okay, I can see that. But surely your authority as CISO counts for something?

Sophia: Of course, it does, and there are times when I need to use that authority. But true leadership isn't about exercising power; it's about influence. Remember the quote by Lao Tzu, "A leader is best when people barely know he exists, when his work is done, his aim fulfilled, they will say: we did it ourselves." That's exactly what we want to achieve here.

Alex: So, you're saying that by involving people in the process, we're more likely to get genuine support and better results?

Sophia: Spot on. And here's another thing to consider: our value chain and resilience index aren't one-time implementations. They need to be living, evolving systems that adapt to new threats and organizational changes. For that, we need ongoing engagement and input from across the organization.

Alex: I see. So, while it might seem faster to mandate it from the top down, in the long run, building relationships and getting buy-in is more effective. That's what you are essentially saying, right?

Sophia: You've got it. It might take more time up front, but it leads to more robust, sustainable change. Plus, the relationships you build in this process will serve you well in future initiatives too.

Alex: Okay, I can see the wisdom in that approach. But it still sounds challenging. How do I start building these relationships effectively?

Alex: You know better than me that there are quite a few "difficult" colleagues. They simply don't want to cooperate, they are resisting change, I would even dare to say that some of them simply avoid workload, with no offense!

Sophia: I understand. You are not far from truth, and indeed I have witnessed such cases. For the sake of this dialogue, can you think of a specific challenge you've faced?

Alex: Let's reuse the same case with the head of operations. He is a "tough cookie" overall! Every time we try to implement a new component of the index or simply try to pitch new ideas, he keeps pushing back hard.

Sophia: Okay, and you mentioned that you are trying to overwhelm him with data, showing why the security measures are necessary and so forth, but still that doesn't work, right?

Alex: Correct. He sticks to his own views, which, by the way, are on the wrong in this threat-informed approach specifically for various reasons.

Sophia: I see. Let's approach this differently. Instead of focusing on why he's wrong, try to understand his perspective. What's driving his resistance?

Alex: I don't know. Perhaps that his team is under a lot of pressure to improve performance metrics? I suppose our security measures might be seen as slowing them down on this task.

Sophia: Excellent observation. Now, how could we reframe the index or the value chain to address his concerns?

Alex: Perhaps... we could show how improved security enhances efficiency in the long run? Fewer breaches mean less downtime and disruption.

Sophia: That's a great start. You're beginning to think strategically about relationships. You are now addressing the "what's in it for me" part. Let's talk about building alliances. In the context of the cyber resilience index, who do you think would be valuable allies?

Alex: The CFO could be powerful. If we can demonstrate the financial benefits of the index, that could help win over other departments.

Sophia: Good thinking. How would you go about building that relationship?

Alex: I could start by scheduling a meeting to discuss how the index can help mitigate financial risks. Maybe prepare a presentation translating our cybersecurity metrics into financial terms?

Sophia: Excellent. You're applying your communication skills here too. In chess, each piece supports the others. In the same way, each relationship you build can support your overall strategy.

Alex: That makes sense. But how do I balance all this relationship building with the actual technical work of implementing the index?

Sophia: That's exactly the art of leadership. One approach is to integrate relationship building into your technical processes. For example, when you're designing parts of the value chain, involve stakeholders from different departments in the planning stages.

Alex: I see. So instead of developing it in isolation and then trying to "sell" it to them, we're involving them from the start?

Sophia: Correct. This not only builds relationships but often results in better solutions. Now, let's discuss trust. How do you think we can build trust around this initiative?

Alex: I would say, primarily, delivering on our promises would be key. If we say the index will improve our security posture, we need to show measurable results.

Sophia: Absolutely. Consistency and follow-through are crucial. But there's another aspect of trust building that many technical leaders overlook: vulnerability.

Alex: Vulnerability? In cybersecurity, that word usually sets off alarm bells.

Sophia: (Laughing) In this context, it's a good thing. Being vulnerable means being open about challenges and uncertainties. If you're struggling with an aspect of the index implementation, sharing that with your team or peers can build trust.

Alex: Really? I always thought I needed to project confidence and certainty.

Sophia: There's a time for that, certainly. But thoughtful vulnerability can be powerful. It shows authenticity and invites collaboration. Ultimately, the cyber resilience index is a complex undertaking. No one expects you to have all the answers all the time.

Alex: That's... actually a relief to hear. I like that. So how do I practice this "thoughtful vulnerability"?

Sophia: Start small. In your next team meeting, you could share a challenge you're facing with a part of the value chain. Ask for input. Show that you value their expertise.

Alex: I can try that. It's a bit out of my comfort zone, but I see the value in this.

Sophia: That's the spirit. Now, let's do another role-play to practice some of these skills. I'll play the role of that difficult head of operations we discussed. You try to build a better working relationship with me, keeping in mind what we've discussed about understanding perspectives and finding common ground, okay?

Alex: Okay, let's do it. "Hi Sophia, thanks for meeting with me. I know we've had some disagreements about the security measures we're implementing to help increase our cyber resilience and have that visualized in the index. I wanted to talk with you to better understand your concerns and see if we can find a way forward that meets both our needs. Can you tell me more about the challenges your team is facing?"

Sophia: (In character) "Alex, every time you implement a new security measure, it seems to slow down our processes. We're under a lot of pressure to improve efficiency and showcase value, and these constant changes are making it hard to meet our targets. I understand the value chain concept and how transformative it can be, but I have my own targets to hit as well. I am under constant pressure to demonstrate value and return on investment."

Alex: "I appreciate you sharing that with me. It helps me understand your perspective better. What if we could find a way to implement these security measures that improves your efficiency in the long run and help you demonstrate value at the same time? For example, by reducing downtime from security incidents, that will also inherently increase our cyber resilience index. Would you be open to exploring that together?"

Sophia: (Breaking character) Excellent, Alex! You showed empathy, sought to understand, and proposed a collaborative solution. That's exactly the kind of approach that can turn a difficult relationship into a productive one.

Alex: Thanks... It felt a bit unnatural at first, but I can see how this approach could be more effective.

Sophia: It will feel more natural with practice, and every interaction is an opportunity to build a stronger relationship, which in turn supports our overall project objectives.

Alex: This is very helpful. But I have to admit, it still feels like a lot to manage on top of all the technical aspects of my role.

Sophia: It is a lot. Leadership, in fact, is complex, especially in a field like cybersecurity. But here's something to consider; as you move up in your career, your technical skills become less about doing the work yourself and more about guiding and enabling others. Your ability to build relationships, navigate corporate dynamics, and lead change becomes increasingly important.

Alex: I can see that. It's a big shift in mindset.

Sophia: It is. But I have confidence in you. You've already shown great adaptability in learning these new skills. Keep practicing, keep reflecting, and don't be afraid to ask for help when you need it.

Alex: Thanks, I appreciate your guidance.

Sophia: You're welcome. Now, for your "homework" this week, I want you to create a stakeholder map for the cyber resilience index. Identify key players, their interests, their current stance on the index, and potential strategies for building stronger relationships with each of them. We'll review it together next week and discuss your action plan.

Alex: That sounds like a challenging but valuable exercise. I'll get started on it right away.

Sophia: Excellent. In chess as in leadership, the key to victory often lies in how well you position your pieces before the main action even begins.

Change Starts from Within: Empowering and Developing Your Team

Sophia: So, assuming you got good positioning and it's time for action. For instance, your team is your front line. If they're not fully prepared and empowered, how can we expect to convince and collaborate with other departments effectively?

Alex: How does this tie into my role as a leader exactly?

Sophia: Empowering and developing your team first means you're setting the stage for effective delegation. And effective delegation is key to freeing up your time for broader leadership responsibilities.

Alex: (Nodding slowly) So, if I invest time now in developing my team, I'll have more time later to focus on strategic aspects of the threat-informed defense overall?

Sophia: Exactly! Lao Tzu said, "Give a man a fish and you feed him for a day. Teach him how to fish and you feed him for a lifetime." Equally, empowering your team means you are not just solving immediate problems, but you are building a sustainable model to effectively increase our cyber resilience index.

Alex: Okay, got it. How do I start this internal empowerment process?

Sophia: Let's break it down step by step. First, we need to assess your team's current capabilities and alignment with our cyber resilience index goals. Then, we'll look at how to motivate and inspire them, identify and nurture talent, mentor potential leaders, and create a culture of continuous learning.

Alex: If I do all this, it is very likely that I will not have time for actual cybersecurity work.

Sophia: (Smiling) That's the beauty of it! Investing time now in your team's development means that you're creating more time for yourself in the long run. It's like developing your chess pieces early in the game; it might seem like you're not making immediate progress, but you're setting yourself up for success in the endgame.

Alex: Alright... Where do we start with this team empowerment journey?

Sophia: Let's begin by discussing how to motivate and inspire your team around the cyber resilience index goals. After all, a motivated team is the foundation of everything else we want to achieve.

Alex: Sounds good, though I hope I won't need to break out in a motivational song about firewalls and intrusion detection.

Sophia: (Laughing) No song required. Though I wouldn't stop you if you felt so inclined! Now, let's start with empowerment.

Sophia: Empowering your teams is crucial for the success of our initiative. Remember what management guru Peter Drucker said: "The best way to predict the future is to create it." In our case, we create our future cybersecurity posture by developing our teams.

Sophia: That makes empowerment an art. You need to provide your team with the tools, knowledge, and authority to make decisions. Think of it like setting up your chess pieces; you position them strategically, but then you need to trust them to play their roles.

Alex: Okay, but how do I build that trust?

Sophia: Start by clearly communicating the goals of the value chain and the resilience index and how each team member's role contributes to those goals. Then, provide opportunities for them to take ownership of specific aspects of the implementation.

Alex: But what about team members who seem resistant to change?

Sophia: Ah, the immovable pieces on our chessboard. Resistance often comes from fear or uncertainty. Your job is to understand the source of that resistance and address it. Sometimes, you must reframe the change in a way that resonates with them.

Alex: Can you give me an example?

Sophia: Let's say you have a team member who's resistant to adopting new threat intelligence processes as part of the first input toward the threat-informed value chain. Instead of focusing on the change itself, highlight how it will make their job easier or more impactful. Show them how it fits into the bigger picture of our cyber resilience strategy.

199

Alex: I see. It's about helping them see the value in the change.

Sophia: Correct, you got this. Now, let's talk about developing your team. What do you think is the most important aspect of team development within the broad context of a threat-informed defense?

Alex: (Thinking) I suppose... ensuring everyone has the technical skills needed to contribute effectively?

Sophia: Technical skills are important, yes, but there's more to it. Development isn't just about skills; it's about mindset and leadership. Ralph Nader once said, "The function of leadership is to produce more leaders, not more followers."

Alex: Not more followers... which means...? Fostering a culture of independence and initiative?

Sophia: Precisely. Your goal should be to develop a team that can drive the resilience index implementation forward even when you're not in the room. This means creating opportunities for team members to lead projects, make decisions, and, yes, even make mistakes.

Alex: I understand the importance of fostering independence and initiative, but I have a concern. If I'm empowering my team to take on more responsibilities and lead projects, what about my own visibility in the organization? How do I showcase my value as a leader if my team is doing all the work?

Sophia: That's a very honest and important question. It's a common concern among leaders transitioning from technical roles. The key is to understand that your value as a leader isn't diminished when your team succeeds, it's enhanced.

Alex: Can you elaborate on that? It seems counterintuitive.

Sophia: Think of it this way: in chess, who gets the credit for a victory? Is it the individual pieces or the player who strategically positioned them?

Alex: No, the player, I suppose.

Sophia: Exactly. As a leader, your role is to strategically position your team for success. Your value lies in your ability to cultivate a high-performing team that drives the cyber resilience index implementation forward. That's a skill set, and it's highly visible to upper management.

Alex: I see. But how do I make sure my contributions are recognized?

Sophia: You need to change the narrative. Instead of saying "I did this," start saying, "My team accomplished this under my leadership." Highlight how you've developed your team members, improved processes, and driven results through others. These are hallmarks of strong leadership.

Alex: Okay. What if I'm not the one presenting our team's accomplishments to upper management?

Sophia: That's where you need to create opportunities for your team members to shine while ensuring your role is acknowledged. For instance, when your team presents to management, you could introduce the session, outlining the strategic direction you've set, then let your team members present the details. This showcases both your leadership and your team's expertise.

Alex: I like that approach. But now I'm wondering about the flip side. What if I have team members who feel I'm taking credit for their work?

Sophia: That's a sharp observation. It's a fine balance, and in principle, failing to give credit where it's due can lead to demotivation and resentment within the team.

Alex: How do we prevent that?

Sophia: First and foremost, always give credit to your team members for their contributions, both publicly and privately. When presenting to management, explicitly name the team members who worked on various aspects of the project. For example, you might say, "Our threat intelligence team, led by Maria, developed this innovative approach to threat actor profiling." This acknowledges both the individual contribution and your role in guiding the overall strategy.

Alex: That sounds like a good approach. But what if I'm a subject matter expert and I feel my manager is taking credit for my work?

Sophia: That's a challenging situation many professionals face. If you're a subject matter expert feeling undervalued, there are several steps you can take.

Sophia: First and foremost, document your contributions clearly. Keep a record of your ideas, projects, and outcomes. Next, communicate proactively with your manager. Don't assume they're intentionally taking credit; they might not be aware of how you feel.

Sophia: Then, you can also look for opportunities to present your work directly to higher-ups when appropriate. Furthermore, you should build relationships across the organization so others are aware of your contributions. Ultimately, if the issue persists, consider having a frank, professional conversation with your manager about your career goals and the importance of visibility for your growth.

Alex: Those are helpful strategies. It seems like open communication is key.

Sophia: Yes, correct. A truly great leader shines not by diminishing others, but by amplifying their light. Andrew Carnegie said, "No man will make a great leader who wants to do it all himself or get all the credit for doing it."

Alex: I'm beginning to see how complex leadership really is. It's not only the technical expertise but more about balancing various human dynamics.

Sophia: Exactly. Leadership, especially in a field as complex as cybersecurity, requires a fine balance of technical knowledge, strategic thinking, and emotional intelligence.

Alex: Hmm, I'll need to reflect on how I can better empower my team while also ensuring everyone's contributions, including my own, are appropriately recognized.

Sophia: That's a great takeaway, and it's an ongoing process. Keep the lines of communication open with your team, continually seek feedback, and always strive to create an environment where everyone feels valued and motivated to contribute to the cyber resilience index.

Alex: Got it, but previously you said it's also fine to make mistakes, right?

Sophia: (Smiling) Correct. Glad you got that too and didn't let it slip by. In chess, even grandmasters make mistakes. The key is to create an environment where mistakes are seen as learning opportunities, not failures. This encourages innovation and calculated risk-taking, which are crucial for advancing a threat-informed defense.

Alex: I get the points, but how do I balance that with the daily need for security and compliance?

Sophia: We need to create a framework for "safe" experimentation. Set clear boundaries and risk tolerances, but within those, allow your team the freedom to explore and innovate. It's like in chess – you have rules that govern how pieces can move, but within those rules, there's infinite room for creativity and strategy.

Alex: Okay, perhaps I see how this all fits together. But how do I measure progress in team development? It seems less straightforward than measuring technical KPIs.

Sophia: Indeed, it's more nuanced. Look for indicators like increased initiative from team members, more diverse perspectives in resilience index–related discussions, and improved problem-solving capabilities. You might also see better collaboration across different parts of our value chain.

Alex: Are there any specific strategies you'd recommend for developing these qualities in the team?

Sophia: Perhaps consider implementing a mentorship program within your team. Pair less experienced members with seniors for knowledge transfer. Rotate responsibilities for leading work packages or even bigger index-related projects. And importantly, create a culture of continuous learning.

Alex: Continuous learning? We're already so busy with day-to-day security operations and the value chain work packages.

Sophia: (Nodding) I understand the time pressure, but continuous learning is crucial in our field. Alvin Toffler said, "The illiterate of the 21st century will not be those who cannot read and write, but those who cannot learn, unlearn, and relearn."

Alex: That's a powerful quote. How can we apply it practically?

Sophia: Think about setting aside time each week for team learning sessions. These could be internal knowledge-sharing presentations, discussions about new threat actor tactics, or even collaborative problem-solving exercises based on scenarios that would potentially improve the overall score of the resilience index.

Alex: I like that idea. It could help keep everyone engaged with the cyber resilience index.

Sophia: Exactly. Now, let's talk about motivation. How do you currently motivate your team?

Alex: Mostly through setting clear expectations and deadlines. How does that sound?

Sophia: It's a start, but there's so much more we can do, for example, intrinsic motivation is powerful. Help your team members connect their work to the larger purpose of enhancing our organization's cyber resilience and improving the index's score. Then, celebrate wins, even the small ones. How does that sound instead?

Alex: I see. You are suggesting helping them find meaning in their work, right?

Sophia: Precisely. Also, keep in mind that different team members may be motivated by different things. Some might be excited by the technical challenges of some work packages in the value chain, others by the opportunity to learn new skills, and others by the chance to contribute to the organization's overall resilience index.

Alex: So, I need to understand what drives each team member and tailor my approach accordingly?

Sophia: Exactly. It's like understanding the strengths of each chess piece and using them strategically. Now, let's do a quick exercise. Think about three members of your team. For each one, tell me what you think motivates them and how you could leverage that. Again, don't think about it from a pure technical perspective. Don't stick to work packages that must be processed through the value chain; the cyber resilience index is not just that.

Alex: (Thinking) Okay... For Maria, our threat intelligence analyst, I think she's motivated by intellectual challenges. I could involve her more in designing our threat actor profiling and monitoring process.

Alex: For John in our SOC, he seems to really care about making a tangible impact. I could show him how his work directly improves the resilience index score when building detection rules for specific TTPs.

Alex: And for Lisa, our newest team member, I think she's motivated by learning and growing. I could assign her to work with different parts of our value chain to broaden her understanding of our cyber resilience strategy.

Sophia: Excellent start. You've started thinking like a leader who empowers and develops their team. Eventually, the goal is to create a team that's not just technically proficient but also engaged, motivated, and aligned with our cyber resilience index objectives.

Alex: This is a lot to digest... I need to constantly and consciously practice every day. But indeed, I can see how crucial it is for the success of the cyber resilience index implementation.

Sophia: Indeed, it is; mind you this is an ongoing process. As you continue to empower and develop your team, you'll find that the index implementation becomes smoother, and our overall cyber resilience strengthens. It's like training a chess team, as each player improves, the whole team becomes stronger.

Alex: Thanks, feels like I have a much clearer picture of how to approach team development now. I'm looking forward to putting these ideas into practice.

Sophia: I'm glad to hear that. I bet you know this one, "The greatest leader is not necessarily the one who does the greatest things. He is the one that gets the people to do the greatest things." Your job is to create an environment where your team can excel in implementing, maintaining, and even advancing the cyber resilience index concept.

Alex: I'll keep that in mind. I suppose my next move is to start having one-on-one discussions with team members to understand their motivations and aspirations better.

Sophia: That's an excellent place to start. And don't forget to share your own vision for the team. Your enthusiasm can be contagious.

Alex: Will do, thank you. I'm starting to realize that mastering the human side of leadership is just as complex and rewarding as mastering the technical side of the threat-informed defense.

Sophia: (Smiling) Welcome to the next level of the game. I'm confident you'll excel here too.

Conflict Resolution, Negotiation, and Feedback

Sophia: You look like you just came from a tough negotiation. Weren't you supposed to have one-on-one discussions with your team? Everything okay?

Alex: Not really. We were discussing the implementation of new security measures as part of the index's improvement plan, and things got... heated. The ops team feels we're slowing them down, and I feel like they're not taking our security concerns seriously.

Sophia: Ah, the classic security versus operations conflict. It's as old as the first firewall. But you know, I believe conflicts like these can be opportunities for growth if handled correctly.

Alex: Growth? It feels more like a stalemate to me. Like we're both playing defense and no one's making any progress.

Sophia: I understand that feeling. Mary Parker Follett said: "All polishing is done by friction." In other words, these conflicts, when resolved constructively, can lead to better solutions and stronger relationships.

Alex: That's an interesting perspective. But how do we get there? Right now, it feels like we're speaking different languages.

Sophia: That's often the case in cross-departmental conflicts. The key is to find common ground. In chess terms, think of it like controlling the center of the board; it's a territory that's valuable to both players.

Alex: Okay, I hear that, and I recognize that. What's our "center of the board" in this situation?

Sophia: In this case, it's the overall success of the company. Both security and operations want the company to thrive, right? Your job is to show how these new security measures contribute to a shared goal, improving the cyber resilience of the organization.

Alex: I see. So instead of framing it as security versus speed, I should focus on how we can work together to make the company more resilient and successful?

Sophia: Exactly. Now, let's talk about some specific strategies for resolving these kinds of conflicts. We talked about active listening being crucial, remember that? So, before you present your case, make sure you fully understand their concerns. Can you tell me what the ops team's main objections were?

Alex: They said the new measures would slow down their processes and make it harder for them to meet their performance targets.

Sophia: Good. Now, did you validate their concerns or immediately jump to defending your position?

Alex: I... may have gone straight into explaining why the security measures are necessary.

Sophia: Don't worry; that's a common reaction. But next time, try acknowledging their concerns first. Something like, "I understand these measures might impact your processes. That's a valid concern. Let's work together to find a way to implement them that minimizes disruption to your workflows."

Alex: Okay, I can see how that would set a more collaborative tone.

Sophia: Exactly. It's much like in chess; sometimes, you need to give up a pawn to gain a better position, right? In this case, you might need to be flexible on the implementation timeline or offer additional support to help them adapt.

207

Alex: That makes sense. What other strategies can I use?

Sophia: Another powerful technique is reframing. Instead of seeing it as a conflict between security and operations, try framing it as a joint problem-solving exercise. You could say something like, "We have two important goals here: maintaining operational efficiency and improving our cyber resilience. How can we work together to achieve both?" Thus, it becomes a matter of perspective.

Alex: I like that approach. It feels less confrontational.

Sophia: Precisely. And another important aspect in resolving conflicts as such is giving and receiving feedback. In fact, it will also improve performance of the teams. The key here is to be specific, objective, and constructive. Instead of saying "Your team is always resistant to security measures," you might say, "I've noticed some hesitation about implementing the new access controls. Can you help me understand the specific concerns?"

Alex: That does sound less accusatory. But what if I'm on the receiving end of feedback that feels unfair?

Sophia: When receiving feedback, the first step is to listen without immediately becoming defensive. Take a deep breath and remember the words of Marcus Aurelius: "You have power over your mind – not outside events. Realize this, and you will find strength."

Alex: So, don't let my ego get in the way of hearing potentially valuable input?

Sophia: Exactly. After listening, paraphrase what you've heard to ensure you've understood correctly. Then, if you disagree, you can calmly present your perspective. Feedback is an opportunity for growth, not a personal attack.

Alex: That's a helpful way to look at it. But what about when I need to have a really difficult conversation, like addressing poor performance regarding a work package delivery to the value chain?

Sophia: Ah, the dreaded difficult conversations. These are like complex endgame scenarios in chess, tricky, but manageable with the right approach. First, prepare thoroughly. Know the specific issues you need to address and have concrete examples ready.

Alex: Okay, yes, it makes sense. What else?

Sophia: Start the conversation by stating your positive intent. For example, "I want to discuss some concerns I have because I value your contribution to the value chain and I want to see you succeed." Then, be direct but empathetic. Describe the behavior or issue, explain the impact, and listen to their perspective. Lastly, work together to create an action plan for improvement.

Alex: That sounds like a constructive approach. But how do I handle it if emotions run high?

Sophia: If emotions escalate, it's okay to take a break. You might say, "I can see this is a sensitive topic. Let's take a few minutes to collect our thoughts and then continue." So, in chess and in leadership, sometimes the best move is to pause and reassess.

Alex: Right. You've given me a lot to think about. But I'm curious, how does all this tie back to the cyber resilience index and the threat-informed approach?

Sophia: I was wondering when you will ask! Effective conflict resolution and feedback are crucial for the success of a threat-informed approach and a unified metric build on top of it, like the cyber resilience index. They help create a culture of open communication and continuous improvement, which is essential for defending against evolving cyber threats.

Alex: Can you give me an example?

Sophia: Certainly. Let's say your threat intelligence team identifies a new type of attack. It went through the value chain, scored in the cyber resilience index, and ultimately there are some action points for improvement. However, our counterparts for implementing these mitigating measures do not agree because of various reasons. This will be a point of friction with them as well as with other departments that may act as the next input/output. Using these conflict resolution skills, you can more effectively collaborate to implement necessary changes, ultimately improving the index's score and overall cyber resilience.

Alex: I see. So, these soft skills are actually critical for the technical success of our cybersecurity strategy, right?

Sophia: Sun Tzu said, "The supreme art of war is to subdue the enemy without fighting." Remember that one? In our context, it's about aligning everyone toward our cybersecurity goals without creating unnecessary conflict, so, yes, they are absolutely critical.

Alex: That's a powerful way to look at it.

Sophia: Leadership is as much about managing relationships as it is about managing technology. Keep practicing these skills, and you'll see improvements in both the resilience index implementation and your overall effectiveness as a leader.

Alex: I will. And who knows? Maybe I'll become a grandmaster of conflict resolution as well as cybersecurity!

Sophia: (Laughing) Indeed! In both chess and leadership, every move is an opportunity to learn and improve.

Sophia: Okay, is that all for today or you have more concerns?

Alex: There is one more thing. I was thinking about the challenges we might face as we roll out the value chain across different departments. It's not just about one-on-one conflicts; we're talking about aligning multiple teams with different priorities.

Sophia: You're right, and that's where more advanced negotiation skills will come into play.

Alex: Such as?

Sophia: Such as the idea of a "secure base."

Alex: Secure base? Like a secure network?

Sophia: Similar idea, but in human terms. In negotiations, a secure base is a person, place, goal, or object that provides a sense of protection, comfort, and energy. In our context, the cyber resilience index itself can serve as a secure base for negotiations across our cyber resilience activities.

Alex: Interesting. How so?

Sophia: Well, the cyber resilience index provides an objective measure that all parties can refer to. It's not about one department's opinion versus another; it's about what will improve our overall cyber resilience. This can help reduce personal conflicts and focus discussions on concrete goals.

Alex: That makes sense. But what about when different departments interpret the index-related data differently?

Sophia: That's where the principle of "bonding before bargaining" comes in, which briefly means before diving into the technical details, take time to establish a personal connection with the other department heads. Understand their challenges, their goals. Show them how the value chain and the cyber resilience index can help them achieve their objectives.

Alex: Aha, this is valuable. But sometimes it feels like we're speaking different languages. IT security, operations, finance... everyone has their own jargon and priorities.

Sophia: Exactly, and that's where you need to become a "cultural translator." Your role is to bridge these different organizational cultures. For instance, when talking to finance, focus on how the index can help quantify and mitigate financial risks. With operations, emphasize how a more resilient security posture can improve system uptime and performance.

Alex: That's helpful. Any other negotiation tactics I should keep in mind?

Sophia: Yes, one powerful technique is "expanding the pie." Often in negotiations, people assume it's a zero-sum game. But when implementing the value chain way of working, look for ways where collaboration can create win-win scenarios.

Alex: Can you give me an example?

Sophia: Let's say the marketing department is resistant to new security measures because they're worried it'll slow down their campaigns. Instead of just enforcing new rules, work with them to see how improved security could actually be a selling point for customers. Suddenly, what was a conflict becomes a collaborative opportunity to improve both security and marketing outcomes.

Alex: I like that approach. It's like finding a move in chess that improves both your attack and defense simultaneously.

Sophia: Exactly! Now, let's assume we are already scaling out the value chain and we are forming cross chains or parachains, as you nicely described them. This is where your ability to build coalitions becomes crucial.

Alex: Coalitions? Sounds political again.

Sophia: In a way, it is. You are not just implementing a technical solution; rather, you are leading an organizational change. For that to succeed, there is one more effective approach you may find useful: the "cascading sponsorship" model.

Alex: What's that?

Sophia: It's about getting buy-in at each level of the organization. Start with top-level executives, then work your way down. Each level becomes a sponsor for the level below them. This creates a cascade of support for your initiatives.

Alex: I can see how that would be powerful. But how do I get that initial buy-in?

Sophia: Utilizing effective communication and practicing the skills we discussed before. You need to tailor your message for each audience. For executives, focus on how the resilience index impacts business objectives and risk management. For middle managers, focus on how it can help them meet their departmental goals. For frontline employees, show how it makes their daily work more effective and efficient.

Alex: Okay, I see. It's not just about the technical details, but about what it means for each group.

Sophia: Precisely. Now, let me share an original idea that I think could be powerful in your context. I call it the "Resilience Simulation Workshop."

Alex: Sounds intriguing. What is it?

Sophia: It's a hands-on workshop where representatives from different departments come together to simulate cyber-attack scenarios. Using the cyber resilience as a guide, they work collaboratively to respond to the threat. This accomplishes several things.

Sophia: It creates a shared understanding of cybersecurity challenges. Moreover, it helps different departments see how their actions impact overall resilience. It also builds relationships across departmental boundaries. Such workshops also provide concrete examples of how the value chain and the cyber resilience index work in practice.

Alex: That sounds really powerful. It's like a fire drill, but for our entire cybersecurity ecosystem. But this time, we have a formed value chain and the index to guide us.

Sophia: You got it. And here's another original idea: the "Cyber Resilience Impact Map."

Alex: What's that?

Sophia: It's a visual tool that shows how different initiatives across the organization impact the cyber resilience index. It helps everyone see how their work contributes to overall cyber resilience. You could use it in negotiations to show the ripple effects of different decisions.

Alex: I love that. It would make the abstract concept of cyber resilience much more tangible for everyone.

Sophia: Glad you like it. Implementing the value chain way of working, improving the cyber resilience index, and ultimately mastering the threat-informed defense isn't just a technical challenge. It's a human one. Your ability to navigate relationships, build consensus, and inspire collaboration is just as important as your technical expertise.

Alex: Indeed. This conversation has really opened my eyes to the broader aspects of my role. I've been so focused on the technical side of the index and value chain that I barely touched upon the human element.

Sophia: That's what leadership is all about. You mentioned a nice quote by Aristotle: "The whole is greater than the sum of its parts." Remember? Your job is to bring all these parts together into a cohesive, resilient whole.

Alex: Yes, I remember that! And who knows? Maybe these negotiation skills will come in handy next time I'm in a tough chess match too!

Sophia: (Laughing) I wouldn't be surprised. In both chess and cybersecurity leadership, the key is to always think several moves ahead, right?

Alex: Spot on!

Self-Awareness and Continuous Improvement

Sophia: Today, you look like a chess player who's just realized they've overlooked a critical move. Am I right? Is there something troubling you?

Alex: I've been reviewing our value chain metrics and our progress on implementing this way of working. On paper, we're making good progress, but...

Sophia: But?

Alex: But I can't shake this feeling that I'm missing something. We're improving our technical capabilities, our threat intelligence is solid, and the team is working well together. Yet, I feel like there's a gap between where we are and where we could be.

Sophia: I see. You know, this reminds me of a quote by the Roman emperor Marcus Aurelius: "Look within; within is the fountain of good, and it will ever bubble up, if thou wilt ever dig."

Alex: That sounds profound, but I'm not sure I follow. What does introspection have to do with our resilience index and value chain implementation?

Sophia: Everything. You've done an excellent job focusing on the technical aspects of our cybersecurity strategy. But have you considered that the next level of improvement might come from looking inward?

Alex: You mean... working on myself as a leader?

Sophia: Exactly. In chess, once you've mastered the basic moves and strategies, what separates the good players from the great ones?

Alex: Things like foresight, adaptability, good decision-making under the pressure of time, understanding your own strengths and weaknesses in your positioning...

Sophia: (Smiling) Precisely. And the same is true in cybersecurity leadership. Have you taken the time to introspect?

Alex: Not really. I've been so focused on the technical aspects and team management that I haven't really thought about my own development as a leader.

Sophia: How about we take some time to discuss self-awareness and continuous improvement? I think you'll find it's the key to taking our cyber resilience to the next level.

Alex: Okay, let's do it. Where do we start?

Sophia: Let's begin with the importance of self-awareness in leadership. Aristotle once said, "Knowing yourself is the beginning of all wisdom." Meaning, understanding your own strengths, weaknesses, and biases is crucial for effective cybersecurity leadership.

Alex: I understand that. But how does self-awareness translate to better cybersecurity outcomes?

Sophia: Think of it like this. Just as we use threat intelligence to understand our adversaries, we need to use self-reflection to understand ourselves. A leader who is aware of their own tendencies and blind spots can make more balanced decisions, especially in high-pressure situations like security incidents.

Alex: That's a good one. I assume it's like a chess player who knows their own habits and can therefore anticipate and counteract them?

Sophia: Exactly! Now you're thinking on the right track. But be mindful, don't overthink... And I can tell now you look like you're deep in thought. What's on your mind?

Alex: I'm just reflecting on everything we've discussed about leadership. It's a lot to digest, and I'm wondering how I can effectively apply it all while still managing our day-to-day cybersecurity operations. Sometimes, it feels like I'm playing simultaneous chess games – one with our team, one with potential threats, and now one with my own leadership development.

Sophia: I get it; it's a suitable analogy. And it's a great place to start our discussion on self-awareness and continuous improvement. Lao Tzu said, "Knowing others is intelligence; knowing yourself is true wisdom." So, understanding the security posture and the related cyber threats is crucial, but understanding yourself as a leader is equally important.

Alex: Sounds logical, in theory, but how do I make time for self-reflection when there's always another security alert to address or another value chain metric to improve?

Sophia: How about making it a habit? Just like you've made reviewing our threat intelligence a daily habit. Even just ten minutes at the end of each day can make a big difference. Here's a practical exercise. At the end of each day, ask yourself these three questions:

1. What leadership action am I most proud of today?

2. What could I have handled better, and how?

3. How did my actions today contribute to our cyber resilience index goals and value chain effectiveness?

Alex: That sounds doable. I suppose it's like analyzing your chess games after you play them.

Sophia: Exactly! And to make it even more concrete, try keeping a leadership journal. Each entry doesn't have to be long, just a few bullet points addressing those questions. Over time, you'll start to see patterns and areas for improvement.

Alex: I like that idea. But how do I make sure I'm not just reinforcing my own biases?

Sophia: You need to seek feedback. It's like having a chess coach review your games; they'll spot things you might miss.

Alex: I get that, but it's not always easy to hear criticism, especially when it comes to my leadership style.

Sophia: I understand. Remember our previous discussion, feedback isn't a personal attack; it's a gift that helps you grow. What I find helpful is the "Start, Stop, Continue" method. Have you heard it before?

Alex: No, can you explain?

Sophia: Ask your team members to provide feedback in these three categories:

1. What should I start doing to be a more effective leader?

2. What should I stop doing that might be hindering our progress?

3. What should I continue doing that's working well?

This structure makes it easier for people to give constructive feedback and for you to receive it.

Alex: Okay, good. Let's assume I got this feedback; how do I turn it into actionable improvements?

Sophia: Then you develop a personal growth plan. Think of it like creating a strategy for your own development, just as you've created strategies for improving our resilience index. Makes sense?

Alex: Hmm... it's a bit fluffy. Can you make it concrete?

Sophia: Look, a step-by-step plan, here is what you can do.

Sophia: Your first step is to assess your current state. Use your self-reflection and the feedback you've received to identify your strengths and areas for improvement.

Sophia: Second step, you set SMART (Specific, Measurable, Achievable, Relevant, and Time-bound) goals. For example, "Improve my ability to communicate technical cyber resilience index concepts to nontechnical stakeholders by delivering three presentations to the board or management teams over the next quarter."

Sophia: Third step, you must identify learning resources. These could be books, courses, mentors, or even specific projects that will help you develop the skills you need.

Sophia: Fourth step, break down your goals into specific actions. For the communication goal, actions might include "Take a course on presenting technical information to nontechnical audiences" and "Practice each presentation with a nontechnical colleague for feedback."

Sophia: Fifth and last step, set review points. Namely, schedule regular times to review your progress and adjust your plan as needed.

Alex: That's very helpful. It's like developing a game plan for my own growth as a leader, right?

Sophia: Exactly! Such a plan should evolve as you grow and as our cybersecurity landscape changes. Now that I remembered, the same way that we adapt to the changes of the cybersecurity landscape, likewise you need to adapt your leadership style to different situations and team members. How does that sound?

Alex: It sounds great, and it makes sense. However, sometimes what works with one team member doesn't work with another. It's like different chess pieces require different strategies.

Sophia: Great analogy, I'll give you that. But just as you wouldn't use a pawn the same way you'd use a queen, you shouldn't use the same leadership approach with every team member or in every situation.

Alex: So how do I know which approach to use?

Sophia: It starts with observation and empathy. Pay attention to how different team members respond to various communication styles and motivations. Here's another practical exercise: create a "leadership cheat sheet" for your key team members. For each person, note

- Their preferred communication style (e.g., direct, diplomatic, detailed, big picture)

- What motivates them (e.g., public recognition, new challenges, job security)

- Their strengths and how they best contribute to the team

- Areas where they need more support or development

This "cheat sheet" can guide your interactions and help you tailor your leadership approach.

Alex: Seems like a valuable exercise, I will try it. But what about adapting to different situations?

Sophia: In chess, your strategy might change depending on whether you're in the opening, middle game, or endgame. Similarly, your leadership style should adapt to the situation at hand. For example:

In a crisis situation, like an active security breach, you might need to be more directive and decisive.

Sophia: During strategic planning sessions for our value chain, a more collaborative and facilitative approach might be appropriate.

When dealing with interdepartmental conflicts about implementing cyber resilience index guided measures, you might need to be more of a mediator and negotiator. The key is to be flexible and read the situation, just as you read the chessboard.

Alex: I see. What you are saying is that I need to have a repertoire of leadership styles and knowing when to use each one, correct?

Sophia: Very good. And on top of that, you need to understand that even when adopting the best leadership style, things can still go wrong. And that's exactly the moment where you need personal resilience.

219

Alex: Personal resilience? Like our cyber resilience?

Sophia: Similar concept but applied to you as a leader. In cybersecurity, we're constantly dealing with new threats, high-pressure situations, and the need for rapid decision-making. This can take a toll if you're not prepared.

Alex: I've certainly felt that pressure. There are days when it feels like we're under constant attack, both literally and figuratively.

Sophia: That's why building personal resilience is so crucial. Think of it as building your own firewall against stress and burnout.

Alex: Got it, but how do I build personal resilience in practice?

Sophia: Personal resilience is something you need to cultivate slowly. I can tell you some steps that worked for me; perhaps you could try them:

- Develop a growth mindset. View challenges as opportunities to learn and improve. When you face a setback, ask yourself, "What can I learn from this?"

- Practice stress management techniques. This might be deep breathing exercises, meditation, or even just taking short walks during the day. Find what works for you.

- Build a support network. This is about finding mentors, peers in other organizations, or even a professional coach. Having people you can turn to for advice or just to vent is incredibly valuable.

- Set boundaries. It's easy to be "always on" in cybersecurity, but that's a fast track to burnout. Set clear work hours and try to stick to them most of the time.

- And finally, celebrate small wins. In cybersecurity, it's easy to focus on what went wrong. Make a conscious effort to recognize and celebrate successes, no matter how small. That's one of my personal favorites.

Alex: Those are great suggestions. I admit I sometimes neglect self-care when work gets intense.

Sophia: Many leaders do, including myself sometimes. So, it's imperative to remind ourselves what Epictetus said: "He is a wise man who does not grieve for the things which he has not but rejoices for those which he has." In simple words, don't stress about the threats you can't control, but take pride in the resilience you're building.

Alex: Good one, I'll try to remember that. Something else now, you mentioned earlier about ethical decision-making. How does that fit into self-awareness and continuous improvement?

Sophia: Ethical decision-making is important in cybersecurity. We often face complex dilemmas, balancing privacy with security, deciding how much information to disclose about a breach, or even whether to pay a ransom in a ransomware attack, right?

Alex: Yes, correct. What's the message here though? How do you achieve balance when facing such ethical dilemmas?

Sophia: First things first, identify the ethical issue. What's the core ethical question at stake? Then you need to gather relevant information. What are the facts? What are the potential consequences of different actions? Next, consider your options. For instance, what are all the possible courses of action? Then evaluate the options. How do they align with our organizational values and ethical standards? What are the potential impacts on different stakeholders? And finally, make a decision and implement it. Choose the best course of action and follow through.

Sophia: How does that sound? Did I miss something...?

Alex: I don't think so; it sounds like a comprehensive decision-making tree for such cases. Very helpful I would say. Oh, wait! Where is the self-reflection?!

Sophia: Excellent!! The very last step as always, reflect on the outcome. What can you learn from this decision for future situations?

Alex: Great, that's complete now. How do I make sure I'm considering all perspectives though?

Sophia: One technique is to use an "ethical roundtable." When facing a complex ethical decision, gather a diverse group of stakeholders, perhaps including legal, HR, different departments affected by the decision, and even an external ethics expert if appropriate. Use the steps we discussed to guide your dialogue while making sure all voices are being heard.

Alex: That would lead into more robust decision-making, right? Sounds like consulting different chess masters for advice on a particularly tricky position. Although I must admit that all these leadership things sound like another world. One must devote a lot of time to learn them and practice them.

Sophia: Exactly! That's why it is important to build a learning culture for yourself and for your teams.

Alex: Indeed. How do I do that effectively to get real value out of it and not on "a checklist approach"?

Sophia: You can start by "modeling" the behavior you want to see. Share your own learning experiences, admit when you don't know something, and show how you go about finding answers. In my experience, I have seen some steps that usually work very well. For instance, you could implement a "Learning Fridays" program. Dedicate a few hours each Friday for team members to pursue learning related to their role or interests. You could also create a team knowledge base. Encourage team members to document their learnings, interesting articles, or solutions to tricky problems in a shared repository.

Sophia: Another good practice is to rotate responsibilities. This allows team members to take on new roles in projects to broaden their skills. Another very important one, don't forget to celebrate learning, not just achievements. Recognize team members who have acquired new skills or knowledge, not just those who have completed projects. And something on the retrospective sessions that you already do, after each major project or incident, hold a retrospective that focuses not just on what went wrong, but on what was learned.

Alex: Those are all great ideas; thank you. I see how this could help us stay ahead of emerging threats and continuously improve ourselves while sharpening our knowledge and skills. Actually, I already know that some people in our CTI team do feel very stressed when faced with technical challenges because they do not have a technical background. That would be a game changer for every team member to start sharpening their skill set.

Sophia: Exactly! And since you brought it up, mindfulness and stress management are critical skills for any leader or subject matter expert. I've been so focused on the technical aspects and team management that I haven't really thought about my own development as a leader.

Alex: Mindfulness? Isn't that about meditation and such?

Sophia: It can be about meditation, but it's primarily about being present and aware. It means maintaining focus and clarity even in crisis situations. For example, have you heard of the "STOP" technique before? When you feel overwhelmed, STOP – Stop, Take a breath, Observe your thoughts and feelings, Proceed mindfully.

Sophia: It is also about mindful decision-making. Before making important decisions, take a few deep breaths and consciously check in with yourself. Are you reacting from a place of stress or clear-headed analysis?

Alex: Thought-provoking things, I must admit. I can see how this different perspective could add value and help decision-making.

Sophia: Good to hear. William James said, "The greatest weapon against stress is our ability to choose one thought over another." In cybersecurity, we can't always choose our challenges, but we can choose how we respond to them.

Sophia: Just as in chess, mastery in leadership is a lifelong journey. Keep reflecting, keep learning, and keep growing. Your development as a leader will directly impact our team's effectiveness and our overall cyber resilience.

Alex: Thank you. I'm going to start working on my personal growth plan right away. Perhaps these mindfulness techniques will help me in my next chess match too!

Sophia: (Laughing) That's the spirit! In chess as in cybersecurity leadership, the grandmasters are always thinking ahead and constantly improving their game.

Alex: Sounds great. I think I'll start with that leadership journal. Who knows? Maybe one day it'll be a bestseller: "Confessions of a Cyber Chess Master: Leadership Lessons from the Security Frontlines."

Sophia: I'd certainly read that!

Your Move: Leadership Scenario Challenge

In this exercise, you'll navigate a series of decisions as you implement the value chain way of working in your organization. After each decision, you'll see the outcomes and receive guidance on the effectiveness of your choice, based on the leadership principles we've discussed in this chapter.

Scenario: Implementing the Value Chain

You're a cybersecurity team leader tasked with implementing the new value chain approach. You've encountered resistance from the security operations center (SOC), particularly from the process owner of security monitoring.

Decision 1: Initial Approach

How do you initiate the conversation with the security monitoring process owner?

A) Schedule a formal meeting to present the benefits of the value chain approach.

B) Invite them for an informal coffee chat to understand their concerns.

C) Send a detailed email explaining why the change is necessary.

[First, make your choice]
[Then read the Outcomes and Analysis below]
Outcomes and Analysis:

A) Formal Meeting

- Outcome: The process owner arrives looking defensive. They listen to your presentation but remain unconvinced.

- Analysis: This approach is less effective. While it demonstrates your preparation, it doesn't allow for open dialogue and may make the process owner feel their opinions aren't valued.

B) Informal Chat

- Outcome: Over coffee, the process owner opens up about their concerns. They reveal that their team is already overwhelmed with current responsibilities.

- Analysis: This is the most effective approach. It aligns with the principles of emotional intelligence and building relationships we discussed in this chapter. By creating a relaxed environment, you've encouraged open communication.

C) Detailed Email

- Outcome: Your email is met with a brief reply: "Received. Will review when I have time." A week passes without further response.

- Analysis: This is the least effective approach. It doesn't allow for immediate feedback and may be perceived as impersonal, failing to address the emotional aspects of change management we discussed.

Decision 2: Addressing Concerns

Based on the informal chat, you've learned about the team's current workload concerns. How do you address this?

A) Offer to provide additional resources for the transition.

B) Suggest breaking the implementation into smaller, manageable phases.

C) Propose a joint workshop to identify efficiency gains in the new system.

[First, make your choice]
[Then read the Outcomes and Analysis below]
Outcomes and Analysis:

A) Additional Resources

- Outcome: The process owner appreciates the offer but points out that new team members would require training, potentially slowing things down further.

- Analysis: While this shows you're willing to invest in the change, it doesn't address the root of the concern and may create new challenges.

B) Phased Implementation

- Outcome: The process owner shows interest in this approach, asking for more details on how it would work.

- Analysis: This is an effective solution. It demonstrates strategic thinking and adaptability, key leadership qualities we discussed. It shows you're willing to be flexible in your approach to achieve the overall goal.

C) Joint Workshop

- Outcome: The process owner agrees enthusiastically, seeing it as an opportunity for their team to shape the new process.

- Analysis: This is the most effective approach. It aligns with the principles of collaborative leadership and empowering team members. It also demonstrates your commitment to continuous improvement and valuing the team's expertise.

Decision 3: Communicating with the Broader Team

Now that you've made progress with the process owner, it's time to address the entire SOC team. How do you approach this?

A) Hold a large team meeting to announce the changes and the implementation plan.

B) Have the process owner communicate the changes to their team.

C) Schedule smaller group sessions to discuss the changes and gather feedback.

[First, make your choice]
[Then read the Outcomes and Analysis below]
Outcomes and Analysis:

A)   Large Team Meeting

- Outcome: The meeting becomes chaotic with many questions and concerns raised simultaneously.

- Analysis: While this approach ensures everyone gets the same information at once, it's less effective for managing change. It doesn't allow for addressing individual concerns and may overwhelm team members.

B)   Process Owner Communicates

- Outcome: The process owner presents the changes, but some team members feel the leadership team is avoiding direct communication.

- Analysis: This approach leverages the relationship between the process owner and their team, which is good. However, it might be perceived as you avoid responsibility or not being fully committed to the change.

C)   Smaller Group Sessions

- Outcome: Team members appreciate the personalized approach and feel more comfortable expressing their concerns and ideas.

- Analysis: This is the most effective approach. It aligns with the principles of emotional intelligence and adaptive leadership we discussed in this chapter. It allows for more meaningful dialogue and demonstrates that you value each team member's input.

Decision 4: Handling Unexpected Resistance

During the group sessions, you discover that a few influential team members are actively resisting the change, potentially undermining the implementation. How do you handle this?

A) Have one-on-one meetings with these individuals to address their concerns.

B) Remind the team of the importance of this initiative and the potential consequences of failure.

C) Adjust the implementation plan to incorporate some of their suggestions.

[First, make your choice]
[Then read the Outcomes and Analysis below]
Outcomes and Analysis:

A) One-on-One Meetings

- Outcome: The individuals feel heard, and some soften their stance, though they're not fully convinced yet.

- Analysis: This is an effective approach. It demonstrates emotional intelligence and conflict resolution skills we discussed in this chapter. It shows you're willing to engage with differing viewpoints and address concerns personally.

B) Remind of Importance and Consequences

- Outcome: The team becomes quieter, but there's an undercurrent of resentment and stress levels increase.

- Analysis: This is the least effective approach. While it might achieve short-term compliance, it doesn't address the underlying issues and could damage team morale and trust in leadership.

C) Adjust Implementation Plan

- Outcome: The team becomes more engaged and starts offering constructive suggestions for making the change work.

- Analysis: This is the most effective approach. It demonstrates adaptability and collaborative leadership. By showing you're willing to incorporate their ideas, you're building buy-in and leveraging the team's expertise to improve the implementation.

Decision 5: Measuring Success

As you progress with the implementation, you need to establish how you'll measure its success. What approach do you take?

A) Focus solely on quantitative metrics like changes in the CRI score.

B) Use a balanced scorecard approach, including both technical metrics and team satisfaction measures.

C) Ask the SOC team to define what success looks like to them.

[First, make your choice]
[Then read the Outcomes and Analysis below]
Outcomes and Analysis:

A) Focus on Quantitative Metrics

- Outcome: You see improvements in the CRI score, but team morale seems to be declining.

- Analysis: While this approach provides clear, objective measures of technical success, it neglects the human aspect of change management. It doesn't align with the holistic leadership approach we've discussed.

B) Balanced Scorecard

- Outcome: You gain a comprehensive view of the implementation's impact, allowing you to make data-driven decisions while also addressing team concerns.

- Analysis: This is the most effective approach. It aligns with the strategic thinking and holistic leadership principles we covered in this chapter. It allows you to track technical success while also monitoring the human factors critical to long-term success.

C) Team Defines Success

- Outcome: The team appreciates being involved, but their metrics don't fully align with organizational goals.

- Analysis: This approach has merits in terms of building engagement, but it may not provide a complete picture. While involving the team is important, as a leader, you need to ensure that success metrics align with broader organizational goals.

Reflection

After completing this extended scenario, reflect on your decisions:

1. How did your choices align with the leadership principles we discussed in this chapter?

2. In what ways did you balance the technical aspects of implementing the value chain with the human elements of change management?

3. How do you think your decisions would impact the long-term success of the value chain implementation and the organization's CRI?

4. What did you learn about adapting your leadership style to different situations and team members?

5. If you were to go through this scenario again, what would you do differently and why?

Effective leadership in cybersecurity requires a combination of technical knowledge, strategic thinking, and strong interpersonal skills. The goal is to implement changes that improve your organization's cyber resilience while also fostering a positive and collaborative team culture.

Conclusion: The Cybersecurity Chess Match

Congratulations on completing this leadership challenge! Implementing the value chain approach is much like playing a complex chess match. Just as in chess, you need to think several moves ahead, anticipate your "opponent's" reactions (in this case, potential resistance or unforeseen challenges), and be ready to adapt your strategy as the situation evolves.

Keep in mind that in both chess and cybersecurity leadership

- Every piece (or team member) has a crucial role to play.

- A well-executed strategy is more important than any single "move."

- The ability to see the whole board (or the bigger picture of your organization's cyber resilience) is key to success.

- Sometimes, you need to sacrifice a pawn (or a less critical objective) to achieve a more important goal.

- The game isn't over until it's over – persistence and adaptability are crucial.

As you continue to develop your leadership skills and implement the value chain approach, keep this chess analogy in mind. Each challenge is an opportunity to refine your strategy and become a grandmaster of cybersecurity leadership.

And remember, even grandmasters sometimes find themselves in a tough spot.

Which brings us to our final lesson:

A CISO, a SOC analyst, and a penetration tester decide to test their skills against each other at a bar.

The CISO confidently orders a vodka martini, saying, "I've implemented 17 different security controls on this drink. It's un-hackable."

The SOC analyst gets a whiskey sour and declares, "I've got real-time monitoring on this glass. I'll know the second anyone tries anything funny."

The pen tester just sits there with a smug smile, sipping water.

After a while, the CISO and SOC analyst start to feel woozy.

"Did you... hack our drinks?" the CISO speaks.

The pen tester smiles and replies, "Nope. I hacked the bar's AC system and pumped in laughing gas an hour ago. By the way, you're both drinking water. I switched your drinks when you were arguing about new year's budget!"

In all seriousness, leading in cybersecurity is no joke, but maintaining a sense of humor can help you and your team navigate the challenges ahead. Keep learning, stay adaptable, and don't forget to enjoy the game!

CHAPTER 5

Endgame

The Cyber Chess Endgame: Preparing for Future Moves

Sophia: Still trying to outsmart that chess engine, Alex?

Alex: (Smiling) You know me too well. I was just thinking about how our cybersecurity journey is a bit like this game. We've made some strong moves, but the endgame is never easy. In fact, it is more complex than ever.

Sophia: Speaking of which, let's reflect on how far we've come. Remember the old days of cybersecurity when our strategy was all about building a strong perimeter and patching primarily the Internet-facing assets?

Alex: Ah yes, the good old days of static castle-and-moat defenses. Like a chess player who only knows how to castle and hope for the best.

Sophia: Exactly. But we've moved well beyond that now, haven't we? Our threat-informed approach with the value chain way of working and the cyber resilience index have transformed our strategy entirely.

Alex: True. We've shifted from just reacting to threats to actively anticipating them. It's like we've gone from defensive play to controlling the entire board, where we anticipate moves several steps ahead; thus, we can defend against current and emerging attack vectors.

© Lampis Alevizos 2025
L. Alevizos, *Cyber Resilience Index*, https://doi.org/10.1007/979-8-8688-1122-7_5

Sophia: Socrates once said, "The secret of change is to focus all of your energy, not on fighting the old, but on building the new." That's essentially what we've done with the threat-informed defense and the index implementation on top.

Alex: Indeed. But personally, I can't help feeling that the game is changing faster than we can learn the rules. Every day I hear about new technologies that could reshape our entire cybersecurity landscape.

Sophia: And I believe you're not wrong. The pace of technological change is accelerating at an unprecedented rate. It's like we're playing chess, but every few moves, new pieces with different capabilities are added to the board, right?

Alex: Yes, exactly, and that sounds incredibly challenging. How do we defend against threats we can't even imagine yet?

Sophia: That's the million-dollar question. The philosopher Alfred North Whitehead once said, "The art of progress is to preserve order amid change and to preserve change amid order." Our cybersecurity landscape symbolizes this constant balance. You get it?

Alex: I see what you mean. We've come a long way from the days of simple perimeter defenses.

Sophia: Indeed, we have. Do you also remember when our biggest concern was adversaries exploiting Internet-exposed protocols directly and then trying to pivot to our on-premises internal network? Now we're dealing with complex, borderless environments, oftentimes residing on cloud infrastructures.

Alex: Right, and the adversaries have evolved too. They're cloud-conscious now, often pivoting from cloud instances to on-premises environments. It's a whole new game.

Sophia: Exactly. And our approach has had to evolve just as dramatically. We've moved away from the fear-driven culture of buying products just because "the next disaster can happen to us."

Alex: (Nodding) Instead, we've developed this fact-based cyber value chain. It allows us to back our understanding of adversaries with real data, doesn't it?

Sophia: Precisely. We can now trace their activities all the way down to the effectiveness of our security controls. It's given us a much stronger basis for decision-making.

Alex: But our decisions still aren't perfect, are they?

Sophia: No, and they never will be. But that's where the beauty of our approach comes in. The value chain and the resilience index allow us to steer our defenses through imperfect decision-making with confidence. We can course-correct when needed.

Alex: So, it's not about achieving perfect security, but about being able to adapt and respond effectively, right?

Sophia: Exactly. Considering the cyber threat landscape, adaptability is one of the greatest tools in our arsenal.

Alex: But this provokes the following question: How do we defend against threats we can't even imagine yet?

Sophia: That's a very good question, indeed. Remember Heraclitus quote? "No man ever steps in the same river twice, for it's not the same river and he's not the same man." Our cybersecurity landscape is that ever-changing river.

Alex: So, what you're saying is that there's no real "endgame" in cybersecurity? No point where we can say, "We've won, we're secure."

Sophia: Precisely. The great paradox of our field is that the moment you think you can defend against every possible threat, the moment you think you've won, is exactly the moment when you're most vulnerable. So, we can't ever win in the traditional sense; it's rather about staying ahead and in the game.

Alex: So instead of trying to achieve perfect security, we should focus on building adaptability and resilience into our systems and processes?

Sophia: Exactly. Nassim Nicholas Taleb calls this being "antifragile," not just robust enough to withstand shocks, but actually able to grow stronger from them.

Alex: How do we even begin to build that kind of adaptability?

Sophia: Well, that's what we need to figure out. We need to consider how our cyber resilience index can evolve to measure not just our current security posture, but our capacity to adapt to new threats. We need to explore the potential of AI and machine learning in our defenses while also preparing for AI-powered attacks.

Alex: And I suppose we need to think about how our roles as cybersecurity leaders will change in this new landscape.

Sophia: True, we're not simply tech experts anymore. We need to be strategists, futurists, and maybe even a bit of philosophers.

Alex: (Laughing) Philosophers? Should I start quoting Plato in our team meetings?

Sophia: (Smiling) It couldn't hurt. But seriously, we need to grapple with some deep questions about the nature of security in a world constantly changing. Socrates said, "I know that I know nothing." That humility, recognizing that we can never know everything, might be our greatest asset in facing future challenges.

Alex: Okay, I'm intrigued. And a little overwhelmed. Where do we start with all of this?

Sophia: Let's cross one bridge at a time. First bridge, start figuring out how we can evolve our cyber resilience index for this new era.

Alex: Agreed, although I have a feeling this game is going to be a lot more complex than chess.

Sophia: (With a wink) Just wait until we start discussing quantum computing. You might start wishing for a nice, simple chess game instead.

The Future of Threat-Informed Defense and the Cyber Resilience Index

Sophia: Now that we've reflected on our journey, I'm curious about the future. How do you see our cyber resilience index evolving onward?

Alex: Here's what I am thinking. If we're dealing with constant change, shouldn't the resilience index be constantly updating too? It's like a chess clock that never stops ticking.

Sophia: Interesting analogy. Are you suggesting real-time updates? How would that work?

Alex: It would require integrating various data streams, threat intelligence, system logs, network traffic, validated security control effectiveness, architecture patterns and diagrams, MITRE's ATT&CK and D3FEND coverage heatmaps, into our resilience index calculations. Ultimately, the goal is to have a continuously updating picture of our cyber resilience. Imagine if in chess, you could get real-time updates on your position strength as the game progresses. That's where we need to take the cyber resilience index.

Sophia: That could be incredibly powerful. We'd be able to see the impact of our security measures almost immediately, right?

Alex: Exactly. And here's where it gets really interesting. We can leverage AI and machine learning to make this happen.

Sophia: AI? Are we not opening ourselves up to new vulnerabilities by relying on AI? I recently read about adversarial machine learning attacks, data poisoning, or overfitting models.

Alex: It is a valid concern, indeed. Bertrand Russell said, "The fundamental cause of trouble in the world today is that the stupid are cocksure while the intelligent are full of doubt." We need to be intelligent and cautious, but not paralyzed by doubt.

Sophia: Fair point. So how exactly would AI and machine learning fit into our index?

Alex: Think of it this way. AI could analyze vast amounts of datasets, such as system logs, network traffic, and behavioral analytics to identify patterns and anomalies that humans performing manual analysis might overlook.

Alex: Thus, it would enhance our resilience index by providing dynamic, real-time updates based on continuously evolving data points from threat intelligence feeds and attack simulations. So, it could help us calculate our index metrics more accurately and quickly than ever before. Moreover, we could develop a predictive cyber resilience index one that doesn't just tell us our current resilience, but anticipates future resilience based on emerging threats.

Sophia: Predictive cyber resilience index would be a game changer. Can you give me a concrete example?

Alex: Certainly. Imagine we're tracking a new ransomware strain targeting cloud environments. Our AI-enhanced resilience index could automatically assess our current cloud configurations against the ransomware's known attack vectors, simulate or even emulate potential attack scenarios based on our specific infrastructure, and suggest immediate mitigation strategies, prioritized by their impact on our overall resilience score.

Sophia: Impressive. And I assume it could do all this in near real time? We're talking minutes, not days or weeks, right?

Alex: Exactly. But, of course, we'd implement a human-in-the-loop system. The AI makes recommendations, but experienced security professionals would review and approve them before implementation.

Sophia: Makes sense. What about the predictive aspect? How far ahead could we look?

Alex: I believe we could look 8–12 months out, with decreasing confidence as we look further ahead. For example, we might predict emerging attack trends based on current geopolitical events, potential vulnerabilities in upcoming software releases, or how our resilience score might change if we adopt or don't adopt certain security measures. That could be achieved using Bayesian networks or time series forecasting. Our system would practically track evolving threat landscapes, anticipate potential vulnerabilities, and model future resilience with confidence metrics.

Sophia: That's quite a vision. But how do we manage all this data?

Alex: We'd need to implement a robust data lake architecture, possibly leveraging cloud services for scalability, with strong data governance and privacy controls. This would allow for a secure and compliant way of handling several data streams like network traffic, security logs, and external threat feeds, all processed in near real time for continuous monitoring. It's like creating a grand chess library, but one that's constantly updating and reorganizing itself.

Sophia: That would transform our day-to-day operations I believe. What might that look like?

Alex: We could start each day with an AI-generated briefing highlighting changes in our cyber resilience index score overnight, emerging threats relevant to our industry, and suggested focus areas based on predicted impact on our resilience. From a strategic perspective, the predictive index could help justify security investments by showing the potential impact on our resilience score.

Sophia: Interesting. Can you give me an example of how we might use that for budget discussions?

Alex: We could show that investing in a new endpoint detection and response solution could improve our ransomware resilience by 15% over the next quarter, for instance. It's like choosing which chess piece to develop next based on a quantifiable improvement in position.

Sophia: This all sounds incredibly exciting, but I can't help feeling we might be getting caught up in the hype. It seems like every vendor is slapping "AI enabled" on their products these days. How do we ensure we're not just chasing a trend?

Alex: I totally agree with you on this point. You're right; there's a lot of AI washing going on in the industry. The philosopher Søren Kierkegaard said, "There are two ways to be fooled. One is to believe what isn't true; the other is to refuse to believe what is true." Navigating in between these extremes is the key here I believe.

Sophia: But how do we do that with our cyber resilience index?

Alex: We need to be very careful and selective about where and how we apply AI. We can't use AI for everything; rather, we must identify where it can truly add value. For instance, in processing vast amounts of threat intelligence data, AI can be genuinely transformative. But for high-level strategy decisions? That's where human judgment remains crucial, for now.

Sophia: Can you give me an example of where AI might not be the answer?

Alex: Take ethical decisions about data usage or privacy trade-offs. An AI might optimize for security at the expense of user privacy, but it can't make the nuanced, value-based judgments that we as humans can. It's like in chess, an AI might suggest sacrificing your queen for a positional advantage, but it can't understand the psychological impact that move might have on your opponent. Or from a more practical perspective, an AI could recommend actions that optimize threat detection but inadvertently create surveillance concerns, highlighting the need for human oversight in balancing security and privacy.

Sophia: That makes sense. So, it's about finding the right balance?

Alex: Exactly. We should view AI as a powerful tool in our cybersecurity arsenal, but not as a panacea. It's augmenting human intelligence, not replacing it. As we develop our AI-enhanced index, we need to continuously ask ourselves: Is this adding genuine value, or are we just adding complexity following a hype train?

Sophia: I like that approach. It's more measured than just jumping on the AI bandwagon.

Alex: Indeed. And let's not forget, the threat actors are using AI too. Our challenge is to stay ahead, using AI smartly and strategically. It's an arms race, but one where wisdom in application matters as much as the technology itself.

Sophia: Well said. Let's make sure we keep this balanced perspective as we move forward. Please explain to me, how do we approach this?

Alex: Given these considerations, I think we could break it down into high-level phases. We could start by enhancing our current index with real-time data inputs, such as threat profiles and others mentioned before. Then gradually introduce AI for anomaly detection and pattern recognition, POMDP calculation automation, security control effectiveness testing, and so on, always ensuring we're adding real value. After that, we could develop and test predictive models on historical data and finally pilot the system in a controlled environment before full deployment.

Sophia: That's a good high-level plan. It makes the whole project seem much more manageable.

Alex: Indeed. The solid foundation we have now and the data sources are the key to enhance something with AI. And as we develop this system, we need to remember that it's a tool, not a solution. I'm reminded of what Martin Heidegger said: "Technology is a way of revealing." Our AI-enhanced cyber resilience index will reveal insights, but we'll still need human wisdom to act on them effectively.

Sophia: Very well said. But you've also mentioned that the index can be predictive. How would it anticipate our future resilience based on emerging threats?

Alex: The predictive resilience index would use machine learning algorithms to analyze trends in threat actor behaviors, emerging technologies, and our own system changes. It would then forecast potential future vulnerabilities and resilience scores.

Sophia: Wow, sounds like a bold statement. How accurate can these predictions really be?

Alex: Niels Bohr once said, "Prediction is very difficult, especially about the future." We're not aiming for perfect predictions, but rather for informed foresight. The cyber resilience index might tell us, for instance, that based on current trends, we have a 70% chance of facing a new type of supply chain attack in the next six months.

Sophia: I see. And how would this help us in practical terms?

Alex: It allows us to be proactive rather than reactive. We could allocate resources to shore up our defenses in areas where we predict increased risk. It's like in chess, where you don't just respond to your opponent's last move, but try to anticipate and prepare for their strategy several moves ahead.

Sophia: Okay, it makes sense. What about new technologies? How do we adapt the index to account for emerging tech and attack vectors that we might not even be aware of yet?

Alex: That's where the real challenge lies. We need to build flexibility into the very foundation of the index. It needs to be able to incorporate new parameters as new technologies emerge.

Sophia: Can you give me an example of how that might work?

Alex: Let's say quantum computing becomes a practical reality sooner than expected. Our cyber resilience index would need to quickly adapt to include quantum resistance as a factor in our overall resilience score. We'd have algorithms continually scanning for emerging technologies and new attack vectors, ready to incorporate them into our model.

Sophia: But how do we defend against threats we can't even imagine yet?

Alex: We should not try to predict specific unknown threats, but we should start building adaptability into our systems. The cyber resilience index would measure not just our current security controls, but our capacity to rapidly adapt to new scenarios. It's like training a chess player not just in current strategies, but in the ability to quickly analyze and respond to never-before-seen positions.

Sophia: I see. So we're not just measuring resilience against known threats but also our adaptability to unknown ones?

Alex: Exactly. Think about what Seneca said, "Luck is what happens when preparation meets opportunity." Our goal is to be prepared for whatever opportunities – or threats – the future might bring.

Sophia: Cybersecurity adaptability is fascinating.

Alex: Indeed, in this rapidly evolving digital landscape, adaptability is our greatest asset. The cyber resilience index of the future won't just tell us how secure we are today, but how ready we are for tomorrow's challenges.

Sophia: Given how this discussion is going, we should start making a road map at least and put something in; otherwise, these nice ideas will be forgotten soon.

Alex: Yeah, we could, indeed. Mapping out our current data sources and identifying gaps, for instance, and starting to think about the ethical implications of using AI in this way as the very first two items on that road map. After all, we don't want to create a system that's all bishops and no pawns; we need a balanced approach.

Sophia: (Laughing) Ah, nice you brought back the chess! But you're right. Let's get to work on this grand strategy. Who knows, maybe one day we'll be playing interdimensional chess with our AI assistants.

Alex: If they don't insist on playing the Sicilian Defense every time... I hear AIs are rather fond of it!

The Rise of AI-Enhanced Cyber Value Chains

Sophia: You've mentioned that the AI-enhanced value chain could automate the POMDP calculations and even... automated mitigations. This in short means... we are headed toward a fully automated cyber defense, right?

Alex: That's exactly right. On a conceptual level, imagine a system that starts with continuous attack surface monitoring, incorporates specifics of our IT landscape like network traffic, endpoints, and cloud environments. Then, AI algorithms analyze the data in real time, looking for anomalies. If a potential threat is detected, the system automatically initiates a response.

Sophia: What kind of response?

Alex: That could range from isolating affected systems to deploying patches or updating firewall rules. For instance, if the AI detects a new strain of malware, it could automatically update our endpoint protection systems with new configurations, all without human intervention.

Sophia: That's impressive. But how do we know such system is not causing more harm than good with these automated responses?

Alex: The system would operate within predefined parameters and risk tolerances that we set. High-risk actions would still require human approval. It's like setting the difficulty level in a chess program; we decide how much freedom the AI has to make moves on its own.

Sophia: Aha! And what about the adversaries? Do they have automated adversarial value chains you think? They set the aggressiveness level, set a target, and attack?

Alex: I believe that we evolve somehow in parallel. Think of it as a dark mirror of our defensive chains. Attackers are developing systems that can automatically probe for vulnerabilities, exploit them, and adapt their tactics based on the defenses they encounter. Some advanced malwares can already alter its code to evade detection. Others are developed to automatically change behavior once they understand they are under forensic investigation and so on.

Sophia: That sounds concerning. How do we defend against something that's constantly changing?

Alex: This is where our own AI comes in. We need systems that can adapt just as quickly as the threats. It's like a chess AI that can learn and adjust its strategy mid-game. Our defenses need to be able to recognize new patterns and evolve their responses in real time.

Sophia: It seems like we are about to enter a new era of cybersecurity given the developments in AI. How do we prepare our team for this?

Alex: The new era is already here, at least for the adversaries who face zero ethical dilemmas. For us, defenders, things are a bit more complicated because we have to abide by regulations, privacy laws and rules, ethics, biases... but you are right; it is a new era.

Alex: Nonetheless, this is nothing to scare us off. Ultimately, it is about being well prepared. We need to focus on training our team to work alongside these AI systems. They'll need to understand how to interpret AI outputs, when to trust automated decisions, and when human intervention is necessary. It's about developing a new set of skills that blends technical knowledge with strategic thinking and ethical consideration.

Alex: But anyhow, right now we're on the cusp of a major shift toward fully automated defensive value chains. At least we have built the foundation, and we are ready to move toward a fully automated and AI-enhanced value chain. You could envision that as our entire cybersecurity workflow, from threat detection to analysis and response, operating like a well-oiled machine, with minimal human intervention in the near future.

Sophia: All these things sound... exciting but also a bit unsettling. We are basically talking about an... autonomous chess player, right? Where this player, or better say the system, would continuously monitor our networks, using AI to detect anomalies and potential threats in real time. Once a threat is identified, it would automatically analyze the situation, determine the best course of action, and implement defensive measures. Am I getting this right?

Alex: Very well said; that's exactly the concept.

Sophia: Impressive. How reliable is AI-driven threat detection and analysis? We've had our fair share of false positives with traditional systems.

Alex: You're right to be cautious. Karl Popper said, "Science may be described as the art of systematic over-simplification." We need to ensure our AI doesn't oversimplify complex threats. However, AI has shown remarkable accuracy in pattern recognition and anomaly detection, often surpassing human capabilities.

Sophia: Okay, but what about response? Isn't that too critical to leave to an automated system?

Alex: It's a valid concern. Think of it like a chess engine's suggested moves. The AI would provide recommended actions, but we'd still have human oversight for critical decisions. It's about augmenting our capabilities, not replacing human judgment entirely.

Sophia: I see. How about these automated adversarial value chains? I can't wrap my head around it. How would our opponents use those? Are they so well organized, you think?

Alex: I believe that we are entering an era where we might see AI-powered attacks facing off against AI-powered defenses. It's like two chess engines playing against each other, each trying to outmaneuver the other at superhuman speeds. And yes, they are automating things as much as possible.

Sophia: That sounds like a cybersecurity arms race. How do we stay ahead?

Alex: It is indeed an arms race, but not just about having the most powerful AI. It's about having the most adaptable, intelligent systems. We need to focus on developing AI that can learn and evolve faster than our adversaries.

Sophia: This all sounds incredibly advanced. Where do humans fit into this automated landscape?

Alex: Humans remain crucial. We're the grandmasters overseeing these AI chess matches, at least for now. However, our role shifts toward strategic oversight, ethical decision-making, and creative problem-solving. AI can crunch numbers and execute tactics, but it can't replicate human intuition and strategic thinking.

Sophia: Can you give me an example of where human oversight would be essential?

Alex: Let's say our AI detects a sophisticated attack and recommends shutting down a critical system as a defensive measure. A human operator would need to weigh the AI's recommendation against broader business implications. It's like a chess player deciding whether to accept the engine's suggestion for a bold sacrifice.

Sophia: Okay, I see how that human element remains crucial. But with all this automation, how do we ensure our team's skills don't atrophy?

Alex: That's a great point. We'll need to focus on continuous learning and skill development. Our team should be like chess players who use engines to enhance their game, not replace their thinking. We'll train them to work alongside AI, interpreting its outputs and making strategic decisions.

Sophia: Sounds fascinating… if we reach that level. Let's assume we do though, then we would need to consider how we'll utilize the time and resources freed up by these AI systems. What strategic initiatives could we focus on with this increased capacity?

Alex: Nice question. With AI handling more of our routine tasks, we have a unique opportunity to elevate our cybersecurity efforts. I would see several key areas where we could invest our newly freed resources. For instance, strategic threat modeling. We could dedicate more time to anticipating future threats and developing proactive defense strategies. It's like a chess grandmaster spending more time studying emerging strategies rather than practicing basic moves. Or we could devote time in original research and innovation, exploring cutting-edge technologies and developing custom security solutions tailored to our specific needs.

Sophia: Indeed. I was thinking that we could also start building more meaningful industry partnerships. We could focus on strengthening our relationships with other organizations, sharing threat intelligence, and participating in collaborative defense initiatives.

Alex: Yes, indeed. Partnerships would play a critical role in tackling the inherent ethical and regulatory needs on the topic. As AI becomes more prevalent, we'll need to dedicate resources to ensuring our use of these technologies aligns with ethical standards and regulatory requirements.

Sophia: However, we need to be cautious. Nassim Nicholas Taleb warns, "The largest gains come from risk management." We must ensure that as we pursue these initiatives, we're not inadvertently creating new vulnerabilities by overrelying on our AI systems.

Alex: I fully agree with that. We need to keep in mind that automation is a powerful tool, but it's not a remedy. As we move forward, we need to strike a balance between leveraging AI's capabilities and maintaining human insight. Much like in chess, the best players are neither pure humans nor pure machines, but a combination of both.

Sophia: Always with the chess analogies, but right on point! Looks like our next move is to start planning for this automated future while keeping our human expertise sharp.

Alex: Exactly. And who knows? Maybe one day we'll be overseeing AI versus AI cyber battles like grandmasters watching the most complex chess game ever played.

Sophia: Let's just hope we don't end up in a stalemate!

Cybersecurity Foresight and Innovation

Sophia: On a second thought, if we are heading toward a stalemate, how can we foresee that so to speak? How can we prepare? How do we stay ahead of emerging threats that we can't even imagine yet?

Alex: That's where cyber foresight and innovation come in. Søren Kierkegaard said, "Life can only be understood backwards; but it must be lived forwards." In cybersecurity, we need to understand past threats but innovate for future ones. This is the essence of cybersecurity foresight and innovation.

Sophia: That's an interesting perspective. Can you give me a more concrete definition of what you mean by cybersecurity foresight and innovation?

Alex: Cybersecurity foresight is our ability to anticipate and prepare for future threats, trends, and challenges in the digital landscape. It's about looking beyond the horizon of current threats to envision what's coming next.

Alex: Innovation, in this context, refers to the development and implementation of novel, cutting-edge, or simply effective and efficient solutions to address these future challenges. Together, they form a proactive approach, which ultimately helps us to stay ahead of cyber adversaries and continuously evolve our defenses.

Sophia: Okay, got it, so it's not just reacting to current threats, but actively shaping our security posture for the future? Trying to foresee what is coming our way and act accordingly, right?

Alex: Exactly. It's like being a chess grandmaster who's not just thinking about the next move, but envisioning entirely new strategies that haven't been played before. We're not just defending against known attacks; we're anticipating and preparing for the threats of tomorrow.

Sophia: Okay. Sounds good in theory, but how do we actually develop these predictive capabilities?

Alex: Think of it like a grandmaster in chess who can anticipate moves several turns ahead. We're developing systems that analyze vast amounts of data, from threat intelligence feeds, global events, and technological trends, to forecast potential future threats.

Sophia: But how accurate can these predictions really be?

Alex: It's not about pinpoint accuracy, but about probability and preparedness. Niels Bohr once said, "Prediction is very difficult, especially if it's about the future." Our goal is to identify what is coming our way, slow or fast, long term, or short term, provide an actionable early signal to senior leadership, and therefore prepare accordingly. In other words, we are trying to be well prepared for multiple futures that might be shaped due to different scenarios materializing. Let me show you a simple slide I have:

Cyber Security Foresight

Planning for MULTIPLE Futures

Scenario 1   Scenario 2

Scenario 4   Scenario 3

Uncertainties/Unknowns

What we know today

Sophia: Can you please explain this to me? Give me a concrete example of how this might work.

Alex: Yes, let's say our research and analysis of credible literature sources indicate that quantum computing is approaching faster than many anticipate, though still in a longer-term horizon. We've taken this external foresight and contextualized it within our company, gathering internal insights.

Sophia: That sounds like a thorough approach. How does this combination of external and internal analysis help us?

Alex: It's a powerful combination that illuminates our path forward. For instance, we know our infrastructure heavily relies on Public Key Infrastructure (PKI), which will certainly be impacted by quantum computing advancements.

Alex: Now, even if quantum computing is years away, we are becoming aware about the "capture now, decrypt later" threat, which refers to the possibility that adversaries could collect and store currently encrypted data, with the intention of decrypting it in the future when sufficiently powerful quantum computers become available, potentially compromising sensitive information that was considered secure at the time of capture.

Sophia: I see. So, what does this mean for us in practical terms?

Alex: It means we need to act now, not later. This foresight allows us to provide an actionable early signal to start our preparedness. We can begin exploring quantum-resistant cryptography, assessing our most critical PKI-dependent systems, and developing a phased approach to upgrade our cryptographic standards.

Sophia: That's impressive. We're essentially preparing for a threat that doesn't fully exist yet?

Alex: Exactly. It's like a chess player preparing for a new opening that's still being developed. By the time quantum computing becomes a real threat to our cryptography, we'll already be several moves ahead in our defenses.

Sophia: I can see how this kind of foresight could give us a significant advantage.

Alex: Since I mentioned this example, quantum computing in principle is like introducing a new, incredibly powerful piece to the chess game. It has the potential to break many of our current encryption methods, but it also offers new ways to secure our systems.

Sophia: That sounds both exciting and terrifying.

Alex: FYI, as part of our value chain work packages but with a low priority label, we're working on quantum-resistant cryptography. Briefly, that means we are looking for algorithms that even quantum computers can't easily crack. We're also exploring how quantum technologies could enhance our threat detection capabilities. Imagine being able to process and analyze threat data at speeds that make our current systems look like they're standing still.

Sophia: Fascinating. Are there other innovative defense mechanisms we should be considering?

Alex: One of the most exciting areas we're exploring is bio-inspired cybersecurity systems. In simple terms, defenses that mimic biological immune systems.

Sophia: Bio-inspired systems? That sounds intriguing. Can you elaborate?

Alex: Think about how our immune system works. It doesn't need to know about every possible pathogen to defend against it. Instead, it recognizes patterns of "self" and "non-self" and responds accordingly.

Sophia: And how does that translate to cybersecurity?

Alex: We're developing systems that can learn what "normal" behavior looks like in our network. Anything that deviates from this norm is flagged as potentially malicious. Much like how your body might react to a new virus, it doesn't need to have seen that specific virus before to know something is wrong.

Sophia: Sounds fascinating, but how effective are these systems?

Alex: They're showing a lot of promise. In tests, they've been able to detect and respond to novel threats that traditional signature-based systems missed. But what's really exciting is their adaptability. Like a biological immune system, they can "learn" from each attack and become stronger.

Sophia: This sounds like it ties into the concept of self-healing systems you mentioned earlier. Can you tell me more about that?

Alex: Self-healing systems take this biological analogy a step further. Imagine a network that can automatically detect damage or breaches and repair itself, minimizing downtime and reducing the need for human intervention.

Sophia: Can this work in practice?!

Alex: Let's say a part of our network is compromised. A self-healing cyber defense would automatically isolate the affected area, much like how your body might form skin over a wound. It would then work to neutralize the threat, perhaps by reverting to a known good state or by deploying countermeasures. Finally, it would repair any damage and reintegrate the healed part back into the network.

Sophia: That sounds almost too good to be true. What are the challenges in implementing such systems?

Alex: The main challenges are complexity and ensuring the system doesn't cause unintended disruptions. We need to carefully define what "healthy" looks like for our network and set appropriate thresholds for action. It requires balance, much like in the human body where an overactive immune response can sometimes cause more harm than good.

Sophia: Such innovations could be game changers. We should not work in isolation when it comes to such topics. Are you aware of other organizations exploring similar ideas?

Alex: I don't know about industry, but certainly academia. I surely agree with your point, however. Cross-industry collaboration and information sharing are more important than ever. As the saying goes, "If you want to go fast, go alone. If you want to go far, go together." Right?

Sophia: Indeed, although the key there is to foster this collaboration while protecting our own interests. Is that doable?

Alex: I think it's a matter of balance again. We're participating in industry forums, sharing anonymized threat data, and collaborating on research projects. For example, we're part of a consortium working on standardizing bio-inspired cybersecurity approaches. By pooling our knowledge and resources, we can advance these technologies faster than any single organization could alone.

Sophia: This all sounds incredibly forward-thinking. I am wondering if we could justify the investment in these futuristic technologies to the board?

Alex: We should frame it in terms of long-term resilience and competitive advantage. Wayne Gretzky said, "I skate to where the puck is going to be, not where it has been." Meaning, our cyber defense is not just protecting against today's threats, but it helps positioning ourselves to thrive in tomorrow's threat landscape.

Sophia: I like that perspective.

Alex: It's important to keep in mind that as we innovate, we must consider the ethical implications of these advanced technologies. When topics as such are being discussed and developed, we must understand that we're not just playing a game of chess; we're shaping the future of digital security. Our innovations must align with our values and societal responsibilities. For instance, as we develop more autonomous systems, we need to ensure they operate within ethical boundaries and respect privacy concerns.

Sophia: Well said. It seems like our cybersecurity strategy could be evolving into something far more complex and forward-thinking than I initially imagined.

Alex: Indeed. The digital world is changing rapidly; therefore, cybersecurity foresight and innovation are not simply advantages, they are necessities. We're not just playing the game; we are helping to write its future rules.

Sophia: Alright, that's a lot to think about already. Perhaps we could start planning how we can implement some of these innovative approaches into our cybersecurity strategy and get in touch with the right people to form cross-industry working groups.

Alex: Sounds great. As the saying goes: In chess the best move is always the next one. Much like in cybersecurity I would add, so let's make it count altogether.

The Changing Roles of Cybersecurity Leaders

Alex: All these technological advancements we've discussed – AI, automation, predictive systems, self-healing cyber defenses – they are not simply technological changes. They're bound to change how we lead in cybersecurity; don't you think?

Sophia: Correct. The role of cybersecurity leaders is evolving dramatically. We're moving from being purely technical experts to becoming strategic visionaries.

Alex: That sounds like quite a shift. What do you think it means in practice?

Sophia: How about if we think of it like the evolution of chess grandmasters? In the past, being a great player was all about memorizing openings and calculating moves. Now, top players need to be strategists, psychologists, and even physical athletes to handle the stress of high-level play, right?

Alex: Interesting analogy. So, what do you believe are the new skills cybersecurity leaders need to develop?

Sophia: First and foremost, we need to become adept at translating technical risks into business language. We're not only the technical guardians of the network anymore; we're key business enablers. We need to understand corporate strategy, finance, and risk management as much as we understand firewalls and encryption.

Alex: That makes sense. But I do not hear something new so far. This is a core skill expected by us since the last decade. So, the question is how do you see our roles as cybersecurity leaders changing in a few years?

Sophia: I believe future cybersecurity leaders will need to become what I call "digital ethicists" and "cyber-sociologists."

Alex: Intriguing terms. Can you elaborate?

Sophia: As digital ethicists, we'll need to be able to handle complex moral dilemmas in real time. Imagine a scenario where our AI defense system identifies a potential insider threat. We'll need to make split-second decisions balancing security, privacy, legal implications, and employee rights.

Alex: That sounds very challenging. And what about being a cyber-sociologist?

Sophia: As cyber-sociologists, we'll need to understand how cybersecurity impacts and is impacted by social dynamics. This goes beyond just user behavior. We'll need to anticipate how cyber threats could exploit societal trends or how our security measures might inadvertently affect different social groups.

Alex: Fascinating...

Sophia: I also believe "cyber-diplomacy" will become crucial. As cyber threats increasingly blur national boundaries, CISOs might need to engage in cross-border collaborations, traversing through complex geopolitical landscapes.

Alex: That's another interesting perspective. You got more?! I am curious!

Sophia: Maybe two more. I think "technology forecasting" will become a core skill, which means not simply understanding current tech but predicting how emerging technologies like neuromorphic computing or digital twins could reshape the threat landscape.

Alex: I see, interesting perspective and sounds very much aligned with the cybersecurity foresight, although I know forecasting is slightly different. What's the second one?

Sophia: The second one is about cybersecurity leaders becoming... "cyber philosophers."

Alex: Oh! So, we should start reading about Aristotle's views on living off the land techniques or Socrates' thoughts on deepfakes and vishing?

Sophia: Jokes aside, by "cyber-philosophers," I mean professionals who can think critically and draw insights from various fields to solve complex cybersecurity problems.

Alex: Ah, I get it now. Though I have to admit, the image of Diogenes searching for an honest user with his lantern is pretty amusing.

Sophia: (Laughing) Now that would be an interesting approach to threat hunting! But let's keep our feet on the ground. Before we get too philosophical, we need to ensure we have a solid grasp of the basics.

Alex: Exactly my concern. Don't you think there's a risk of getting too abstract if we start bringing cross-disciplinary problem-solving approaches and theories into our field? Shouldn't we first ensure a solid foundation in the basics, as you nicely highlighted?

Sophia: Absolutely, and that is a critical point. These approaches should proceed in tandem. But I agree, these advanced concepts and philosophies should be backed by solid fundamentals. In fact, we must master the fundamentals. Solid practitioners need a strong grasp of networking, system administration, basic coding understanding, and current security protocols. It's only when we've mastered these basics that we can effectively apply more advanced and philosophical approaches.

Alex: Yes, okay, that makes sense. So, we need to build on a strong foundation to reach these higher-level skills and perspectives.

Sophia: Exactly, I agree. After all, it's as a pyramid. The base is formed by solid technical skills and understanding. As we move up, we layer on these more abstract and interdisciplinary approaches. But without that strong base, the whole structure becomes unstable.

Alex: Agreed, so the journey to becoming these multifaceted cybersecurity leaders is a long one and starts by having a solid base. But now the question arises; how do we even begin to prepare for such changes in our roles?

Sophia: Having a solid foundation, we should start with expanding our knowledge base far beyond traditional IT and security domains. We should be engaging with futurists, ethicists, sociologists, and even science fiction authors to broaden our perspectives.

Alex: That's a great perspective, and I can't agree more, really. I also believe we need to push the boundaries of what it means to be a cybersecurity leader. It seems we're evolving from guardians of data to shapers of our digital future.

Sophia: Exactly. The philosopher Marshall McLuhan said, "We shape our tools and thereafter our tools shape us." Therefore, as cybersecurity leaders, we're not simply protecting systems; we are actively shaping the digital world of tomorrow.

Alex: Now, here's a bit of challenge for you... With all this automation that we discussed before, how do we balance that with human intuition and decision-making?

Sophia: I think we need to figure out how we blend the analytical power of our AI systems with the evolving human wisdom and intuition.

Alex: Agreed, but how do we do that in practice?

Sophia: How about if we start figuring out when to trust the AI and when to rely on human judgment? For routine tasks and data analysis, we can lean heavily on automation. But for strategic decisions, ethical considerations, and novel situations, human oversight is imperative.

Alex: So, a matter of balance again.

Sophia: Yes, it is. We need to cultivate what I call "augmented intuition," namely, the ability to quickly interpret AI-generated insights and combine them with our human experience and contextual understanding.

Alex: I like your terminology; it's creative and spot on. Just before, you mentioned ethical considerations. How does that fit into our evolving role?

Sophia: As cybersecurity becomes more intertwined with every aspect of business and society, we need to grapple with complex ethical questions. For instance, how do we balance privacy with security? How do we ensure our AI systems don't perpetuate biases?

Alex: Those are big questions. It sounds like we need knowledge beyond just technology yet again.

Sophia: Exactly. The cybersecurity leaders of tomorrow need interdisciplinary knowledge. We need to understand technology, of course, but also psychology to grasp human behavior in cybersecurity, ethics to navigate moral dilemmas, and even aspects of law and policy perhaps.

Alex: That's a lot. I am wondering how we develop all these skills.

Sophia: I think it boils down to continuous learning and broadening our horizons. We should be reading not just technical manuals but also books on strategy, psychology, and philosophy. Engaging with diverse teams and seeking mentorship outside our field can also be very valuable.

Alex: This all sounds exciting, but also challenging. We should prepare our current teams for these changes. How about if we start by creating cross-functional projects that expose our technical experts to business strategy? For instance, the cyber value chain. We could encourage our teams to pursue diverse educational opportunities, maybe a course in business ethics or organizational psychology.

Sophia: I like that approach, and yes, I will support that. Anything else before we wrap this up?

Alex: A quote for wrapping up our sessions is always nice, right?

Sophia: Ah, indeed; go on!

Alex: The poet T. S. Eliot said, "We shall not cease from exploration, and the end of all our exploring will be to arrive where we started and know the place for the first time." Our journey as cybersecurity leaders will continuously evolve, but our core mission remains the same, to protect and enable our organizations in an increasingly digital world.

Never-Ending Chess Game

Sophia: Thinking back to when you first proposed the cyber resilience index, I was as skeptical as a grandmaster facing an unusual opening move. Now that we've implemented it, I'd like to hear your reflections.

Alex: (Smiling) It's been quite a chess match, hasn't it? Remember when I said we could quantify and steer our cyber defenses like a stock market index?

Sophia: I do, and I admit it seemed as improbable as predicting every move in a chess game.

Alex: Yet here we are. The cyber resilience index acting like a grandmaster's intuition, guiding our moves across the entire board of our operations.

Sophia: You are right. It has transformed our conversations with the board, firstly, and on a technical level, we are no longer moving pieces reactively; we really started anticipating threat actors' moves.

Alex: Exactly right. Remember that new ransomware strain that made the news last month? We had our defenses set up before they even made their opening move. So, I presume for the first time you had a ready answer when the leadership team called in a panic after reading the news, asking how well are we doing against such threat actors, right?

Sophia: That's correct. I have to admit, you were right about it being attainable. But "simple"? That might have been an optimistic gambit.

Alex: Perhaps I underestimated the complexity of the game. But like chess, the rules are simple; it's the strategy that's profound.

Sophia: Fair enough. You know, I've learned so much through this process. From understanding the value chain to appreciating the power of predictive analytics, the threat-informed defense, and the tools available out there that we barely scratched the surface. I feel like I've gone from a casual player to a serious contender in the cybersecurity arena. Thank you.

Alex: I'm glad to hear that. And I must say, your guidance on leadership and communication has been extremely valuable. I've learned that being a good cybersecurity leader is far more than just knowing the technical moves; it's about inspiring and guiding the entire team. Thank you very much.

Sophia: It seems we've both grown in this journey. What's your thoughts for our next moves now?

Alex: The beauty of our approach is that it's designed for continuous evolution, like a chess AI that learns from every game. We are not at checkmate; we are entering a new phase of the game.

Sophia: You've certainly made a believer out of me. Here's to our ongoing cybersecurity chess match.

Alex: Indeed, in this game, we are not just players, we are reshaping the board with every move.

As they concluded their conversation, Sophia and Alex gathered their things and prepared to leave the office. It was a rainy Friday evening, the kind that makes you reflect on your professional journey. They stood at the entrance, watching the city lights reflect off the wet pavement.

Sophia: You know, Alex, I think the future of cybersecurity leadership is a blend of both our strengths, your technical expertise and innovative thinking and my focus on strategy and communication.

Alex: I agree. The threats we face are too complex for a one-dimensional approach. We need leaders who can play both on the technical chessboard and the chess-boardroom with equal skills.

Sophia: And who aren't afraid to draw inspiration from philosophy, biology, or even an occasional game of chess!

They shared a knowing smile, both realizing how far they'd come and how much further they could go together.

Sophia: So, are you ready for our next move, partner?

Alex: Always. Let's show them how the game is really played.

As they stepped out into the rain, their umbrellas unfolding like shields against the elements, Sophia and Alex knew they were more than just colleagues now. They were pioneers on two fronts: on one hand, creating a single metric that served as a lighthouse for cybersecurity leaders guiding cybersecurity decision-making at strategic, tactical, and operational levels; on the other, charting the course for a new generation of multidisciplinary cybersecurity leaders. They stood ready for the next challenge in their never-ending chess game against cyber threats, armed with both precision and vision.

Afterword

Within the rapidly evolving cybersecurity landscape, transformative ideas rarely emerge in isolation. For me, the concept of the cyber resilience index took shape through multiple interactions and insights. In fact, the Cyber Resilience Index and the Threat Intelligence Based Security Assessment concepts were conceived, designed and developed during my time at ABN AMRO Bank N.V., where the innovative cybersecurity environment and collaborative culture provided the perfect foundation for transformative thinking. The bank's commitment to pioneering cybersecurity approaches enabled the development of these concepts through extensive collaboration with exceptional leaders and practitioners at the bank.

The journey began with a late-afternoon conversation with a colleague about the limitations of our compliance-driven approach to cybersecurity. This spark ignited a series of insightful discussions on threat-informed defense concepts with forward-thinking peers at ABN AMRO Bank N.V. The development of these ideas was significantly shaped by Martijn Dekker, whose pioneering approach to managing uncertainty aligned perfectly with the threat-intelligence based security assessment concept. Martijn's insights helped establish a solid conceptual framework and clear methodology that underpinned the entire project. Our discussions extended far beyond the initial scope, exploring fascinating areas such as bio-inspired cybersecurity and biomimicry, as well as the leadership skillset for the future and boardroom challenges. The concepts of the TIBSA, CRI, and the cyber value chain have been a testament to this collaborative spirit. The introduction of the CVC concept with its associated index within ABN AMRO Bank N.V, can be traced back to the

© Lampis Alevizos 2025
L. Alevizos, *Cyber Resilience Index*, https://doi.org/10.1007/979-8-8688-1122-7

ambition of Coen Klaver to have a full orchestrated value chain and being able to report out with 1 encompassing KPI. His leadership and foresight played a crucial role in bringing this idea to fruition within the bank. Designing the CVC was part of a collaborative effort, where the collective expertise and insights of the ABN AMRO Cyber Defence colleagues were instrumental in making it a reality. The CRI is implemented in practice at ABN AMRO Bank N.V and is still being used to steer cyber resilience.

The concept further evolved through engagements with academia, where fellows and researchers helped refine my views. The groundbreaking work of MITRE Engenuity and the Center for Threat Informed Defense provide great foundations with their collaborative R&D efforts. Then, it was the pressing challenge of bridging the gap between security professionals and leadership teams or executives that fueled my passion. This drive led to endless research and learning, gradually modeling the cyber resilience index into a tool that could reshape our approach to digital defense.

But my vision extended beyond mere communication. I became driven by the idea of seamlessly uniting cybersecurity elements into a single, cohesive entity, "a well-oiled engine" where every part works in perfect harmony. This engine would evolve into an automated cyber defense center where humans maintain decision-making authority while computers execute all technical changes. Thus, I believe that by working together, rather than in isolation, we can maximize our chances of defending against cyber threats.

Looking ahead, it is highly likely that we see a future – if not already happening by now – where adversarial AI and defensive AI would face off, with humans overseeing the digital battlefield. In this scenario, the first critical step is to start forming cyber value chains – interoperable systems of defense that can be empowered and evolved. As such, we can strengthen our current cybersecurity posture and improve cyber resilience massively, but we also lay the groundwork for a future where we can effectively produce and manage AI-driven security landscapes.

While writing this book, I chose to present these ideas through a dialogue between Sophia and Alex. This format allowed me to explore the doubts, challenges, and "eureka" moments that come with adopting a new paradigm in cybersecurity. It is my hope that through their conversations, readers will find echoes of their own thoughts and experiences.

As it becomes evident from the narrative, embracing the concepts of threat-informed defense, the value chain way of working, and ultimately the cyber resilience index is not a simple task. There are points that may make one want to resist, ideas that seem counterintuitive, and proposals that might appear overly ambitious. Yet, it is precisely these challenges that make the journey worthwhile. Ultimately, the ideas presented in this book help in shaping a path from reactive defense to proactive resilience, from siloed operations to an integrated cyber value chain, and from abstract risk assessments to quantifiable metrics.

In closing, I would like to express my deep gratitude to the countless cybersecurity professionals whose insights and experiences have shaped this work. To my mentors, who encouraged me to think beyond conventional boundaries. To my teams and colleagues, who patiently listened to my evolving ideas and helped refine them. And to my family, for their endless support during the long hours of writing and reflecting.

Lastly, my sincere thanks go to you, the reader. Your willingness to explore new ideas and challenge the status quo is what drives our field forward. The future of cybersecurity is not just only in the pursuit of new technologies and trends, but in our ability to adapt our thinking and approaches.

Concluding this book, in cybersecurity as in chess, the game is never truly over. There is always a next move, a new strategy to explore, a novel threat to counter. I believe that the key is to keep learning, keep adapting, and have the courage to dream, speak about, and lead the change regardless of the result.

Thank you for joining me on this journey. Now, it's your move.

Checkmate Reflections
Chapter 1

♟ Key Concepts:

1. Cyber Resilience Index (CRI): A unified metric quantifying an organization's ability to anticipate, prepare for, respond to, and recover from cyber threats. The equivalent of a stock market index, but for cyber resilience.

2. TIBSA (Threat Intelligence–Based Security Assessment): A methodology for integrating actionable threat intelligence into security assessments.

3. Known Unknowns Versus Unknown Unknowns: Understanding the difference between threats we know exist but lack complete information about and threats we don't even know exist.

4. Ellsberg Paradox: Illustrating how people tend to prefer known risks over unknown risks, even when the known risk can be potentially worse.

5. CTEM (Continuous Threat Exposure Management): Coined by Gartner in 2022, a cyclical approach to managing cyber threat exposure, comprising of scoping, discovery, prioritization, validation, and mobilization stages.

♟ Key Takeaways:

1. Traditional, compliance-driven approaches to cybersecurity are no longer sufficient in today's rapidly evolving threat landscape.

2. The cyber resilience index provides a comprehensive view of an organization's cybersecurity posture, allowing for data-driven decision-making.

3. TIBSA helps align cyber defenses with the evolving threat landscape, making the security assessments more relevant and effective.

4. Understanding both known unknowns and unknown unknowns is crucial for comprehensive risk, threat, and uncertainty management in cybersecurity.

5. A unified metric like the CRI can help bridge the gap between technical teams and executive leadership, improving communication and resource allocation.

6. The CRI builds upon and enhances existing approaches like CTEM, providing a more comprehensive and dynamic view of an organization's cybersecurity posture.

7. CTEM is valuable, but the CRI and TIBSA provide a more proactive, threat-intel driven approach as opposed to CTEM's primarily asset-driven focus.

♟ Strategic Analogies:

1. Chess Game: Cybersecurity is like a complex chess game where the CRI acts as a grandmaster's "engine" and "intuition" combined, guiding strategic decisions across the entire "board" of operations.

2. Chess Pieces: Different security measures are like different chess pieces, each with their own strengths, contributions to the game, and ways of operating.

3. Chess Openings: Implementing TIBSA is like studying your opponent's favorite openings to inform your strategy.

4. Chess Strategy Evolution: The shift from CTEM to CRI is like evolving from a defensive chess strategy to a more dynamic, proactive approach that anticipates and counters the opponent's moves.

♟ Next Moves:

1. Assess your current cybersecurity metrics and consider how they might be integrated into a unified index.

2. Evaluate your organization's current threat intelligence capabilities and how they inform your security strategy.

3. Conduct a self-assessment of your organization's cyber resilience using the provided exercise.

4. Begin discussions with leadership about the benefits of a unified cybersecurity metric and how it could improve decision-making and resource allocation.

5. Consider how your organization currently handles known unknowns and unknown unknowns in your risk and threat management processes.

6. If you're currently using CTEM, assess how it could be enhanced or complemented by the CRI approach.

7. Consider how a threat-intel driven approach (as opposed to an asset-driven one) might change your current cybersecurity strategies.

Chapter 2

♟ Key Concepts:

1. Cyber Threat Intelligence (CTI): The science of gathering, analyzing, and interpreting information about potential cyber threats, turning them into actionable intelligence, essentially extracting the signal from the noise.

2. Threat Intelligence Versus Threat Information: The distinction between raw data (information) and analyzed, contextualized insights (intelligence).

3. Possible, Probable, and Plausible (PPP) TTPs: A strategic element of TIBSA for categorizing and prioritizing tactics, techniques, and procedures based on likelihood and relevance.

4. Causal Graphs: Visual representations of cause-and-effect relationships in cybersecurity, used to map out complex attack scenarios in a probabilistic way.

5. Attack Trees: Hierarchical structures showing different ways an attacker might compromise a system.

♟ Key Takeaways:

1. Effective cyber threat intelligence is crucial for proactive cybersecurity strategy.

2. The shift from an asset-driven to a threat-intel driven approach enhances cybersecurity effectiveness.

3. Understanding PPP TTPs will allow for a more nuanced and effective threat assessment and prioritization.

4. Causal graphs provide a comprehensive view of attack scenarios as opposed to traditional attack trees.

5. Risk scoring in a threat-intel context enables more accurate and relevant security assessments.

6. TIBSA methodology enhances traditional approaches like CTEM by incorporating threat intelligence more dynamically.

♟ Strategic Analogies:

1. Chess Intelligence: Cyber threat intelligence is like studying your opponent's past games and strategies in chess.

2. Chess Move Prediction: PPP TTPs are like categorizing potential chess moves as possible, probable, or plausible based on the current board state and opponent's style.

3. Chess Game Tree: Causal graphs are like complex game trees in chess, showing various possible sequences of moves and countermoves.

4. Piece Positioning: The shift to a threat-intel driven approach is like moving from simply defending your pieces to strategically positioning them based on your opponent's likely strategies.

♟ Next Moves:

1. Assess your current threat intelligence capabilities and how they inform your security strategy.

2. Begin incorporating the PPP concept into your threat assessment processes.

3. Experiment with creating causal graphs for key threat scenarios relevant to your organization.

4. Evaluate how you can shift from an asset-driven to a threat-intel driven approach in your security operations.

5. Practice the TIBSA methodology by conducting a threat intelligence–based security assessment for a critical system or process. Ideally, start with an applicable threat actor relevant to your organization.

6. Engage in the "Operation Conti Counteract" exercise to apply the concepts learned in a practical scenario.

Chapter 3

♜ Key Concepts:

1. Cyber Value Chain: A collaborative network of cybersecurity capabilities within an organization.

2. Expert Panel: A cross-functional team responsible for assessing and prioritizing cybersecurity efforts.

3. Confidence Score: A baseline metric derived from historical data to inform cybersecurity decisions.

4. Interoperable Capabilities: The seamless integration of various cybersecurity functions.

5. Cyber Resilience Index (CRI) Trends: Visual representations of an organization's cybersecurity posture over time.

♜ Key Takeaways:

1. The cyber value chain approach transforms siloed security operations into a cohesive, collaborative system.

2. An expert panel is crucial for making informed, cross-functional cybersecurity decisions.

3. The confidence score provides a data-driven foundation for cybersecurity assessments and decisions.

4. Interoperability between different security capabilities enhances overall cyber resilience.

5. The CRI provides a clear, actionable metric for tracking and improving cybersecurity posture.

6. Effective communication and collaboration across departments are essential for implementing the value chain approach.

7. The cyber resilience index can be used to drive strategic decision-making and justify cybersecurity investments.

♜ Strategic Analogies:

1. Chess Team: The cyber value chain is like a chess team where each member (capability) has unique strengths but works together toward a common goal.

2. Chess Clock: The CRI acts like a chess clock, keeping the organization focused and on track in its cybersecurity efforts.

3. Chess Strategy Evolution: Implementing the value chain is like evolving from individual piece tactics to a comprehensive board strategy in chess.

4. Grandmaster Oversight: The expert panel functions like a chess grandmaster, overseeing and coordinating the moves of all pieces on the board.

♖ **Next Moves:**

1. Begin mapping your organization's cybersecurity capabilities to identify potential components of your cyber value chain.

2. Assemble a cross-functional expert panel to guide your cybersecurity efforts.

3. Start collecting historical data to establish your organization's confidence score.

4. Identify and prioritize areas where greater interoperability between security functions could be achieved.

5. Implement a pilot version of the cyber resilience index for a specific and relevant set of threats and threat actors, for example, ransomware and the top 5 of ransomware threat actors relevant to your organization.

6. Develop a communication plan to explain the value chain approach and CRI to various stakeholders in your organization.

7. Conduct a workshop to explore how the CRI could inform and improve your organization's cybersecurity decision-making process.

Chapter 4

♛ Key Concepts:

1. Emotional Intelligence in Cybersecurity Leadership: Understanding and managing emotions in high-stress cybersecurity situations.

2. Effective Communication: Translating technical concepts into business language for various stakeholders.

3. Bidirectional Understanding: Bridging the gap between technical teams and leadership in cybersecurity discussions.

4. Change/Resistance Management: Implementing new cybersecurity approaches while managing resistance.

5. Conflict Resolution and Negotiation: Addressing disagreements and finding common ground in cybersecurity initiatives.

6. Self-Awareness and Continuous Improvement: Ongoing personal development for cybersecurity leaders.

♛ Key Takeaways:

1. Technical expertise alone is not sufficient for effective cybersecurity leadership.

2. Emotional intelligence is crucial in managing teams and stakeholders in high-pressure cybersecurity environments.

3. Effective communication requires tailoring messages to different audiences, from technical teams to the board.

4. Creating a culture of continuous learning is essential for staying ahead in the rapidly evolving cybersecurity landscape.

5. Successful implementation of new approaches like the cyber resilience index requires strong change management skills.

6. Resolving conflicts and negotiating effectively are key skills in aligning different departments toward common cybersecurity goals.

7. Self-awareness and continuous personal development are fundamental to growing as a cybersecurity leader.

♛ Strategic Analogies:

1. Chess Grandmaster: A cybersecurity leader is like a chess grandmaster, needing to think several moves ahead and adapt strategies as the situation evolves.

2. Multidimensional Chess: Leading in cybersecurity is like playing multidimensional chess, managing technical, human, and business aspects simultaneously.

3. Chess Coach: Effective leadership involves being like a chess coach, developing team members' skills and helping them see the bigger picture.

4. Chess Diplomacy: Traversing organizational dynamics is like chess diplomacy, building alliances and negotiating moves to achieve strategic objectives.

♛ **Next Moves:**

1. Assess your emotional intelligence and identify areas for improvement in the context of cybersecurity leadership.

2. Practice translating a complex cybersecurity concept into simple terms for nontechnical stakeholders.

3. Initiate discussions with board members or executives to understand their perspective on cybersecurity and how it aligns with business objectives.

4. Develop a plan for managing change as you implement new cybersecurity approaches like the cyber resilience index.

5. Identify a current conflict or negotiation challenge in your cybersecurity efforts and strategize how to approach it using the principles discussed.

6. Create a personal development plan focusing on both technical and leadership skills in cybersecurity.

7. Organize a workshop or team-building exercise to enhance collaboration and shared understanding across different cybersecurity functions.

Chapter 5

♛ Key Concepts:

1. AI-Enhanced Cyber Resilience Index: Integrating artificial intelligence to provide real-time, predictive cybersecurity metrics.

2. Automated Cyber Value Chains: Fully automated defensive systems that can detect, analyze, and respond to threats in real time.

3. Quantum Computing in Cybersecurity: The potential impact of quantum technologies on both cyber threats and defenses.

4. Bio-inspired Cybersecurity Systems: Defense mechanisms that mimic biological immune systems.

5. Cybersecurity Foresight and Innovation: Anticipating and preparing for future threats and technological advancements, providing early signals to stakeholders.

6. Evolving Role of Cybersecurity Leaders: The shift toward more strategic, multidisciplinary leadership in cybersecurity.

♛ Key Takeaways:

1. The future of cybersecurity requires a shift from reactive to proactive, predictive defense strategies.

2. AI and machine learning will play a crucial role in enhancing the cyber resilience index and automating cyber defense.

3. Quantum computing presents both significant threats and opportunities for cybersecurity.

4. Bio-inspired systems show promising new approaches to adaptive, self-healing cyber defenses.

5. Cybersecurity leaders of the future will need to be strategists, ethicists, and innovators, not just technical experts.

6. Continuous adaptation and innovation are essential to stay ahead in the ever-evolving cybersecurity landscape.

7. Ethical considerations become increasingly important as cybersecurity systems become more autonomous and powerful.

♛ Strategic Analogies:

1. Evolving Chess Rules: The changing cybersecurity landscape is like chess where new pieces and rules are constantly being introduced.

2. AI Versus AI Chess Matches: Future cybersecurity battles may resemble AI versus AI chess games, with humans overseeing strategy.

3. Quantum Chess: The advent of quantum computing in cybersecurity is like introducing quantum mechanics to chess, fundamentally changing the game.

4. Chess Ecosystem: The future cybersecurity environment is like a complex chess ecosystem where multiple games are played simultaneously across various boards.

♛ **Next Moves:**

1. Start exploring how AI could enhance your current cybersecurity metrics and decision-making processes.

2. Begin discussions about the potential impact of quantum computing on your organization's cybersecurity strategy and how that could be captured and shown through the cyber resilience index.

3. Investigate bio-inspired or self-healing systems and their potential application in your cybersecurity infrastructure. Experiment with how much that would contribute to your resilience index.

4. Develop a long-term plan for evolving your cybersecurity leadership skills to meet future challenges.

5. Initiate a cybersecurity foresight program to anticipate and prepare for emerging threats and technologies.

6. Consider the ethical implications of advanced cybersecurity systems and start developing guidelines for their use.

7. Engage with cross-industry working groups or academic institutions to stay ahead of cutting-edge cybersecurity innovations.

Index

A

AI-powered attacks, 238, 248
Asset-driven approach, 5, 6,
    54–56, 58, 125

B

Bio-inspired cybersecurity,
    255, 265
Bio-inspired cybersecurity systems,
    254, 279
Bio-inspired or self-healing
    systems, 281
Bio-inspired systems, 254, 280

C

"Cascading sponsorship"
    model, 212
"Castle-and-moat" model, 11, 235
Check/countercheck
    awareness/improvement,
      214–224
    continuous learning, 188
    corporate dynamics and
      relationships, 190–197
    counter resolution/negotiation/
      feedback, 206–213

cybersecurity mentor, 186
    leaders, 179–184
    leadership, cybersecurity,
      171–179
    leadership skills, 187, 188
    senior leadership
      meeting, 189
    team empowering and
      developing, 198–205
    value chain, 185, 186
    value chain implementation
      broader team,
        communication, 227, 228
      CISO, 233
      human elements, 232
      initial approach, 224–226
      leadership, 232, 233
      measuring success, 230, 231
      unexpected resistance,
        229, 230
      workload concerns, 226, 227
Checklist approach, 222
Chess Game Tree, 272
Chess intelligence, 272
Cloud chessboard, 3
Configuration management
    database (CMDB),
    38, 40, 134

L. Alevizos, *Cyber Resilience Index*, https://doi.org/10.1007/979-8-8688-1122-7

Printed in the United States
by Baker & Taylor Publisher Services